BIBLE STUDY COMMENTARY

# 1, 2 Peter, Jude

Curtis Vaughan, Thomas D. Lea

1, 2 PETER, JUDE: BIBLE STUDY COMMENTARY


Lamplighter Books are published by the Zondervan Publishing House
1415 Lake Drive, S.E., Grand Rapids, Michigan 49506

**Library of Congress Cataloging-in-Publication Data**

Vaughan, Curtis
1, 2 Peter, Jude

(Bible study commentary)
"Lamplighter books."
Bibliography: p.
1. Bible. N.T. Peter—Commentaries. 2. Bible. N.T. Jude—Commentaries. I. Lea, Thomas D. II. Series: Bible study commentary series.
BS2795.3.V37 1988 227'.9207 88–17330
ISBN 0-310-44161-7

The authors wish to express special thanks to Susie Sanders, who labored with uncommon dedication in typing the manuscript of this work, and to Carol Bratton, who kindly assisted her.



Other versions used include the American Standard Version, ASV; the Good News Bible, GNB; the King James Version, KJV; the New King James Version, NKJV; the New American Bible, NAB; New English Bible, NEB; the Modern Language Bible, MLB; the Revised Standard Version, RSV; the Twentieth Century New Testament, TCNT; the Today's English Version, TEV. The abbreviation ZPEB stands for the Zondervan Pictorial Encyclopedia of the Bible.



*Printed in the United States of America*

88 89 90 91 92 93 / CH / 10 9 8 7 6 5 4 3 2 1

# Contents

# Introduction to 1 Peter

Robert Leighton, writing in the seventeenth century, described 1 Peter as "a brief, and yet very clear summary both of the consolations and instructions needful for the encouragement and direction of a Christian in his journey to heaven." It belongs to that group of epistles sometimes called "Catholic." This is a transliteration of a Greek word that has been used of them since the beginning of the third century. There is difference of opinion about the precise meaning of the term in reference to the epistles, but most interpreters think it means something like "general." The thought is that these letters were addressed to Christians in general or (what is more probable) to groups of churches, and not (as was the case with most of Paul's letters) to certain individuals or particular churches.

The *writer* of this book identifies himself as Peter (1:1), and evidence from within the book supports this claim. There are several references within the epistle, for example, that must have been prompted by remembrances of Jesus (cf. 1 Peter 2:13–17; Matthew 17:24–27; 1 Peter 1:20; Acts 2:23). In addition, the statements concerning Jesus' death in 1 Peter 2:22–25 sound like the words of an eyewitness who actually viewed Jesus as He died. Some scholars have questioned the Petrine authorship of the letters. Their objections have focused mainly on the refined Greek that the epistle exhibits, its seeming dependence on Paul, and the nature of the persecution to which it refers. All of these objections have been ably dealt with by a great array of biblical scholars who contend that there are no compelling reasons for questioning the letter's claim of apostolic authority. On the contrary, there is overwhelming supporting evidence suggesting that claim. In fact, no book of the New Testament has earlier, better, or stronger attestation in the post-apostolic period.

Assuming (as we do) that Peter was the author of this book, we may place the writing of it just before the outbreak of the Neronian persecution (A.D. 64). Paul, a few years earlier, had been brought to Rome to face the charges against him, and James, the Lord's brother, had been martyred in Jerusalem. Peter knew that a storm of opposition against the church was looming on the horizon, and he felt it necessary to prepare his far-away brothers for the coming turmoil.

The letter was written from "Babylon." It is also improbable that Peter was referring to Old Testament Babylon (5:15). It is unlikely that the term refers to the Old Testament Babylon, for there is no evidence that Peter ever traveled to that location. In northern Egypt there was a military outpost known as Babylon, but this little-known location has no defensible claim to being the place of writing. It is therefore likely that Peter used the term "Babylon" as a symbolic reference to Rome. The name seems to symbolize the arrogant idolatry and raw power that characterized the city of Rome in the first century (cf. the designation of Rome as "Babylon" in Revelation 17–18).

In 5:12 reference is made to Silas (Silvanus), who assisted Peter in the writing of this epistle. It is probable that he fulfilled the role of an amanuensis (secretary) whose responsibility it was to put Peter's dictated message into writing. Silas may therefore have been responsible for the style and quality of the Greek that the epistle exhibits. He is to be identified as the Silas who accompanied Paul on his second missionary journey (Acts 15:39–41; 1 Thess. 1:1; 2 Thess. 1:1).

The *recipients* of 1 Peter are called "God's elect strangers in the world" (1:1). The description may at first appear to refer to Jewish Christians (and many scholars interpret in this fashion). However, the readers are also described as having practiced idolatry (4:3), as having "lived in ignorance" (1:14), and as being at one time "not a people" (2:10). All of these things lend support to the view that most of the readers were Gentile

Christians. The epistle describes them as "scattered throughout Pontus, Galatia, Cappadocia, Asia and Bithynia" (1:1). These five provinces were located in the part of the world that we know as Turkey.

The *purpose* of the letter, as suggested by 5:12, was to encourage the readers. The emphasis on suffering, found in several passages of the letter (e.g., 3:13; 4:12–19), indicates that they were passing through difficult times. Peter's message must have heartened them to endure their sufferings triumphantly. Robert Leighton writes that the three principal "heads of doctrine" in the book are "faith, obedience, and patience." It seeks to establish [the readers] in believing, to direct them in doing, and to comfort them in suffering."

Among the special characteristics and emphases of 1 Peter are its stress on hope; the prominence of exhortation (being almost a continuous chain of imperative verbs); its consolatory tone; the frequency of OT quotations (on a proportionate basis more here than in any other NT book); the emphasis on suffering (of Christ and of Christians) and on doing good; and the prominence of the idea of submission.

**Outline of 1 Peter**

I. Introduction to 1 Peter
II. Address: The Writer and His Readers (1:1–2)
III. Obligations of Christians as a Privileged People (1:3–2:10)
   A. The Privileges of God's People: A Prayer of Thanksgiving (1:3–12)
      1. The Mercy of the New Birth (1:3–5)
      2. The Possibility of Joy in the Midst of Present Trials (1:6–9)
      3. The Greatness and Glory of Salvation (1:10–12)
   B. The Obligations Inherent in Those Privileges: Appeals for Holy Conduct (1:13–2:10)
      1. Cultivation of Hope (1:13)
      2. Cultivation of Holiness (1:14–16)
      3. Cultivation of Godly Fear (1:17–21)
      4. Cultivation of Love (1:22–25)
      5. Nurture of the New Life (2:1–10)

- IV. Obligations of Christians as a Pilgrim People (2:11–3:12)
  - A. A General Appeal for Proper Conduct toward Unbelievers (2:11, 12)
    1. The Negative Appeal (2:11)
    2. The Positive Appeal (2:12)
  - B. Special Appeals Addressed to Various Classes among the Readers (2:13–3:7)
    1. Duties of Citizens (Subjects) to Those Who Govern Them (2:13–17)
    2. Duties of Servants (Slaves) to Their Masters (2:18–25)
    3. Duties of Wives to Their Husbands (3:1–6)
    4. Duties of Husbands to Their Wives (3:7)
  - C. Appeals Addressed to Christians Generally (3:8–12)
    1. Christians in Relation to Other Christians (3:8)
    2. Christians in Relation to Unbelievers (3:9)
    3. These Appeals Enforced by Scripture (3:10–12)
- V. Obligations of Christians as a Persecuted People (3:13–5:11)
  - A. General Counsel for Those under Persecution (3:13–4:19)
    1. Cultivate a Proper Attitude with Reference to Suffering (3:13–17)
    2. Look to Christ, Whose Vicarious Death and Triumphant Resurrection Are the Basis for the Christian's Confidence and Encouragement in Suffering (3:18–4:6)
    3. Live in Awareness of the Approaching End (4:7–11)
    4. See Suffering in Proper Perspective; Understand Its Place and Its Meaning in the Christian Life (4:12–19)
  - B. Special Counsel for Elders, for Young Men, and for the Whole Christian Community (5:1–11)
    1. Counsel for Elders (5:1–4)
    2. Counsel for Younger Believers (5:5a)
    3. Counsel for the Entire Christian Community (5:5b–11)

VI. Conclusion (5:12–14)
   A. A Summary Description of the Letter (5:12)
   B. The Final Greetings (5:13)
   C. A Request (5:14a)
   D. The Benediction (5:14b)

Selwyn sees three cycles in the arrangement of the body of the work, each cycle containing a doctrinal section and a hortatory section, the first consisting of 1:3–2:3; the second, 2:4–3:12; the third, 3:13–5:11. Dalton understands the letter to contain three major units: 1:3–2:10, the dignity of the Christian vocation and its responsibilities; 2:10–3:12, obligations of the Christian life; and 3:1–5:11, the Christian and persecutions. Graham Scroggie divides the book similarly and, along with several other interpreters, uses three words to sum up these sections, respectively: salvation, submission, and suffering. He explains that the vocation of the Christian is salvation; his behavior is marked by submission; and his discipline is through suffering.

**For Further Study**

1. Notice the name "Silas" that appears in 1 Peter 5:12. Some describe Silas as an amanuensis. Using the *Zondervan Pictorial Encyclopedia of the Bible* (ZPEB), look under the article "Silas" for information on the kind of activity in which Silas (Sylvanus) might have been engaged.

2. Some have questioned the Petrine authorship of 1 Peter on linguistic, theological, and historical grounds. Most evangelicals feel that Peter was the author. For further information see the article "Peter, First Epistle" in the ZPEB.

3. Early Christian tradition locates Peter's residence and death at Rome. For information on this tradition see the article "Peter, Simon" in the ZPEB.

# Chapter 1

## Address: The Writer and His Readers

(1 Peter 1:1–2)

The address of this epistle, like others in the New Testament, follows the accepted style of letter writing current in the first century. A typical example of this style, outside of the epistles, may be found in Acts 23:26. In the present passage the name of the writer and the identity of the readers, each with appropriate descriptive phrases, are followed by a distinctive Christian greeting.

### A. The Writer

The writer identifies himself as "Peter, an apostle of Jesus Christ" (v. 1a). The name is the Greek equivalent of the Aramaic "Cephas" (meaning "Rock"), the surname given to our writer by Jesus (Matt. 16:18; Mark 3:16; John 1:42). Before this time he was called Simon (or Simeon) Bar-jona (i.e., Simon son of Jonah—Matt. 16:17).

"Apostle of Jesus Christ" designates the office of Peter and at the same time indicates his authority for writing this letter. Apostles were thought of as being directly commissioned by Christ. They therefore stood in a unique relationship to Him. The word "apostle" occurs approximately seventy-five times in the New Testament, with most of these occurrences clustered in the writings of Luke and Paul. Essentially it means "one sent forth" by another, hence a messenger. (In John 13:16 the NIV translates it "messenger"; NASB has "one who is sent.") In most of its occurrences in the NT the word means something like "authorized ambassador." All of those who were apostles in the strict sense of the word had seen the Lord (and so could bear witness to His resurrection [cf. Acts 1:21–22; 1 Cor. 9:1; 15:8–9]) and had received a personal commission from the risen Christ. The marks of a true apostle were the performance of signs, wonders, and miracles (cf. 2 Cor. 12:12). Peter's use of the word reflects his consciousness of a commission from the Lord, his sense of dependence upon and responsibility to the Lord, and his sense of authority to speak for the Lord.

**B. The Readers**

The readers are identified as "God's elect, strangers in the world, scattered throughout Pontus, etc." (v.1; cf. ASV, "the elect sojourners of the Dispersion in Pontus, etc."). From this designation we see that they are described from three points of view.

First, their relation to God: they are "elect."[1] This word, which Cranfield calls "a theme-word" of 1 Peter (cf. 2:4, 6, 9; 5:13), is generally used in the Bible of those chosen out by God for a special relation to Him and with a view to special service in His behalf.

In the NT, it is the third most frequent term for Christians, exceeded only by "disciples" and "saints." The word speaks of privilege: believers are chosen to salvation in Christ, destined to be sons of God, holy and blameless before Him (Eph. 1:3–4). It also speaks of responsibility: believers are chosen to carry out God's purpose of grace in the world, sent forth to proclaim abroad the praises (or excellencies) of Him who called them (cf. 1 Peter 2:9). The word does not refer to anything special that believers are in themselves or to anything special that they have done, but rather to something special that God has done to and for them.

Hiebert calls the doctrine of election "a 'family truth' intended to foster the welfare of believers" (p. 34). It has been the occasion of much controversy among believers, and many

[1]It is debated whether "elect" in this passage has reference to the eternal decree by which God, before time began, set apart His people or has reference to the actual, historical selection of them in time—their call to conversion. John Brown (a thoroughgoing Calvinist) favors the latter, but most interpreters (Calvinist and non-Calvinist) prefer the former view.

people feel uneasy when it is mentioned. It must be remembered that the Bible represents it as a truth designed to make us humble, give us comfort and encouragement, and elicit from us thanksgiving and praise to God. The writers of Scripture do not attempt to harmonize the insistence on divine sovereignty with the equally biblical insistence on human responsibility. When asked how he reconciled divine sovereignty (and election) with human responsibility, Charles H. Spurgeon is said to have replied, "I never try to 'reconcile' friends."

This election/selection is defined in three particulars. These set forth respectively its origin or basis, the means by which it becomes effective, and its end or purpose.

*1. It was done "according to [in accordance with, on the basis of] the foreknowledge of God the Father."*

Foreknowledge, represented here as the basis or foundation on which election rests, means more than a knowledge beforehand of facts or events. As Cranfield explains, it "includes the distinct though closely related ideas of divine purpose, divine choice, divine providence, and carries with it the assurance that [the] destiny [of those foreknown] shall be accomplished." The teaching then is that Christians were chosen by God, not because they were seen to possess merit that others did not have, but because it lay within the deliberate plan of God to save them. Awareness of this would have a steadying and strengthening effect on Peter's troubled readers.

*2. Election is "by the sanctifying work of the Spirit" (lit., "in [by means of] sanctification of the Spirit";*[2] *cf. 2 Thess. 2:13).*

The words show that the sanctifying work of the Holy Spirit is the means by which our election has, in time, been made effective. In sanctifying—the Greek word literally denotes "a setting apart"—the **Spirit** convicts the sinner, draws him to Christ, and gives him saving faith.[3]

---

[2]Brown and a few others understand "spirit" to be a reference to the human spirit, not the Holy Spirit. In this interpretation, the Greek word for "spirit" is construed as an objective genitive, and the meaning is that the human spirit is that which is sanctified or set apart. But the majority of modern commentators explain the case of the word for "spirit" as a subjective genitive; the reference then is to the Holy Spirit, and He it is who *does* the sanctifying.

[3]Cranfield quotes Luther ("I believe that I cannot by my own reason or

3. *Election is "for obedience to Jesus Christ and sprinkling by his blood" (lit., "unto [with a view to] obedience and sprinkling of the blood of Jesus Christ").* In these words that describe the aim and purpose of election there is an allusion to the establishment of Israel's covenant relation to God as recorded in Exodus 24:3–8.

**a.** The primary meaning of the passage before us is that believers were chosen by God with a view to His bringing them into a (new) covenant relationship with Himself, a relationship in which obedience and sprinkling by blood are notably conspicuous.[4] The inference to be drawn is that Christians are a part of the Israel of God.

**b.** Second, the readers are described in terms of their status in the world: they are "strangers in the world, scattered throughout Pontus, Galatia, etc." "Strangers" (RSV, "exiles") translates a word used of foreigners who settled for a while in a town or region without making it their permanent home. They were "resident aliens." The word occurs in only three places in the NT: here; 1 Peter 2:11; and Hebrews 11:13. The underlying thought in our text is that Christians' true home is heaven, and so long as they are in this world they are living in an alien environment. The idea is illustrated in this quotation from the *Epistle to Diognetus* (2nd cent.):

> Christians are not distinguished from the rest of mankind by either country, speech or customs. . . . They reside in their respective countries, but only as aliens. They take part in everything as citizens and put up with everything as foreigners. Every foreign land is their home, and every home a foreign land. . . . They find themselves in the flesh, but do not

strength believe in Jesus Christ my Lord or come to Him," and adds that faith in Christ is not the achievement of one's "own superior moral character or intellectual insight . . . , but rather a miracle wrought by the Holy Spirit (cf. 1 Cor. 12:3)."

[4]The idea in "sprinkling of the blood of Jesus Christ" is understood by many to be the cleansing effected by Christ's blood (cf. TCNT). We understand the phrase to teach that Christ's blood is that which brings us into a covenant relationship with God. (The reader should observe how the ideas of obedience and blood-sprinkling are combined in the Exodus passage.) The reference to "obedience" points up that a covenant relationship with God involves duty and responsibility as well as privilege. Bigg defines obedience as "obedience to the law of God, faithful service, righteousness."

live according to the flesh. They spend their days on earth, but hold citizenship in heaven.

"Scattered" (ASV, "Dispersion"; cf. James 1:1) is a free rendering of a Greek noun that was almost a technical term for Jews who lived outside of Palestine. They were a "scattered people." Here it seems to be used figuratively (spiritually) to suggest the pilgrim life of believers.[5] Additionally, by applying to Christians a term widely used of the Jews, Peter may have intended to suggest that Christians are an integral part of the Israel of God.

**c.** Third, the readers are described in terms of their geographical locality: "Pontus, Galatia, etc." Of these districts, only Galatia and Asia are mentioned elsewhere in the NT as having Christian converts. We have no information concerning the means by which the others were evangelized. Had Peter preached in these areas? If not, by whom were they evangelized? We have no record of a visit by Paul to Pontus, Cappadocia, or Bithynia. (On one notable occasion "the Spirit of Jesus would not allow" Paul and his companions to go into Bithynia [Acts 16:7].) Perhaps we should bear in mind that people from some of these provinces were present in Jerusalem on the day of Pentecost (Acts 2:9).

## C. A Prayer for Grace and Peace

The greeting is a prayer for grace and peace to be given abundantly to the readers. "Grace" is the special favor of God through which the believer experiences forgiveness and divine help. "Peace" describes a condition of wholeness and completeness in fellowship with God.

## For Further Study

1. Using a good map, locate the geographical area in which the recipients of 1 Peter lived.

[5] Moffatt points out that Peter's expression gives "Dispersion" fresh sense and scope: (a) The reassembling of these exiles is to be in heaven, not on earth in Palestine. (b) There is "no touch of pathos ('poor exiles'), but an exulting stress upon the privilege of membership in this community that is soon to be admitted to its proper glory and privileges in heaven." (c) There is an ethical obligation, worked out especially in 2:11f., "of pure detachment from the vices of the pagan world."

2. Peter described his leaders as "scattered" (the term for scattered is a noun that literally means "the dispersion"). Outside of the Book of 1 Peter this word described Jews who lived outside of Palestine. For further information see the article "Diaspora" in the ZPEB.

3. Verses 1 and 2 of 1 Peter 1 are the salutation. Salutations were generally written in this form: writer, readers, greeting. Look for the appearance of these three features in Peter's salutation. Compare this with the salutation in Paul's letters.

4. What is the meaning of the term "foreknowledge"? For further information see the article "Foreknow, foreknowledge" in ZPEB. A brief but very helpful discussion of divine election and human responsibility is J. I. Packer's *Evangelism and the Sovereignty of God.*

# Chapter 2

## Obligations of Christians as a Privileged People

(1 Peter 1:3–2:10)

A salient feature of 1 Peter is its teaching that Christians are a new people of God, a new Israel. The first hint of this is at the outset of the letter, in the mention of the readers' election by God, their exile status in the world, and their being brought into a covenant relation with God through sprinkling of the blood of Jesus Christ (1:1–2). The idea is clearly affirmed in 2:9–10, where language is boldly used to describe Christians that, in the OT, describes Israel. Throughout the letter the thought is not far from the surface.

Mention was made earlier that 1 Peter is mainly hortatory, that it presses upon believers the obligations that are theirs as God's new people. There appear to be three series of appeals, with each series containing a more or less distinctive emphasis. The first division enlarges on the privileges of God's people (1:3–12) and then expounds the obligations that are inherent in those privileges (1:13–2:10). In the second division (2:11–3:12) the readers are reminded of their alien (pilgrim) status in the world, the consequent dangers that confront them, and the obligations incumbent upon them by virtue of their position in a world alienated from God. The last section (3:13–5:10) dwells at considerable length upon the readers' sufferings and closes with detailed instruction for leaders and people as they live their lives under the pressures of persecution.

## A. The Privileges of God's People: A Prayer of Thanksgiving (1:3–12)

The body of the epistle, which was written to believers passing through difficult and trying times, begins with an expression of thanksgiving. In this opening paragraph Peter seems to say, "Remember first of all how much you have to thank God for: new life, new hope, God's sure promises, His keeping power, and the prospect of full salvation soon to come."

The thanksgiving takes the form of a hymn of praise, and in this respect it is much like Ephesians 1:3–14, 2 Corinthians 1:3–11, and 1 Thessalonians 1:3–10. Addressed to "the God and Father of our Lord Jesus Christ," it calls special attention to His great mercy and the rich benefits that accrue to His people. Numerous concepts are woven into it, but the passage appears to fall into three major divisions, each of which gives a distinctive strand of praise to God: the mercy of the new birth and the new life effected by that birth (vv. 3–5); the possibility of joy in the midst of suffering, of gladness in spite of sadness (vv. 6–9); and the greatness and glory of salvation, prophesied by prophets of old and wonderingly admired by the angelic hosts (vv. 10–12). The first stanza of praise has God the Father as its central figure; the second, God the Son; and the third, God the Holy Spirit.

### *1. The Mercy of the New Birth (1:3–5)*

The first unit of the thanksgiving focuses on the readers' experience of the new birth and ascribes praise to God the Father for making this possible through the resurrection of Jesus Christ.[1] The fulsome title ("Lord Jesus Christ") given to the Savior calls attention to His relationship to us (our divine "Lord"), His true humanity ("Jesus"), and His divinely appointed office ("Christ"). The imagery of birth ("has given us new birth"; ASV, "begat us again") suggests the radical nature of

---

[1]The NIV's "Praise be" expresses accurately the meaning of the Greek, that literally reads "Blessed be" (Gr., *eulogētos*, a verbal adjective used in the NT only of God). The formula, "Blessed be God . . . ," was frequently used by the Jews in prayer, and occurs again and again in the Greek version of the OT (cf. Ps. 66:20). Peter uses the familiar formula but gives it a distinctly Christian flavor by describing God as "the God and Father of our Lord Jesus Christ." "Christian worship is . . . addressed . . . to the God Whom Christ has revealed and Whose Son in a unique sense He is" (Kelly).

the experience in Christ. Believers have been brought into a situation so entirely new and different that it is nothing short of a new life. It is as though they had been born a second time (cf. John 3:3–5). The verb, used in the NT only here and in 1:23 (though a similar word is used by Jesus in John 3:3; cf. Titus 3:5), marks a decisive change in status and outlook and denotes the creation in believers of a new and divine life. The reference to God's mercy ("In his great mercy") points up three things:

- God's action in causing us to be born again was in accordance with (Gr., *kata* ) His compassionate character. The Greek word has in it the ideas of mercy, compassion, and pity.
- There is a richness and magnitude in God's mercy: It is "great" or abundant mercy.
- It follows that Christians owe God a great debt of gratitude for making new birth a reality. Not our merit but His mercy (i.e., pity and compassion toward the miserable) is at the root of it.

Peter explains that the new life into which believers are brought involves a hope (v. 3), an inheritance (v. 4), and a salvation (v. 5).[2] As the child of a rich man might be described as born to wealth, the child of a king as born to a throne, so believers have been born to hope, to an inheritance, etc. The sequence of thought seems to be as follows: Christians have been born to a living hope. This hope is explained as involving an inheritance, and the inheritance is more precisely defined as

[2]There is difference of opinion as to how these terms are related to one another and to "given . . . new birth." The Greek reads: *anagennēsas hēmas* (gave us new life, caused us to be born again) *eis elpida* (unto, for hope) . . . *eis klēronomian* (unto, for an inheritance) . . . *eis sotērian* (unto, for salvation). It is generally agreed that "unto (for) hope" and "unto (for) inheritance" are to be construed with "given us new birth" (lit., "caused us to be born again"). The relationship of the last phrase (unto, for salvation; NIV, "until the coming of the salvation . . .") to what precedes it is not so certain. Calvin and others see it as coordinate with the two similar phrases that go before it (cf. NAB). NIV and most recent versions and commentaries construe the phrase in question with "shielded." Beare thinks the phrase has a double connection—not only with "shielded" (which is obvious), but also with "given us new birth" (which is admittedly less obvious). We think there is validity in Beare's suggestion. The idea then is that believers are begotten to salvation, then "shielded" until that salvation is manifested in its fullness at the end of the age.

a full salvation from God. The phrases are not so much to be seen as parallel as they are to be viewed like steps on a ladder, each bringing the reader closer and closer to the climactic concept of salvation.

**a. A Living Hope (v. 3).** Hope, a word occurring five times in this epistle (here, 1:13, 21; 3:5, 15), is understood by some to be the theme of the entire thanksgiving (vv. 3–12). Cranfield, for example, acknowledges that the word itself is used in the thanksgiving only once but writes that "the idea runs through it like a golden thread and holds it together." It is not to be thought of as mere wishful thinking but as a firm conviction concerning the future. Perhaps it is best expressed by such expressions as confident expectation, joyful anticipation. Sometimes the term is objective, denoting that on which our hope (expectation) is set (cf. Col. 1:5). Here it is subjective, having to do with the emotion, the attitude of hope.

We tend to take hope for granted, but it is well to remind ourselves that the pagan world of apostolic times (like the pagan world of our day) was a world without hope (cf. Eph. 2:12). Unprecedented depression had settled over the masses. Life was care-ridden and full of worry. Indeed,

> On that hard pagan world disgust
> And secret loathing fell;
> Deep weariness and sated lust
> Made human life a hell.
> —Matthew Arnold

Two things are said in the text about the believer's hope: First, it is a "living" hope. That is to say, it is a hope that is active (cf. Heb. 4:12), that has reality about it, that will not disappoint, but will be fully realized (cf. Rom. 5:5). "It is a fearful thing when a man and all his hopes die together" (Leighton). Because ours is a living hope, "it is a firm, stable, individable hope, an anchor fixed within the veil" (Leighton). Second, it is a hope made possible "through the resurrection of Jesus Christ from the dead." This implies that the hope of which Peter spoke is essentially the joyful expectation of believers that they will rise from the dead just as Jesus did.

The words under consideration ("through the resurrection,

etc.") may be construed with the word "living," and the order of words in the Greek text lends some support to this view. The meaning then is that the Christian's hope lives by virtue of Christ's resurrection. (Compare NAB: " . . . a birth unto hope that draws its life from the resurrection of Jesus Christ. . . .") Christ's resurrection is indeed, as Kelly writes, "the ground and guarantee of our resurrection hope (i. 21; cf. Rom. viii:10f.; I Cor. xv. 12–22; I. Thess. iv. 14)." However, it is questionable that the total context supports the view that "through the resurrection, etc." is to be construed with "living." It is therefore better to construe the phrase "through the resurrection, etc." with the verb "begat" (NIV: "has given us new birth"), because this is the term that "governs the whole pericope" (Kelly). The idea then is not that Christian hope lives by the resurrection of Christ (true though this is), but that hope is brought to believers by regeneration, and regeneration is made possible by Christ's resurrection.[3]

**b. A Heavenly Inheritance (v. 4).** The hope of Peter's readers is more precisely defined as "an inheritance" (a possession),[4] a term that perhaps alludes to Israel's possession of Canaan as an inheritance from the Lord (cf. Deut. 15:4; 19:10). Elsewhere in the NT Christians are spoken of as "heirs" (Rom. 8:17; Gal. 4:7) and as having an inheritance (as here). This inheritance is variously referred to as eternal life (Mark 10:17; Titus 3:7), glory with Christ (Rom. 8:17), the kingdom of God (1 Cor. 15:50) and of Christ (Eph. 5:5), salvation (Heb. 1:14), the new Jerusalem (Rev. 21:2–7), and so forth. Peter elsewhere in this epistle speaks of it as the grace of life (3:7) and a blessing (3:9). In this passage "inheritance" is a term for the blessedness and glory of heaven, of which the indwelling presence of the Spirit is the foretaste and pledge (Eph. 1:13–14).

Peter uses four descriptive terms of the Christian's heritage. The first three depict the excellence of its nature; the last, the certainty of its attainment. Each of these points up that it is a blessedness "totally unlike ordinary human possessions; neither

[3]There is much to be said for Leighton's view that "by the resurrection, etc." refers both to "begotten again" and to the word "living."

[4]Alford quotes Steinmeyer: "During our pilgrimage we have a living hope: when it is finished, that hope becomes the inheritance of the promise."

catastrophes, nor human sin, nor the transitoriness to which the whole natural order is prey . . . can affect it" (Kelly). It cannot perish, it cannot spoil, it cannot fade, or waste away. Being under the watchful eye of almighty God, it is eternally secure.

*1. It "can never perish."* The Greek word was occasionally used with a military connotation—of a land not ravaged by (or beyond the reach of) enemy armies. Sometimes it was used of a land unscathed by natural calamities. Likely the language here suggests perpetuity: the Christian's heritage is imperishable, not liable to corruption or decay. In short, death cannot reach and destroy it.[5]

*2. It "can never . . . spoil."* The idea is that it is unpolluted, unstained by evil; it is beyond the reach of evil and cannot be contaminated by it. As the first term spoke of perpetuity, this speaks of purity and perfection. The inheritance lasts forever, and forever retains its integrity.

*3. It "can never . . . fade."* That is to say, the Christian inheritance is not subject to the wasting effects of time. The root word was used of the withering of flowers, of the wasting of one's features by illness or age. The word used in the text suggests then a beauty that time does not impair or cause to wither away. It is unchanging.

*4. It is "kept in heaven."* This means that it is divinely preserved and therefore completely safe. The Greek word has the connotation of being watched over or guarded, and then of being preserved (protected from loss or injury). The inheritance is not simply stored safely away (the idea of a similar word used in Col. 1:5), but securely kept under God's careful watch. The readers may endure much hardship and suffering, but they can be sure that their eternal inheritance is secure, for it is in the custody of their God. His eye is ever upon it.

---

[5]Leighton understands the meaning to be that the Christian inheritance, unlike others, "cannot come to nothing, is an estate that cannot be spent." The reader should also read ASV'S rendering of verse 5. If a comma is placed after "through faith," the expression "unto a salvation" is parallel to "unto a living hope" and "unto an inheritance." (The same Greek preposition [*eis*] is used in each of these phrases.) If no comma is employed, "unto a salvation" is to be construed with "guarded." It should be remembered that no marks of punctuation were used in the earliest Greek text.

**c. A Complete Salvation (v. 5).**[6] Not only is the *inheritance* safe; those for whom it is intended are also safe.[7] They "through faith are shielded [NASB, "protected"; ASV, "guarded"] by God's power until the coming of the salvation that is ready to be revealed in the last time." "Shielded"—the same Greek word is used in Philippians 4:7—translates a word that had a military connotation; that is, it suggests being guarded or protected, as by a military garrison. The term brings to mind the picture of people in a fort under siege, but guarded and protected by an invincible detachment of soldiers. In our case the enemy is Satan, who, unwearied in his assaults, is ever raising his batteries against us. Our protection, more than a match for him, is the presence of God. The present tense of the verb shows that the shielding is a continuous activity, in keeping with our continuous need for protection in our lifelong struggle with evil.

"By God's power" expresses the *supreme* cause of our security. Our stability and our perseverance all depend on it.[8] "By" might be rendered "in." If so, the suggestion is that God's power is all around us, like an all-embracing shelter or a fortress. But probably "by" is the better rendering. God's power is the guarding force, the garrison that keeps us safe.

"Faith" (firm, steadfast trust) is the *subordinate* cause of our security. Our faith lays hold on God's power, and His power strengthens our faith, and in this manner we are preserved. Faith, says Leighton, "sets the soul within the guard of the power of God." The NEB expresses this sense: "you, *because you put your faith in God*, are under the protection of his power until salvation comes" (author's italics). Alford calls the power of

---

[6]See footnote 7. The reader should also read ASV's rendering of verse 5. If a comma is placed after "through faith," the expression "unto salvation" is parallel to "unto a living hope" and "unto an inheritance." (The same Greek preposition [*eis*] is used in each of these phrases.) If no comma is employed, "unto a salvation" is to be construed with "guarded." It should be remembered that no marks of punctuation were used in the earliest Greek text.

[7]Bengel: "The inheritance is reserved: the heirs are guarded: neither shall it fail them, nor they it."

[8]"When we consider how weak we are in ourselves . . . and how assaulted, we wonder . . . that any can continue one day in the state of grace; but when we look on the strength by which we are guarded, the power of God, then we see the reason of our stability to the end; for Omnipotence supports us, and the everlasting arms are under us" (Leighton).

God "the efficient cause" of our security; faith, "the effective means."

"Salvation" picks up and defines more precisely the hope and the inheritance already mentioned. It is a term that speaks of a rescue, a deliverance—sometimes from danger, sometimes from disease or death. Here it is a spiritual rescue; more specifically, it denotes the believer's final, complete salvation—the consummation of the saving experience in Christ. Cranfield takes it to mean "the whole sum of what God has in store for us, the enjoyment of our inheritance."

A salvation "ready to be revealed in the last time" is a salvation prepared and complete, awaiting only the proper time for its full manifestation. This future aspect of salvation is a distinctive emphasis of 1 Peter (cf. 2:2, ASV), though the epistle makes clear that we also have a present experience of it (cf. 1:9)—i.e., we are in the process of receiving it. "The last time" is a reference to the endtime, ushered in by the Second Coming of Jesus.

### 2. *The Possibility of Joy in Present Trials (1:6–9)*

The preceding verses looked to the future. Verses 6–9 emphasize the present experience of joy in the Christian life. ("Joy" is another theme-word of this letter.) The opening phrase of the Greek text of verse 6 is made up of a preposition (*en*) and a relative pronoun (*hō*). The phrase is sometimes translated "wherein" (ASV),[9] sometimes "in whom" (understanding the antecedent of the pronoun to be "God," vv. 3, 4, or "Jesus Christ," v. 3). But perhaps it is better to understand the pronoun as neuter and as having its antecedent in the entire concept of verses 3–5, a construction not uncommon in Greek. Viewed in this manner, the phrase (*en hō*) may mean "in which circumstances" or may be seen as equivalent to the English "therefore." The NIV, though not using these words, expresses the same sense by employing the phrase "In this." In effect Peter

[9]This rendering appears to make the antecedent "salvation" (v. 5). However, this is grammatically impossible. In Greek the pronoun must agree with its antecedent in gender, and the pronoun of our text is either masculine or neuter. The Greek words for "salvation," "inheritance," and "hope" are all feminine words.

was affirming that because of the new birth and all that it has brought to believers (hope, inheritance, salvation), they were able to rejoice—even though they had been put to grief for a time by many trials.

**a. The Joy of the Christian.** Two ideas dominate this unit. These are "rejoice" (vv. 6, 8) and "trials" (v. 6). The former translates a word (*agalliasthe*) that expresses "a jubilant and thankful exultation" (Bultmann in TDNT). Since there is no evidence of its use in secular literature, it has been concluded that the word expresses a distinctly religious joy. It may be rendered "exult," "be full of joy," "overjoyed," even "leap for joy." The ASV and NIV have "greatly rejoice." Arndt and Gingrich translate it "shout for joy" in 1 Peter 4:13, where it is used in conjunction with another word for rejoice (*chairō*).

Several matters are taught here about the joy of the Christian. First, it exists in spite of grief (v. 6). Indeed, Peter implies that it is enhanced, not diminished, by grief. Milligan, in his commentary on 1 Thessalonians 1:6, speaks of this union of suffering and joy, so characteristic of New Testament thought, as "marking a new aeon in the world's history." Second, it is "inexpressible" (ineffable) and "glorious" (lit., "glorified," v. 8). "Inexpressible" means that human language is unable adequately to describe it. It is supreme joy. "Glorious" (ASV, "full of glory") may mean that Christian joy in the midst of trial already has the touch of glory (heaven) resting upon it. Cranfield writes that it is "lit up by the light of the future." Hiebert understands the meaning to be that the Christian's joy is "inspired by, and in a remarkable measure already radiant with, the glory that is yet to come." Third, Christians' experience of joy is rooted in two realities: (a) the fact that they have been born again to a living hope, etc. (suggested by "In this," the opening words of v. 6), and (b) the fact that they are, as believers, already in process of receiving (present tense) "the goal" (i.e., the outcome, the consummation) of their faith, namely the salvation of their souls (v. 9). In using the word "souls" the author did not intend a distinction between body and soul, as though salvation were restricted only to the latter. The term is a favorite one with Peter (cf. 1:22; 2:11, 25; 3:20; 4:19), and it regularly has the semitic sense of "man as a living being, as a self or person" (Kelly). The whole phrase, "the salvation of your souls," is equivalent to "your salvation."

**b. The Trials of the Christian.** The word "temptations" (v. 6, KJV )[10] speaks not of enticements to do wrong, but of outward trials: adversities, afflictions, and distresses. The NIV rightly translates it "trials." The Greek word, like "temptation" in the English of 1611, could denote either enticements to sin or outward testings. It is the context that determines the meaning.

At least four things are said about the trials of Peter's readers. (a) They are diverse in kind ("all kinds of") (v. 6). The literal meaning of the Greek word is "many-colored," "variegated." Barclay, alluding to the root meaning of the word, comments, "There is no color in the human situation which the grace of God cannot match." (b) They are "for a little while" (v. 6). The context seems to require that we understand "for a little while" to mean that the Christian's trials will only last as long as he lives on this earth. This is a "little while" when set over against eternity (cf. 2 Cor. 4:17). (c) There is a "need" for all our trials (v. 6; KJV, ASV). The NIV expresses this by the words "you may have *had* to suffer" (author's italics). Moffatt renders it, "though for the passing moment you may need to suffer various trials." "It is consoling to know," writes Hiebert, "that God's people are never needlessly afflicted." The words in our text translate a first class conditional construction, that assumes the actuality of the trials: "if necessary[11] [as is the case]." Though conditional in form, the clause states what is in fact the case. (d) They serve a divine purpose in our lives, namely, to refine our faith, bring out the genuineness (Gr., *dokimion*) of it (v. 7a), so that in the last day our genuine faith will elicit for us praise and honor and glory (i.e., participation in the glory of the eternal age) from God (v. 7b). The NIV states it thus: "These [i.e., all kinds of trials] have come so that your faith . . . may be proved genuine and may result in praise, glory and honor when Jesus Christ is revealed." Peter's words intimate that "our faith

[10]"Trial" in the KJV of verse 7 translates an entirely different word.

[11]The Greek verbal (*deon*) is the same root word that Jesus used when He spoke to Nicodemus of the necessity of the new birth (John 3:7) and when He spoke to His disciples of the necessity of His death and resurrection (Matt. 16:21).

is not to be honoured and crowned by God until it be duly proved" (Calvin).

Two questions need consideration in reference to verse 7. The first has to do with the meaning of *dokimion,* that KJV translates "trial" (cf. Weymouth, "testing"); ASV and NASB, "proof"; TCNT, RSV, and others, "genuineness"; NIV, "genuine." It is generally thought that in James 1:3 the word is used in the active sense of "testing." In 1 Peter it is commonly held that the word is used in the passive sense of "approved after testing," "tested and approved," hence "the genuine part." The Greek combines two nouns ("*genuineness* of your *faith*"), but this is equivalent to "your *genuine faith*" or "your *faith when proved to be genuine*" (cf. note in Calvin's *Commentary*). It speaks of what remains after the refiner's fire has done its work: the approved residue, the genuine element. In the present passage Beare and Kelly render the word "sterling quality"; Selwyn, "the proven part"; Bigg, "the tested residue." We may conclude then that the term denotes the genuine element in our faith, the proven part refined by suffering. This is genuine faith, and it is such genuine faith (tested and found to be true) that is more precious than gold. The latter perishes, even though it is refined by fire, but faith tried and tested by the fires of trial lasts forever. The process of testing and refining is painful, but God's intention is good. He wants to strip our faith of all dross and make its genuineness apparent, so that at the revelation of Jesus Christ it may be "found unto praise, glory and honor" (v. 7b).

The latter terms have a cumulative effect and probably are not to be rigidly distinguished. If such is done, perhaps the sense is this: "praise" is the approval that will come from our righteous Judge; "honor" has to do with rank, positions of distinction and privilege; "glory" (another key word in 1 Peter) points to the privilege God will give His faithful people of sharing in His divine splendor and majesty.

The second question has to do with the structure of the verse. That is to say, how are the several phrases and clauses of the verse related to each other? The NIV construes "faith" as the subject of the sentence and makes "genuine" the predicate and "praise, glory and honor" a sort of secondary predicate. "Of greater worth than gold, etc." is taken to be a parenthetical description of faith. This is true to the essential meaning of the verse, but it obscures the grammatical construction of the Greek sentence. The NEB, though differing in language, sets forth the same thought. Weymouth, who understands *dokimion* to mean "testing," takes that word to be the subject, the parenthesis to be a description of it, and the rest of the sentence to be the predicate. This construction is essentially identical with that of the KJV. The ASV and NASB, though interpreting *dokimion* to mean "proof," set forth the same construction as that found in KJV and Weymouth. Kelly, who interprets *dokimion* to mean "sterling quality," construes that as the subject, "more precious than gold, etc." as the predicate, and "praise and glory, etc." as a secondary predicate: "so that the sterling quality of your faith may be found to be more precious than gold (which is perishable even though it is tried by fire) and so redound to your praise and glory and honour at the revelation of Jesus Christ."

**c. The Concluding Statement (vv. 8, 9).** Verses 8 and 9 round out this second stanza of Peter's doxology. They pick up on the reference to Jesus Christ in the closing words of verse 7 and call attention to the personal relationship of Peter's readers to Him, the key words being "love," "believe," and "joy." They love Him though they have never seen Him. Though not seeing Him at the present time, they still believe in Him and are filled with ineffable and heavenly joy. (Believing is unswerving trust, confidence that though they do not see the Lord now, eventually they will.) The context suggests that the joy that suffering Christians experience is the joy of the end time overflowing into the present. "Receiving" (v. 9) does not mean, as some have contended, "being about to receive" or "receiving in the future." It is a present experience. We do not now receive in full all that salvation means to us, but that which will be consummated in eternity is even now being experienced in foretaste.

### *3. The Greatness and Glory of Salvation*[12] *(1:10–12)*

The concept of salvation has been prominent in the preceding verses. For example, it is mentioned in verse 5 as a salvation for which believers are being guarded and as ready to

[12] Bigg thinks "salvation" in verse 10 is "practically an equivalent for the gospel," but it should probably be understood in its usual NT sense.

be revealed at the last time. It is named again in verse 9 as something believers are already receiving, in foretaste, as the end or outcome of their faith. Verse 10 opens with a reference to this salvation, and the apostle wonderingly lingers over it. Indeed, all else that is said in verses 10 through 12 is in some way related to salvation and points up its surpassing greatness.[13]

The greatness of the salvation we have in Christ is suggested by at least three matters that are brought out in these verses. *First*, it was the theme of Old Testament[14] prophecy and inquiry (vv. 10–12). They prophesied of "the grace that was to come to [was meant for] you" (v. 10). "Grace" perhaps means a gift of grace, a bestowal of favor; specifically, the grace shown in the bestowal of the blessings of the gospel.

Three statements sum up the teaching of these verses relative to the witness of the prophets:

- As instruments of the Spirit, they predicted[15] the sufferings and subsequent glory (lit., "glories") of the Messiah (v. 11). Therefore the messianic salvation proclaimed by the apostles was no novelty. The "sufferings of Christ" suggests sufferings *destined for* Christ. The "glories" (note the plural) of Christ are perhaps the successive manifestations of glory that followed His death on the

[13]There is another line of thought that runs through verses 10–12, namely, that Christians are highly favored of God to be the recipients of so great a salvation. Even the prophets of old, though anticipating and predicting it, were not privileged to share in it. As Moffatt writes, "They could neither experience it nor understand the hour or method of its realization."

[14]Selwyn feels that the prophets of the apostolic church are referred to in this verse, but he has few who follow him in this opinion. Kelly, for instance, answers Selwyn's arguments and concludes that we are "justified in taking **the prophets** in its obvious and natural sense, i.e. as referring to the OT prophets, and indeed to the OT in general, since the Law and the Writings (cf. esp. the Psalms) were regarded by early Christians as prophetic."

[15]Kelly appropriately calls attention to the fact that Peter's reference to the prophets does not take notice of every aspect of Hebrew prophecy. "In their historical setting the prophets were not so much concerned to peer into the future as to announce God's verdict on the world in which they lived. Inevitably, however, with their eschatological approach to history, their attention was directed to the Day of the Lord, when the condemnation of the wicked and the salvation of God's chosen would be finally accomplished, and they scanned the horizon for signs of its advent."

cross—as in the resurrection, the ascension, the enthronement, and His second coming.

- The prophets, having spoken of these things, made earnest inquiry as to the time when they would happen (v. 11). "Inquired" and "searched" (ASV) are synonyms, the use of the two words together conveying rhetorical effect. NIV translates, "searched intently and with the greatest care." Both are compound forms and therefore intensive in force. "What time and what kind of time" (NIV: "the time and circumstances" [cf. NEB])[16] means that they inquired as to the time and/or the character of the time that would see the fulfillment of these great events. "The former means, the very date itself: the latter, the kind of period, to be known by various events" (Bengel). They knew what they prophesied; they knew not, and sought to understand, when the prophecy would be fulfilled.
- It was revealed to them that in their prophecies they were serving not themselves but Peter's readers (and, we may add, others like them). "The great revelation [to the prophets] of suffering and glory awakes [in them] an eager desire to know when and how these things shall be, and this is answered by a further revelation" (Bigg). That further revelation was that in their prophecies of the Messiah's sufferings and glory they were ministering not to their own day but to an age to come.

*Second,* the salvation of which the prophets spoke was the substance of Christian preaching (v. 12b). Stress is placed on the fact that those who proclaimed the message acted under the influence of "the Holy Spirit sent from heaven." (Compare Heb. 2:4 for the idea of the Spirit's assisting and confirming the preaching of the gospel.) "Sent from heaven," an allusion to the event of Pentecost, suggests the divinity of the Spirit.

*Third,* the greatness of the messianic salvation is further indicated by the fact that it is the object of angelic inquiry (v. 12c). It is significant that the Greek uses no article with the word for "angels," thus heightening the qualitative force of the

[16]The RSV has "what person or time" (cf. NASB).

term. "Beings such as angels" might capture the meaning. "To look into" translates a word that literally means "to stoop to look into." (It is the word used of the disciples stooping to look into the open tomb from which Jesus had risen [Luke 24:12; John 20:5, 11].) But the word came to suggest "study intently." Here the idea is that the blessings of the gospel "excite the envious interest of the angels" (Hunter; cf. Eph. 3:10).

Charles Wesley's words seem to catch the impact of the present passage:

> Angels in fix'd amazement
> Around our altars hover,
> With eager gaze
> Adore the grace
> Of our Eternal Lover.

### B. The Obligations Inherent in Those Privileges: Appeals for Holy Conduct (1:13–2:10)

The very first word of verse 13 ("Therefore") is of considerable significance, showing that what is said in the verses to follow has a close connection with what has been set forth in the preceding verses. It is open to question whether the backward reference in the word embraces all that was said in verses 3–12 or only what is contained in verses 10–12. We are assuming the former to be true. (Compare Paul's use of "therefore" in Rom. 12:1.) The word points up that the obligations described in this section flow from the believer's experience with God in the new birth (along with the hope, the inheritance, and the salvation accompanying that birth, vv. 3–5), his present joy in Christ (vv. 6–9), and the greatness of the messianic salvation (vv. 10–12). The stress in verses 3–12 was on privilege; here (1:13; 2:10) it is on responsibility.

The preceding paragraph has said much about the future: a hope that looks to the future, an inheritance reserved for us in heaven, and a salvation to be revealed in the last time. The verses now to be considered make it abundantly clear that there is a very practical side to Christianity and that it speaks powerfully to our present situation. They set forth the urgent moral responsibilities that accompany the Christian's exalted privileges.

To present Peter's thought in neat outline form is difficult, for he moves back and forth from appeals about duty to expressions of motive and incentive. The commentaries, though in general agreement as to the main thrust of this unit, arrange its details somewhat differently. Some treat 1:13–25 separately; others include 2:1–3 with these verses; others, whom we are following, take 1:13–2:10 as a single unit.

As the passage is rendered in nearly all of our English versions, it contains numerous appeals or moral demands. (The KJV contains at least eight imperatives in 1:13–2:3; the RSV, nine; the NIV, ten; the ASV, six.) A look at the Greek text, however, reveals that in all of 1:13–2:10 there are only five imperative verbs.[17] These have to do with hope (v. 13), holiness (vv. 14–16), reverence (fear) (vv. 17–21), love (vv. 22–25), and growth (2:1–3). All else that is written in the passage is subordinate to and a development of these ideas. The whole passage amounts to an exposition of the Christian, as opposed to the pagan, way of life.

### *1. Cultivation of Hope (1:13)*

If Paul was the apostle of faith and John the apostle of love, Peter may well be thought of as the apostle of hope. In this epistle the Greek verb meaning "to hope" appears twice (1:13, 3:5), and the noun for hope appears three times (1:3, 21; 3:15).

The central thought of verse 13 is expressed in the words "set your hope" (in Greek a single imperative word, *elpisate*). It is interesting to observe that in 1:3 it is said that believers have been *born* to a living hope. Here they are *commanded* to hope. It is one of many instances of a remarkable blending of indicatives and imperatives exhibited in the New Testament (cf. Col. 2:20, "you died with Christ," and Col. 3:5, "Put to death, therefore . . ."). The essence of it is, "Be what you are! Realize in actual experience what God has made possible by His grace." The tense of the verb (a Greek aorist) gives a note of urgency to

[17]This point is made only to justify the outline of the passage that we are proposing. It is recognized that several of the Greek participles in this passage may have imperative force. But it remains true that the key demands are expressed by the Greek imperatives that occur in the passage; the participles derive their imperative force from the imperative verbs.

the command. It has what the grammarians speak of as "ingressive" force, meaning "start to hope." Thus, "it implies the purposeful adoption of a new attitude of mind and heart" (Beare).

The meaning of hope has been discussed at 1:3. Suffice it to say here that it is a combination of desire and expectancy and suggests waiting with joyful anticipation. To hope "fully" ("perfectly," ASV; "to the end," KJV)[18] means to hope strongly, wholeheartedly, unwaveringly.

"Girding up the loins" of the mind (ASV; "prepare your minds for action," NIV) speaks of intellectual effort, and being "sober" (ASV; "be self-controlled," NIV) speaks of overall discipline of life. Both actions are represented as accompaniments of (perhaps preparation for) hope. Both "prepare" and "be self-controlled" translate Greek participles, and though there is an imperative flavor to both terms in this context, they are actually subordinate to and amplify the command to hope. The idea appears to be that the actions described by these two participles encourage, nurture, and condition Christian hope. "Prepare your minds" ("Girding up," ASV) is an allusion to the dress customs of men in Peter's day. Long, flowing robes were worn, and before a man engaged in strenuous physical activity, it was necessary to gather up his robe and tuck it under his belt at the waist. Expressions like "roll up your sleeves," "pull yourself together" are modern equivalents.

Girding up "the loins of [the] mind" means to prepare one's self mentally, to be alert and ready in one's spiritual and mental attitudes. (NIV's "prepare your minds for action" captures the sense.) More specifically it is a call for preparedness in reference to the Lord's coming (Kelly). The Christian, according to Cranfield, must make a real effort to understand Christian hope, using vigorous concentration and determined resolution.

[18]It is debated whether the adverb "fully" is to be construed with "be self-controlled" (i.e., be fully [perfectly] sober [self-controlled]) or with "set your hope." Hort, Beare, Bigg, and others take the former position. Most interpreters advocate the latter construction (e.g., Selwyn, Kelly, Cranfield, Moffatt, and, among the versions, KJV, ASV, RSV, NIV, etc.). On the basis of the Greek text either construction is possible.

> Such strenuous thinking . . . can seldom have been more urgently needed than today. . . . It is a pathetic feature of contemporary church life that there are still plenty in the pews who clamor for shorter and lighter sermons and bright and easy services, and not a few in the pulpits are prepared to pander to popular taste. . . . Peter's slogan is a call . . . for sermons that teach, not merely entertain, and for church members who will not shirk the discipline of intellectual effort, a call to the strenuous but exhilarating adventure of trying to understand ever more and more deeply the gospel.

Sobriety (NIV: "self-control") is a favorite theme with Peter (cf. 4:7; 5:8). The Greek word primarily denoted abstinence from wine, the avoidance of drunkenness. But it came to have a much broader meaning than this; in the NT it usually denotes overall self-control and clarity of mind—sobriety in conduct, speech, and judgment (things that in fact accompany abstinence from alcoholic beverages). In the NT it usually occurs in contexts having an eschatological connotation (as here), and it rebukes both self-indulgence and reckless fanaticism as we look toward the end. Our eyes are to be turned upward, but our feet must be planted firmly on the ground.

The *object* on which hope must be fixed is "the grace to be given you when Jesus Christ is revealed" (v. 13b). "Grace" here stands for the whole redemptive activity of God in Christ, what was referred to earlier as "the salvation that is ready to be revealed in the last time" (1:5). This grace was inaugurated with the incarnation (Titus 2:11), is in process of being brought to us now (see margin of the ASV text), and will reach its consummation at the last day, when Christ returns in glory (referred to here as "the revelation of Jesus Christ," ASV; NIV, "when Jesus Christ is revealed," NIV).

### 2. *Cultivation of Holiness (1:14–16)*

It seems best to put a period at the end of verse 13 (as in RSV, NIV, and others) and make verses 14–16 a separate unit (broken up in the NIV into three sentences, for the sake of clarity). The grammar of verses 13–16, however, is not at all simple and clear, and were it not for the adversative "but" at the beginning of verse 15, the punctuation of KJV and ASV, making verses 13–16 a single sentence, would perhaps be preferable. It is not a matter of great importance. Either way there appears to be a slight irregularity in the construction. If a new sentence is begun at verse 14, the participial construction translated "do not conform" probably should be taken as an instance of the imperatival force of the Greek participle. The command to holiness of life is stated both negatively (v. 14) and positively (vv. 15, 16).

**a. The Prohibition against Worldly Conformity (1:14).** The negative statement is that the readers "not conform to the evil desires" that had been characteristic of their past pagan lives. This period is described as a time "when you lived in ignorance," the latter being a phrase that suggests that the recipients of this letter were mostly Gentiles. The picture is that of people without knowledge of God ("ignorance") and enslaved to their passions ("evil desires"). Since the word for "conform" is in the present tense, it might be rendered, "do not continue to fashion (conform) yourselves, etc." The total idea is that of turning life in a new direction, ceasing to conform one's self to the manners and morals of pagan society.

The motivation and incentive for the performance of this command is the recollection on the part of the readers that, now that they are Christians, the determining quality of their lives must be obedience (14a; cf. 1:2), for they are "obedient children." In effect Peter was saying, "Remember who and what you are."

In addressing his readers as "obedient children" (lit., "children of obedience") Peter employed an expression Hebraic in character (cf. "children of light" [Luke 16:8; 1 Thess. 5:5; Eph. 5:8]; "sons of wickedness" [2 Sam. 7:10]; "sons of the kingdom" [Matt. 8:12]). In such constructions the genitive does not simply express a quality, but "fastens on an essential property or role of the persons described" (Kelly). Obedience, it should be noted, is another key word of this letter.

**b. The Command to Be Holy (1:15, 16).** The positive command to the readers is: "be holy in all you do." The verb might more literally be rendered, "Begin to be" or "Become." If we remember that these were relatively new converts (cf. 2:1, 2), this emphasis in the verb takes on special significance. The word for "holy," one of the great words of the Bible, denotes separateness, dedication, consecration, and is used for persons and things withdrawn from ordinary use. The opposite of "holy" is "profane" or "common." In Greek the words for "saint," "sanctify," and "holy" are all built on the same root. In itself the word "holy" does not have special ethical or moral connotation. That comes from contextual considerations: the nature of that to which one is dedicated. Women dedicated to the ancient pagan goddess Astarte were said to be "holy," but because of the gross immorality associated with the worship of that pagan deity such women were temple prostitutes. On the other hand, holiness in persons dedicated to the God of the Bible, a God of absolute moral purity, means that they, like their God, are marked by moral purity.

Verse 15a, the second and third words of which ("just as"; Gr., *kata*) convey the idea of moral conformity to a model, represents God as *the standard* for Christian holiness. The command, in effect, says, "Do what is in accordance with the character of God. Conform your mind, will, and conduct to Him." It could be read: "In likeness to the Holy One who called you . . . " (Beare) or "As he who called you is holy . . ." (cf. KJV, ASV, RSV, NIV). Either way, the thought is that God Himself is to be the standard of holiness for His people.

Verse 16 represents the holy nature of God as the incentive or motivation for Christian holiness: "for it is written: 'Be holy, because I am holy.'" (These are words that run like a refrain through Lev. [11:44; 19:2; 20:7, et al.) In the case of God's holiness the pervading idea is that of otherness, difference, complete separateness from evil. The new Israel, to whom Peter addresses his letter, are "saints" (lit., "holy ones") by virtue of a divine call, and as Israel of old was to express holiness in outward conduct, so Christians are to be holy in all they do.

### 3. *Cultivation of Godly Fear (1:17–21)*

The main statement of these verses is: "live your lives as strangers here in reverent fear" (v. 17b). "Live" translates a word (*anastraphēte*) that is often rendered "conduct yourselves" (RSV). The NT uses it of outward conduct, of life in its relations with others. "Your lives as strangers" translates a single word in Greek (ASV, "sojourning"; Gr., *paroikias*, from which the English "parish" is derived). It denotes a temporary stay (a pilgrimage) and is a reference to the Christian's life on earth. Its use of the transitoriness of the Christian's stay on earth is reminiscent of Paul's assertion in Philippians 3:20 that "our citizenship is in heaven."

"Fear," another key word of this epistle (2:17, 18; 3:2, 15; cf. 2:6, 14), suggests reverence, awe, and humility. It is not the cringing terror of a slave before an offended master, but the reverential awe of a son toward a beloved and esteemed father. It is the spirit that shrinks from anything that would grieve God. It is the becoming humility of the creature toward the Creator. It reflects an attitude of dependence, a recognition of our accountability to God. Such fear is the safeguard of holiness. The thrust of the apostle's command is that Christians are not to presume on God's favor but are, with becoming reverence and humility, to stand in awe of Him.

The whole statement implies that since the readers are conscious of a filial relation to God (they "call on a Father"), they might be tempted to expect special treatment from Him.

To encourage his readers to demonstrate godly fear, Peter reminds them of three facts: (1) The life they live on earth is but a brief pilgrimage. The language employed suggests the brevity and transitoriness of life. (See above discussion on "live your lives as strangers.")

Our years are like the shadows
 On sunny hills that lie,
Or grasses in the meadows
 That blossom but to die:

A sleep, a dream, a story
 By strangers quickly told,
An unremaining glory
 Of the things that soon are old.

O Thou who canst not slumber,
 Whose light grows never pale,
Teach us aright to number
 Our years before they fail.

—Beckersteth

(2) The God they invoke as Father (cf. Matt. 6:9; Luke 11:2; Rom. 8:15) is an impartial Judge who takes into account

"each man's work" (v. 17). As an impartial Judge He grants no special indulgence to His children. It is an expression of God's infinite condescension that we are allowed to call him "Father." He continues to be the impartial Judge of all mankind. "The more truly, the more intimately, we know him, the more of awe and reverence we shall feel" (Cranfield).

The people of God should have a healthy dread of God's judgment and shape their lives accordingly, never taking their privileged status as His children to be a license to sin. The privilege of being God's people does not entitle us to sin with impunity. It is a powerful motive for deeper commitment to His will and way.

(3) The redemption they have experienced is transcendently great (vv. 18–21). To point this up, the passage focuses on three aspects of redemption.

• Its great cost to God. The readers were redeemed, "not with perishable things . . . but with the precious blood of Christ" (vv. 18–19). A redemption purchased at such a price must never be treated lightly and should provoke not presumption, but a sense of profound gratitude to God.

This is an immensely important passage requiring careful study. The heart of it is the word "redeem." What does it mean? The basic lexical definition of the Greek term is "set free" or "liberate." Used over a hundred times in the OT (LXX), it occurs only three times in the NT (Luke 24:21; Titus 2:14, and here). However, several words built on the same root are found in the NT: *antilutron* ("ransom"), *lutrōsis* ("redemption"), *lutron* ("ransom," "means of release"), and (the one used with greatest frequency) *apolutrōsis* ("redemption"). In the OT this word group was in early times used of the redemption of property held in mortgage (Lev. 25:25–28) or of a payment made to God for the ransom of the firstborn (Num. 18:15). Later the verb we are considering came to be used in the more general sense of a rescue or a deliverance from enemies, from sin, from death, from exile, and (especially) of God's deliverance of the Israelites from Egyptian bondage.

In our passage that from which believers are delivered is not sin as such but what Peter calls "the empty way of life handed down to you from your forefathers" (v. 18b). "Empty" means worthless, futile, useless, having no goal, no purpose (cf. Eph. 4:17). "Handed down to you from your forefathers" suggests not only that this was the kind of life the readers' ancestors had followed, but also that it was the kind of life in which the readers themselves had been reared. The thought is that through redemption in Christ they had experienced a moral transformation.

Such redemption (deliverance) was effected by the payment of a price (cf. Mark 10:45; Titus 2:14). That price was not perishable things, such as silver or gold, but rather "precious [i.e., of great worth, valuable, costly] blood."

• Its place in the purpose of God. Verse 20, with its assertion that Christ was "chosen before the Creation of the world," teaches what Selwyn calls the "transcendent origin" of our redemption. Christ's sacrifice was not an afterthought with God. It was not an alternate plan that God chose because things had not turned out as He had hoped. It was rooted in eternity, destined before the beginning of history to be offered in our behalf. "Chosen" translates a word that is often rendered "foreknown." (See the discussion of "foreknowledge" at 1:1.) The NIV rendering is felicitous, for the Greek word denotes much more than prescience.

Christ was chosen before Creation "but was revealed in these last times for your sake" (20b). "The last times" denotes the final age of all the periods that constitute time—the last epoch of human history.

There are two very significant implications in Peter's statement. First, there is the thought that with the incarnation, death, and resurrection of Christ the last age of human history has arrived. All of us who have lived since that great cluster of divine activity occurred have lived in the last age (cf. Acts 2:16f, Heb. 1:2; 9:26). We only await its consummation. Second, the language assumes the pre-existence of Christ, that is, that He existed prior to His incarnation (cf. John 1:1ff; 1 Peter 1:11).

• Its divine certification in Christ's resurrection and exaltation (v. 21). The twenty-first verse does two things: First, it describes the readers as persons who through Christ "believe in God." The idea is that their faith has been mediated through Christ, that He who spoke of Himself as the way to the Father is the One through whom Christians have come to know God. "Believers" renders a verbal adjective that may indicate either belief or loyalty. Perhaps both meanings are in the word as it is used here: It is through the agency of Christ that we believe; it is also through Him and the power He imparts that we are kept loyal to God.

Second, this verse characterizes God, the object of Christian faith, as the One who "raised him [Jesus] from the dead and glorified him." The thought seems to be that the Father saw Christ's work as having accomplished its aim and in consequence of this, He raised Christ from the dead and gave Him glory. The resurrection and exaltation of Christ, then, are the glorious proofs of God's having accepted the redemptive work of the Son. The result is that Christians' faith and hope, the fruits of an accomplished redemption, are in God.

### *4. Cultivation of Love (1:22–25)*

The preceding verses have reminded the readers that they live in an alien world (cf. 1:17), and in light of the perils that surround them in such a world they have been urged to let reverent fear of God characterize their conduct. The present paragraph is pervaded with the thought that they are not in complete isolation in this hostile world. They are part of a spiritual community made up of brothers and sisters in Christ. They share a common faith and common interests and are to love each other sincerely and heartily. The nature of the appeal is seen in verse 22b; the grounds for it, in verses 22a, 23–25. The opening words of verse 23 may be seen as parallel to the opening words of verse 22. The main word in both passages is a perfect tense participle that in both instances modifies the verb "love" (NIV 22b). In a way, the two participles complement one another, describing from two points of view what happens when one becomes a Christian. Morally, he experiences inward purification (v. 22a); but, more fundamental than that, he enters upon a new life—a life that is a result of the creative activity of God.

*5. Nurture of the New Life (2:1–10)*

Peter has spoken of the new life communicated to his readers by faith in Christ (1:23). Now he enjoins them to cultivate and nurture that life so that they will be fit for service as the people of God. The structure of the passage is complex, and the imagery employed of the readers changes with bewildering suddenness. First, they are regarded as children in a family, then as stones in a building (temple), then as a company of priests, and finally as members of an elect nation. The OT is cited with such frequency that the entire passage almost forms a mosaic of quotations. Though the word "church" is not employed (either here or anywhere else in the letter), this entire passage is concerned with the church, that is, with believers as constituting the people of God.

The passage may be seen as falling into three parts, consisting of verses 1–3, verses 4–8, and verses 9–10. The dominant idea of the first unit is that believers are children in a family. In the second unit the principal concept is that believers are a company of priests (though this is closely joined to the related idea of their being parts of a temple). In verses 9–10 the most prominent thought is that believers are a chosen race, a holy nation, a people belonging uniquely to God. With each of these motifs there is a duty enjoined that corresponds to the imagery. As children, believers are to nurture the new life and grow "up in . . . salvation." As a company of priests they are to offer up spiritual sacrifices. And as the people of God they are to show forth the excellencies of the God who called them to be His. Thus, there is a personal duty (vv. 1–3), a priestly duty (vv. 4–8), and a missionary duty (vv. 9–10).

**a. Christians as Children in a Family: Grow Up to the Attainment of Full and Final Salvation (2:1–3).** Peter addresses his readers as "newborn babies" (v. 2), suggesting that they had been Christians for a relatively short time. The idea of childhood was perhaps suggested by the reference to the readers' having been "born again" (1:23).

Two appeals are given, one with negative overtones (v. 1) and the other positive (v. 2). The essence of the first appeal (v. 1) is that the readers renounce sin, that is, put away from themselves those things (mainly attitudes) that will hinder growth. "Rid yourselves" translates a participle that, in this context, may be the equivalent of an imperative verb (cf. RSV, NEB, Beare, et al.). The figure in the Greek word is that of stripping off (or away), like the stripping off of a garment from one's body. Sin must not be condoned, excused, covered, or harbored in the heart. It must be dealt with drastically and decisively.

The sins to be stripped away (renounced) represent types of conduct incompatible with the brotherly love described above. They appear to be listed in groups, each group preceded in the Greek text by the modifier "all." Perhaps no special significance is to be read into this. However, the threefold use of "all" may suggest that Peter was differentiating three separate classes of sins. "Malice" is an all-inclusive word, translating the most general word for evil used in the Greek NT. Among its meanings are "ill-will," "spite," and "vicious disposition."

The next grouping includes "deceit, hypocrisy, envy." The first word speaks of treachery or crookedness in dealing with other people. It denotes an attitude that disrupts fellowship. "Hypocrisy" suggests play-acting, pretending to be what one is not. Actually, the word is a plural in Greek, "hypocrisies." The plural calls attention to various expressions or acts of hypocrisy. The Greek word rendered "envy" is also plural. The term may denote envy, jealousy, or spite. Selwyn calls this sin "a constant plague of all voluntary organizations, not least religious organizations."

In the final class a single sin is mentioned: "slander." The Greek word (*katalalias*, lit., "speaking against," "talking down") is understood by some to mean slander or insult. Selwyn thinks it denotes the habit of disparagement rather than open slander, adding that it is "often the fruit of envy" (p. 153). Souter defines it as backbiting. The "all" of the Greek text is perhaps rightly interpreted in the NIV to mean "of every kind."

The second appeal (v. 2), which is positive, alludes to the spiritual infancy of the readers ("newborn babies")[19] and calls

[19] Selwyn, following Hort, thinks we must not extract from the words any allusion to the length of time the readers had been Christians. They are added, he explains, simply to make the imagery more vivid. "What the author wants to

on them to "long for the spiritual milk which is without guile." Having laid aside all that hinders growth, they are to desire that which will promote it. "Crave" translates a very strong Greek word that expresses intense, yearning desire. In the present passage the imagery is that of the infant nestled in its mother's arms and craving with intense desire the nourishment of the mother's breast.

"Spiritual milk" is variously understood, the focus of attention being on the meaning of the Greek word here rendered "spiritual." Used in the NT only here and in Romans 12:1, the term seems to be interpreted by most modern commentators either in the sense of spiritual or rational (cf. Hort, Moffatt, Selwyn, Beare). (These also appear to be the dominant ideas in the renderings of Rom. 12:1; a check of that shows that KJV, Phillips, Montgomery, Knox, and others convey the thought of rational or intelligent; ASV, RSV, NIV, NEB, and others employ "spiritual.")

"Word" should not be taken to refer to Christ, the personal Word (cf. John 1:1), but to the message of the gospel—for all practical purposes, the Scriptures. There seems to be an obvious allusion to 1:23, where God's "word" (*logos*) is denoted as the preached message instrumental in the readers' new birth.

"Milk" is to be understood as a metaphorical term for the divinely-given sustenance derived from the gospel. It is described as being "pure" because it is free from human deceit. The noun form of the root word was translated as "deceit" in verse 1. When used to describe foods, the word used here generally meant unadulterated, uncontaminated, or pure.

Peter's intention in urging his readers to feed on the word was that "by it" they might "grow up in . . . salvation." "By it"[20] refers primarily to the word (i.e., the gospel message), but in light of the thought in the next verse the term may combine an allusion to Christ, the one proclaimed in the word (so Kelly).

The Greek term for "grow" was a common one for the

---

express is the ardour of the suckled child." However, we should not reject altogether the possibility (or probability) that the expression suggests the recency of the readers' conversion to Christ.

[20] It could be translated "in/by him" (i.e., Christ), but the NIV rendering is to be preferred.

growth of children. Selwyn interprets it here with the double sense of thriving on and growing up.

"Salvation"[21] in this context denotes full and final salvation, that is, the consummation of the saving experience begun in the new birth (cf. 1:5; Rom. 13:11; 1 John 3:2). Kelly defines it as "the glory and blessedness which God has prepared for His elect at the End." The growth involved can be experienced only as one receives spiritual nourishment, such nourishment as comes only from God's Word. Surely the main reason for the stunted growth of many modern Christians may be traced to their neglect of that Word.

Two facts are mentioned in verses 1–3 to support Peter's appeals: (1) His readers had been brought into a new life, and (2) they had found the Lord to be gracious. The first is suggested in verse 1 by the word "therefore," which points back to 1:23–25 and the mention of the new birth experienced by the readers. The second is stated in verse 3: "now that you have tasted that the Lord is good."

The earlier reference to "milk" perhaps suggested the term "tasted"; its meaning, however, is not metaphorical ("experience") but literal. The word for "good" may mean kind, loving, good, merciful, etc. However, the context (with its references to food) seems to justify Kelly's paraphrase, "delicious to the taste." The thought is that since our first experiences with Christ have been sweet and pleasant to the palate, this should make us yearn to drink more deeply of His inexhaustible goodness.

**b. Believers as a Spiritual House and as a Company of Priests (2:4–8).** The emphasis of verses 1–3 has been on the individual's responsibility to grow in his salvation. But growth is not just an individual matter. We grow not in isolation but within a society of redeemed people. Therefore, beginning with verse 4, Peter stresses the corporate life of Christians.

Verses 4, 5. These verses are the heart of the unit of which they are a part. They declare that believers in coming to Christ the living stone are themselves transformed into living stones and become a part of God's great spiritual temple (made up of believers); moreover, they become a company of priests who

[21] Some Greek manuscripts do not contain words for "unto ['in,' NIV] salvation." This accounts for their absence from the KJV.

offer spiritual sacrifices to God. The imagery is mixed, combining the ideas of Christians as living stones in a building or temple (vv. 4, 5a) and as a company of ministering priests (v. 5b). The two concepts, however, are not entirely unrelated, for temple and priesthood were intimately bound together, and one readily suggested the other.

Several matters of considerable importance are brought out in verses 4 and 5. First, they tell the means by which believers become a part of God's great spiritual temple and of the company of priests ministering for Him. This is stated in the opening words of verse 4: "As you come to him."[22] "Coming" to Christ suggests being joined to Him, being united to Him in faith at the time of conversion (cf. John 5:40; 6:35, 37, 44, 65, et al.). It may be significant, however, that the Greek participle ("as you come") is in the present tense. Beare, for instance, says the tense suggests that "the Christian keeps coming to Christ" (p. 93).

Second, Christ, who was pictured in the preceding verses as the Christian's sustenance, is represented here as "a living Stone," chosen and honored by God (v. 4). The figure alludes to Psalm 118:22 (cited below, in v. 7), that is here (as elsewhere in the NT [e.g., Acts 4:11]) interpreted as messianic. In the historical setting of the psalm the stone seems to represent Israel, "harried by world-powers and thrown away as useless, but in spite of all given marvelous honor by God" (Kelly, p. 88). Early Christians saw Psalm 118:22 as prophesying Christ's death at the hands of men and His vindication by God in the resurrection. "Living" calls attention to the fact that Christ is the Risen One, able to impart life to those who come to Him in faith. "Stone," a messianic title, suggests strength and stability.

Third, the last half of verse 4 contrasts the world's attitude toward Christ with the attitude of God toward Him. He was rejected by men, but with God He is elect (chosen, choice) and precious (held in honor, esteemed). The context seems to suggest that the readers, persecuted and rejected by their

[22] Some interpreters understand the Greek participle translated "as you come" (Gr., *proserchomenoi*) to have the force of an imperative (cf. RSV, Moffatt, Goodspeed, Bigg), but it seems better to retain the more usual meaning of the participle, as above.

unbelieving neighbors, share in the vindication and honor of Christ. In other words, they too are "chosen and precious" (cf. v. 5, "you also").

Fourth, verse 5a suggests the nature of the Christian fellowship. Two figures are used. In verse 5a it is affirmed that as believers come to Christ, the living Stone, they are, as it were, assimilated to Him and themselves become living stones. As such, they are "being built into a spiritual house, to be a holy priesthood." That is to say, believers by virtue of their union with Christ form the true dwelling place for God (cf. Eph. 2:19–22; 1 Cor. 3:16f; 2 Cor. 6:16f). They are a "spiritual" house (temple) because in contrast with the Jerusalem temple this one is immaterial, not made by hands. Perhaps it is "spiritual" also in the sense that it is indwelt, pervaded by the Spirit of God. The word for "house" combines the ideas of house (temple) and household (family), but the context (with its reference to stones and building) places primary emphasis on the idea of a temple. Perhaps both concepts (household and house) suggest the close-knit unity that characterizes the people of God.

The figure changes quickly from that of a temple to that of priests ministering in that temple. That is to say, the living stones, when they are built into a temple of God, become also the priests who minister in the temple. They are built into a spiritual house, "to be [for the purpose of being] a holy priesthood" (v. 5a). The word behind the term "priesthood" is a collective and means a body (i.e., a company) of priests. The thought is that the entire Christian community constitutes a body of priests. They are a "holy" priesthood in the sense that they are consecrated to God, set apart for His work and worship.

Fifth, the priestly *function* of Christians is expressed in the explanatory words, "offering spiritual sacrifices acceptable to God through Jesus Christ" (v. 5b). The term "spiritual" suggests that these sacrifices are non-material; that is, they consist not in the offering of "the blood of bulls and goats" as a covering for sin. Christ as the Lamb of God has already offered the one necessary sacrifice for sins. That sacrifice cannot be repeated, nor does it need to be. There may be the added notion that the sacrifices are spiritual because inspired by the Spirit. What these sacrifices are may be seen in passages such as Romans

12:1 (our bodies [lives]), Philippians 2:17 (our service), 4:18 (our substance), and Hebrews 13:15, 16 (our praise and our good deeds). Such sacrifices are "acceptable to God through Jesus Christ." Thus it is not in themselves that they are acceptable, but their acceptability to God comes "through Jesus Christ."

Verses 6–8. These verses are for the most part Scripture quotations explaining the word "stone" (v. 4). Three passages are cited: Isaiah 28:16, Psalm 118:22, and Isaiah 8:14. All three passages are seen to be messianic, and in all three the Messiah is likened to a stone. Their common theme, according to Kelly, "is that the destiny of men, and of the readers and their persecutors in particular, is determined by their attitude to Him."

In the first quotation (Isa. 28:16), which represents Christ as "a chosen and precious cornerstone," we see *God's* estimate of Him. "The chief features of a cornerstone," writes Selwyn, "are that it controls the design of the edifice and that (unlike a foundation stone) it is visible." Christ, he explains, is, of course, both cornerstone (here) and foundation stone (1 Cor. 3:11). (References to cornerstones and foundation stones do not mean as much to us as they did to the ancients. It's difficult for us to imagine the immensity of some of the building stones of that age. One stone has been found that was 69′ x 12′ x 13′.)

"Chosen" may mean either "elected" or "choice" (in the sense of "select"). "Precious" may mean either "valuable" (cf. NEB, "of great worth") or "honorable," "held in honor," "esteemed." The latter meaning is preferred by Bigg, Kelly, and others (Kelly: "a choice and honoured corner-stone"). Arndt and Gingrich prefer the former, seeing in the word a reference to "the preciousness of the material" used in the cornerstone. Most versions and commentaries seem to accept this meaning.

Those who see Christ as God does and put their faith in Him "will never be put to shame" (v. 5b; Weymouth, "disappointed"). Stated positively, the thought is that they shall come to honor.

Verse 7a amounts to an exposition of the quotation given in the preceding verse and may be seen as making the point that the "preciousness" (honor) ascribed to Christ is shared by believers (see ASV)—both at the Judgment Day and at the present time.

Verse 7b asserts that for disbelievers—the word suggests a refusal to hear—there are other passages that are applicable. Two of these (Ps. 118:22 and Isa. 8:14) are quoted in verses 7c and 8a. The first quotation suggests that like the faithless builders in the OT passage, all unbelievers will have the mortification of seeing the stone that they rejected as worthless made the head of the corner. "Head of the corner" (KJV), which refers to the chief cornerstone, denotes the most important stone of the building. NIV renders the phrase as "capstone."[23] The second quotation (v. 8a) shows that Christ, the rejected stone, has not only proved to be the most important stone but also a stone over which His enemies stumble and fall into disaster. Christ is thus represented as "the key to all human destiny and the touchstone of all endeavor; faith in Him leads to honour, unbelief to disaster" (Beare). Whereas believers find Christ to be the stay and support of their lives, unbelievers trip over Him and collapse. Human destiny is determined by one's attitude toward Christ.

A "stone that causes men to stumble" is a stone that leads men to trip and lose their balance. "A rock that makes them fall" uses different words but has the same meaning. The two phrases are an instance of Hebrew parallelism, and stone/rock both refer to Christ.

Verse 8b is a comment on "stone of stumbling," explaining the cause of stumbling: "They [unbelievers] stumble because they disobey the message—which is also what they were destined for." This does not mean that God has appointed men to disobedience, but that He has foreordained stumbling to be the punishment of disobedience. "The will of God," writes

[23]Beare, following the *Westminster Dictionary of the Bible,* sees "the head of the corner" as the "massive cornerstone which is set not in the foundation, but at the upper corner of the building, to bind the walls firmly together. A huge stone suitable for this purpose would be useless to the builders in any other position, and would have to be 'rejected' while the walls were going up, yet its very size would make it a continual stumbling block to all concerned with the building as long as it lay on the ground unused."

Beare, "decrees the ruin of unbelief, as surely as the exaltation of faith."[24]

**c. Christians as a Chosen People, Belonging to God in a Special Way (2:9, 10).** As God's special people Christians are to minister as missionaries proclaiming abroad the mighty acts of God. Almost all of verses 9 and 10 is taken from the OT. The passage continues the description of the nature of the Christian community that was begun in verses 4 and 5 and interrupted in verses 6–8 by a somewhat parenthetical explanation of the word "stone."

Four phrases, derived from Exodus 19:5f and Isaiah 43:20f, are used in verse 9 to describe Christians: "a chosen people, a royal priesthood, a holy nation, a people belonging to God." In their original settings these phrases are applied to Israel, but by using them of Christians, Peter suggests that believing people are the new Israel (cf. Gal. 6:16; Rom. 2:28–29). Some think the idea is that Israel has now been supplanted by the Christian community, that the Christian community is the true heir of all the divine promises (Kelly). Others, however, feel the thought is not so much that the church has supplanted Israel as it is that the people of God now form a single community not bound to one nation but encompassing believing people from all nations.

"You" (first word of v. 9) is emphatic in the Greek, contrasting the status of Peter's readers with that of unbelieving people: "you in contrast to the disobedient and unbelieving." "A chosen people," from Isaiah 43:20, may pick up the word "chosen" from verses 4 and 6. It accentuates a certain parallelism between Christ and His people: He is the elect (Chosen One) of God, and His people share with Him in that privileged status. Too much, however, should not be made of this, for the word "chosen" was used of Peter's readers in the opening verse of the epistle. "People" translates a word that calls attention to blood relationship. Applied to the new Israel, blood relationship is no longer in mind; the focus is rather on corporate unity, Christians of all races being "one family in union with Christ" (Arichea and Nida).

---

[24]The same author feels that the divine decree should probably here be thought of as not limited to the consequences of unbelief but as including both the unbelief and its consequences (cf. Rom. 9:17–22).

"A royal priesthood" picks up an idea already given in a slightly different form in verse 5. The same word for "priesthood" is employed in both passages, and in both it is a collective term denoting a body or company of priests. The emphasis is on Christians in their corporate capacity, not as individuals. The Greek word for "priest" is never used in the NT of the church's ministers; "the whole Church, not a part of it, was to be a priesthood. The priestly service of the Church was something in which every member was to share" (Cranfield). Instead of "holy" (v. 5) the word "royal" is now used to describe the priesthood. The Greek word may be either an adjective or a noun. The only other place where it occurs in the NT is Luke 7:25, where it means "king's house" or "palace." Selwyn says that when the word is used as an adjective in the sense of "royal," it connotes a more intimate and personal relationship than the similar term *basilikos,* and is almost equivalent to "of [or belonging to] the king." So Christians may be thought of as a "royal" priesthood because they belong to and are in the service of Christ, their King (cf. TEV, "the King's priests"). Both Selwyn and Kelly prefer to read the word as a noun and see the phrase "royal priesthood" as containing not a single concept but two, each descriptive of the Christian community: "a royal house" or residence—"royal" (because the King dwells in its midst)—and "a company of priests." In designating Christians as a company of priests, Peter calls attention to the nearness of God that they enjoy and to the dedicated service that they are to render.

"A holy nation," a phrase derived from Exodus 19:6, means a nation dedicated to God and His service. "Holy" (see comments on 1:15, 16) does not imply that Christians are "paragons of virtue" but rather that they have been set apart for God's service.

Lastly, the Christian community is called "a people belonging to God." The meaning is that Christians are God's special people, the Greek word for "people" (*laos*) being in the Septuagint almost a technical term for Israel as distinguished from all other nations and calling attention to their intimate relationship with God. The NEB renders the phrase in our text, "a people claimed by God for his own."

In the last part of verse 9 Peter affirms the intention of God for the recipients of this letter in their capacity as God's new people. They exist as "a chosen people, a royal priesthood, etc." that they may declare the praises of him who called [them] . . . out of darkness into his wonderful light." The word "declare" means to proclaim, to make known. The Greek word has a prepositional prefix, that (according to some interpreters) is perfective, making the verb more emphatic: publish widely, etc. Arichea and Nida think the primary idea is proclaiming through speech, but they do not rule out the idea of proclamation through deed and example.

"Praises" translates a Greek word that the philosophers often used in the sense of moral excellence (cf. Weymouth, "perfections"). Selwyn says the plural form, which is rare in the Septuagint, would have suggested to Greeks both "the intrinsic glory of God's character" and the "noble acts" . . . by which He had revealed it throughout history. Arichea and Nida explain that the word was used in the pagan literature of Peter's day "to describe the powerful acts and miraculous deeds which were attributed to a god." Beare translates it "wonderful works."

Perhaps one of the "wonderful works" of God is suggested in the description of Him as the one "who called you out of darkness into his wonderful light." (The reference in these words is the conversion of Peter's readers from paganism [darkness] to Christianity [light]). But it seems that Peter was thinking mainly of the mighty acts of God in raising Christ from the dead and exalting him to the highest heaven (cf. 1:21).

Verse 10, employing language drawn from Hosea (1:6, 9; 2:2, 23), explains what Peter means by "darkness" and "light" and draws a further contrast between the readers' previous pagan state and their present position in Christ. In the past, they were a "no people"; now, they are "the people of God." Once they had not received God's mercy, but now they have experienced it. The word for "mercy," according to Arichea and Nida, "combines the elements of 'pity,' 'compassion,' and 'concern.' "

**For Further Study**

1. Verses 3–4 of chapter 2 affirm that Jesus' resurrection gave Christians a living hope. What other doctrinal or spiritual

help does Christ's resurrection provide? For an answer summarize the following passages of Scripture: Romans 1:3–4; 4:25; 1 Corinthians 15:12–19.

2. In 1:12 Peter said that angels had a desire to look into the things that God was doing. A similar statement referring to angelic activity appears in Ephesians 3:10. Compare Peter's statement with that of the Ephesian passage. For further information on the ministry and activity of angels see the article "Angel" in ZPEB.

3. Use a concordance to study the word "hope." How does hope differ from faith? How does hope function in the life of a human being? For further information, see the article "Hope" in ZPEB.

4. Using a concordance, find other passages in which the topic of redeeming or redemption is discussed. What is the spiritual result of redemption in our life? See the article "Redeemer, Redemption" in the ZPEB.

5. Notice the three Old Testament passages referred to in 1 Peter 2:4–8 (Isa. 28:16; Isa. 8:14; Psa. 118:22). Using an Old Testament commentary, discover the context and meaning of each passage as written by the Old Testament author.

# Chapter 3

## Obligations of Christians as a Pilgrim People

(1 Peter 2:11–3:12)

The concept of Christians as a special (elect) people, the recipients of high and holy privileges, has dominated Peter's epistle to this point. Now we enter upon a section in which the apostle addresses his readers as "aliens and strangers" (ASV, "sojourners and pilgrims") who live in the midst of a pagan society. This notion has by no means been entirely absent from the earlier portion of the book. The opening words, in fact, describe the readers as "strangers . . . scattered" (ASV, "sojourners of the Dispersion"; see comments on 1:1), and 1:17 calls upon them to "live [their] lives as strangers here in reverent fear" (ASV, "pass the time of your sojourning [pilgrimage] in fear"). But although the first section of the letter does indeed mention the idea of pilgrimage, the prevailing theme has been that Christians are a people of privilege. And these privileges carry with them weighty responsibilities.[1]

In the present unit the notion of pilgrimage is expressly mentioned only in 2:11, 12, but these two verses form a kind of general introduction to the unit and set the tone for all the

[1]Both the preceding unit and this give large place to exhortation. But there seem to be differences in emphasis and point of view. One of those differences underlies the above discussion, namely that in 1:3–2:10 the appeals are rooted and based upon the privileges enjoyed by believers. In 2:11–3:12 the appeals arise from Peter's recognition that his readers are living in the midst of a pagan society, that they were like exiles in a strange land. Beare puts it this way: "In the first section . . . the writer has spoken in a general way of the principles of holiness and love which govern the life of those whom God has regenerated and brought into the fellowship of the Church. In this section (2:11–3:12), he deals with particular issues of Christian conduct in a heathen environment."

appeals that follow. Cranfield observes that the "motif of pilgrimage and heavenly citizenship dominates the Christian understanding of life. We are in the world, but not of it; children of light for the time being living as strangers in the darkness" (p. 70).

Three lines of thought may be traced through the passage. There is first a general appeal (2:11, 12) that serves to introduce the entire section. This is followed by specific appeals to various classes within the church (2:13–3:7). Finally, there is a concluding appeal to the church as a whole in which emphasis is given to right attitudes toward one another (3:8–12).

## A. A General Appeal for Proper Conduct toward Unbelievers (2:11, 12)

The apostle has expounded the concept of Christians as the new people of God (2:1–10). Now he begins to explain the behavior that is proper for them as they live out their lives in the midst of a pagan society. The two verses we are now considering form a general introduction to this part of the letter.

The use of the term "Dear friends" at the beginning of verse 11 is thought by some interpreters (e.g., Beare, Arichea and Nida) to be an indication that Peter was consciously entering upon a new section of his letter.[2] It is probably to be taken here as an expression of special affection by Peter for his readers (cf. Goodspeed, NEB, Phillips), not as a simple term of address (cf. TEV: "My friends").

"I urge" is frequently employed in the NT in hortatory passages (cf. Rom. 12:1; Eph. 4:1; 1 Thess. 4:1, et al.). Connoting urgent and strong appeal, it could be rendered "beg" (Goodspeed, NEB) or "implore" (MLB).

In describing his readers as "aliens and strangers" Peter reflects the words of Abraham to the children of Heth: "I am an alien and a stranger among you" (Gen. 23:4; cf. Ps. 39:12). The Greek word for "aliens" (*paroikos;* used elsewhere in the NT only in Eph. 2:19; cf. 1:17, where a related word is used) strictly means "foreigner" or "exile," one who makes his home in a

---

[2] Hort, for instance, sees this word as the key to the structure of the book. Since it occurs both here and at 4:12, he accordingly understands the major divisions to be 1:1–2:10, then 2:11–4:11, and finally 4:12 to the end.

country but does not become a citizen. "Strangers" translates a word (*parepidēmos;* cf. 1:1) that literally denotes one who is a temporary visitor, one just passing through a foreign land with no intention of becoming either a citizen or a permanent resident. KJV, RSV and NKJV translate it "pilgrims."

It is doubtful that Peter intended a sharp distinction to be drawn by these two words. They are substantially the same in meaning. Used together, they produce a certain rhetorical effect, strengthening the one idea of alienation or exile (cf. NEB, "aliens in a foreign land"). The suggestion is that Christians, living as they do among non-Christians, are like aliens living in a foreign land. Their real citizenship is in heaven (Phil. 3:20); and on earth they have no "enduring city" (Heb. 13:14). This concept is not used by the NT writers in an escapist sense. On the contrary, the corollary they draw from it "is that the ideals and motives of the heavenly city should inspire the Christian's daily life" (Kelly).

*1. The Negative Appeal (2:11)*

Two appeals are issued, one negative (v. 11) and the other positive (v. 12). The negative appeal is that the readers "abstain from [lit., 'hold yourselves back from'; TEV, 'do not give in to'] sinful desires." "Abstain" is in the present tense, the idea being that abstinence from sinful desires is to be a continuing thing, a life-habit. Kelly interprets "fleshly lusts" (KJV) to mean "disorderly appetites connected with the body" but cautions against "reading out of [Peter's] words any innuendo that physical appetites are intrinsically sinful." NIV interprets it to mean "sinful desires."

These "sinful desires" are further described by the clause following, "which war against your soul." "Which" translates a qualitative relative pronoun ("which are of such nature that"). It may have explanatory or causal significance ("because" or "for"; cf. TCNT). If this is its significance here, then the clause is giving a reason for abstaining from these desires: they war against the soul.

"War," a very strong verb that suggests the most active opposition, is in the present tense. The thought is that fleshly lusts continually wage war against the soul. The latter word ("soul") appears to stand for the whole person, the essential being of man, not just the immaterial part of one's being (see 1:9, where there is a similar use of the word.

*2. The Positive Appeal (2:12)*

The positive appeal, stated in verse 12, shows Peter's concern for the church's reputation among nonbelievers. (See 1 Cor. 10:32; Col. 4:5; 1 Thess. 4:12; 1 Tim. 3:7; 5:14; Titus 2:5–10, 15; 3:1, 16 for expressions of similar concern by Paul.) The NIV, though not a literal rendering, brings out the meaning clearly: "Live such good lives among the pagans that, though they accuse you of doing wrong, they may see your good deeds and glorify God on the day he visits us." "Live such good lives" is a free rendering of a Greek construction that is more literally translated, "having [have, keep] your conduct among the Gentiles [pagans] good [i.e., honorable]." "Having" translates a Greek participle that most versions read as an imperative. "Conduct" (KJV, "conversation") translates a word that occurs four times in 1 Peter (here, 1:15; 3:1, 16). Sometimes rendered "manner of life" or "behavior" (ASV), it includes all the dimensions of one's life, personal and (especially) social. The Greek word for "good" sometimes means "beautiful." Here it may denote a beauty that is the outward sign of an inwardly good and honorable character.

The last part of verse 12, that is to some degree reminiscent of Matthew 5:16, sets forth the motive for (or purpose in) living this good life: "that, though they accuse you of doing wrong, they may see your good deeds and glorify God on the day he visits us." This is a rather free rendering of a Greek statement whose syntax is somewhat complex. "Accuse" (lit., "speak against") may refer to accusations in a court of law, but probably the word should be understood here in the non-legal sense of slander or malicious talk. At the time Peter wrote this letter it was not a crime to be a Christian, but Christians were often despised by their pagan neighbors and (at a later time) suspected and accused of the most vicious crimes, including disturbing the peace, incest, and cannibalism.

The NT provides insight into the kinds of charges that might have been made against Christians in the pagan world of

Peter's day—things such as interference with trade (cf. Acts 16:16; 19:23), setting slaves against their masters (cf. Philemon), children against parents, wives against husbands, disloyalty to Caesar (cf. John 19:12), and perhaps a revolutionary spirit generally, a disposition to "turn the world upside down" (Acts 17:6).

The Greek of verse 12 contains a prepositional phrase (ASV, "wherein") that is given a concessive meaning ("though") by the NIV. Some interpreters see in it a general temporal sense, "whenever" (cf. Selwyn, p. 170; TEV ("when"). Beare's paraphrase is perhaps best: "in the very matter wherein they slander you, etc." The thought is that the very things that are now the occasion of unbelievers' slander (namely, the Christian's faith and good works) will, as unbelievers reflect on them, bring the enemies of the gospel to "glorify God in the day of visitation."

To "glorify God" essentially means to praise Him, acknowledge His greatness and goodness. Some think the meaning here is that the accusers of the recipients of this letter would, by reflecting on the good deeds of Christians, be converted (and glorify or praise God) when He visits them in mercy. Others contend that glorifying God simply denotes that at the day of judgment the enemies of the gospel will recognize the rightness of the Christians whom they persecuted. "On the day he visits us" (lit., "in the day of visitation") reflects OT language. There, God "visits" to comfort or deliver (Exod. 3:16; 1 Sam. 2:21; Job 10:12), to punish (Exod. 32:24; Ps. 59:6; Job 29:4), or to carry out judicial investigation (Ps. 17:3).

Luke 19:44 affords a parallel, and in that passage the reference is to a visitation in mercy. Indeed, wherever the Greek noun (visitation) or the Greek verb (visit) is elsewhere used in the NT of a divine visitation, the reference is always to a visitation in mercy (cf. Luke 1:68, 78; 7:16; 19:44; Acts 15:14; Heb. 2:6). For this reason we are inclined to see that meaning in the present passage.

### B. Special Appeals Addressed to Various Classes among the Readers (2:13–3:7)

In this section are found the first of Peter's exhortations having to do with the various relationships of daily life: subjects to their rulers (2:13–17), slaves to their masters (2:18–25), wives to their husbands (3:1–6), and husbands to their wives (3:7). The passage should be compared with Romans 13:1–6; Ephesians 5:21–6:9; Titus 2; and Colossians 3:18–4:1. The topics of discussion must have frequently come up in Christian churches all over the Roman Empire; hence the need for instruction such as that given by Paul and Peter. The essential qualities that Peter insisted on are submission, harmonious living, brotherly love, humility, compassion, and a willingness to suffer insult and injury without striking back.

### *1. Duties of Citizens (Subjects) to Those Who Govern Them (2:13–17)*

The general principle laid down in this unit is that it is the duty of Christians to live a law-abiding and honorable life. They are indeed citizens of heaven (and should so regard themselves), but they must remember that they are also citizens upon earth; they are, like others, subject to human government and are to show their fidelity to Christ by being good citizens.

It is perhaps not without significance that this appeal for submission to governmental authorities follows immediately the reference to Christians' being foreigners and strangers in the world (2:11, 12). Recognition of their alien status might easily have led some rash, ill-informed believers to disregard their obligations to civil authority. Where the rulers were themselves pagans (as was the case in the area to which this letter was addressed), there might have been a special tendency to doubt that Christians were obligated to obey them.

**a. The Statement of Duty (2:13–14).** The main duty, stated in verse 13a, is submission.[3] "Submit yourselves for the Lord's sake to every authority instituted among men." Although "submit yourselves" translates a passive imperative, this particular Greek word may (and here does) have a middle (reflexive) force in the passive. This rendering brings out more clearly the voluntary character of the act. The aorist imperative, the form employed here, conveys a note of urgency and suggests that the action is to be undertaken decisively.

[3]This concept dominates the entire passage that extends from 2:14–3:6. See especially 2:13, 18; and 3:1.

The root meaning of the Greek verb, a compound form (*hypotassō*), is "rank yourselves under." The leading ideas here are recognition of and submission and obedience to authority.[4] In the NT it is used of the submission of the Christian to God (James 4:7), to the leaders of the church (1 Cor. 16:16), to civil authorities (Rom. 13:1; Titus 3:1; and here), and to one another (Eph. 5:21). It is also employed of the submission of wives to their husbands (1 Peter 3:1; Eph. 5:22; Col. 3:18), of slaves to their masters (1 Peter 5:5), and of the church to Christ (Eph. 5:24).

The extent of the subordination enjoined is suggested by the words "to every authority instituted among men." The precise meaning of the Greek text, that literally reads "to every human creation [or 'creature']," is much debated. Selwyn understands it to mean "every fundamental social institution, i.e., the state, the household, and the family." Kelly translates it "every human creature." This, he says, is the only sense that in this context can naturally be given to the Greek; "the writer is laying it down that the principle of the redeemed Christian life must not be self-assertion or mutual exploitation, but voluntary subordination of one's self to others." In Kelly's interpretation, for which there is much to be said, the sense is the same as that found in Ephesians 5:21, Romans 12:10, and Philippians 2:3f.

It should be acknowledged though, that the majority of interpreters have taken the view set forth in the NIV, namely, that the phrase in question refers to the institution of government or governmental authority. Assuming this to be the correct interpretation, we are to confine its reference to verses 13–17, not seeing it (as Kelly, Cranfield, and others do) to be a kind of general heading for the larger section including 2:13–3:12.

In verses 13b and 14 the principle of submission is specifically applied to the duty of subordination to the king (i.e., the Roman emperor) and to governors. The emperor is described as "supreme," because at the human level he was

[4]The word always expresses a voluntary subordination of one's self to others. In some contexts, though not here, it denotes simply putting the interests of others above our own and means about what Paul expresses in different language in Rom. 12:10 ("in honor preferring to one another") and Phil. 2:3 ("in lowliness of mind each counting others better than himself").

indeed the supreme authority. It is well to remember that the emperor at the time was Nero, not a particularly noble character! Governors (the officials and ministers sent to govern by the emperor's mandate) are to be obeyed because they are sent (appointed) by the higher authority (the king, emperor) to punish those who do wrong and to praise (commend) those who do right. What is meant by the commending of those who do right is not so easily understood, and it is not explained. Probably we are to see no more in the expression than that the governor looked approvingly on those citizens who behaved well.

This appeal for submission to governmental authority poses serious problems and must be carefully studied if one is to avoid error in applying it to life. A good rule of thumb is that higher authority must take precedence over lower authority. If obedience to a human law or authority would violate our allegiance to God, we must obey God at all costs. In point of fact, the man who wrote the words before us said on one notable occasion, "Judge for yourselves whether it is right in God's sight to obey you [the Jewish authorities] rather than God" (Acts 4:19). Later, under similar circumstances, he put it more bluntly, "We must obey God rather than men!" (Acts 5:29).

**b. The Reasons for the Duty (2:13b, 15).** Two reasons for subordination to governmental authority are given. The first is stated in verse 13a: "for the Lord's sake." Arichea and Nida give two possible meanings to this phrase. It may be understood as a reference to Christ's example: "as he was obedient to established authority, so the Christian must do likewise." If construed in this manner, the meaning is, "because of what the Lord has done" or "in order to follow the Lord's example." On the other hand, the phrase may mean "in order to honor the Lord" (p. 72). The latter seems to be the better way of interpreting the words.

The second reason (or incentive) for submission is given in verse 15: "For it is God's will that by doing good you should silence the ignorant talk of foolish men." The NIV rendering clearly states the essential meaning, and most of the versions agree with the interpretation that it reflects. For example, the GNB reads: "For this is God's will: he wants you to silence the ignorance of foolish men by the good things you do." Beare thinks that in the first part of the verse the word "is" may be more than a mere copula, having the sense of "is given effect" or "is recognized and carried out." Behind the word "it" is a Greek word (*houtos̄* "so," "in this manner") that some interpreters here translate "such." Kelly says that the "drift of the clause might be expressed by such a paraphrase as 'God's will is realized by your being dutifully obedient to the authorities.'" In his interpretation, the last half of the verse ("That by doing good, etc.") is loosely added as a sort of "explanatory afterthought," making the further point that when Christians comport themselves as obedient citizens they will silence those who falsely accuse them. These, however, are not matters of pressing importance, and (as said above), the NIV expresses the essential sense.

The accusations, Peter affirms, arise from ignorance, and those who make them are "foolish men." The Greek term is frequently used in the Septuagint of arrogant unbelievers who set themselves against God.

The spirit in which submission is to be given is set forth in verse 16. Peter perhaps anticipated that some of his readers, who had rightly learned that in Christ there is freedom, would find his insistence on submission somewhat distasteful. This verse is intended to correct wrong interpretations of the believers' subordination to civil authority. It brings out, for one thing, that such subordination is to be exercised in a way befitting free men (v. 16a).[5] Believers submit themselves to authority not as a matter of compulsion and necessity, but rather as a matter of choice. They do it with full recognition that they are truly free in Christ. But they also must recognize that freedom is easily perverted into license. Peter therefore added that his readers must not use their freedom as a cover-up or a pretext (Goodspeed, "excuse") for misconduct.

[5]Verse 16 does not, in Greek, contain a finite verb. Some versions supply a verb (e.g., NIV, "Live as free men, etc."). This is legitimate from a grammatical point of view, but it is possible that the adjective "free" and the participle "using" (NIV, "see") are in a sense loosely connected with the imperative verb of verse 13 ("Be subject"). Viewed in this manner, they explain how, or in what attitude the subjection is to be carried out. The interpretation above assumes the correctness of this latter construction.

But not only must subordination to civil powers be rendered in keeping with the Christian's status as a free man, it must be given in a way befitting persons who are bondservants of God (v. 16b). Though free, Christians must exercise their freedom in a manner commensurate with their relation to God. So on the deepest level they submit to authority not merely as an obligation to men but as an obligation to God, the Master of all. Implied in the apostle's statement is the idea that when Christians submit to the state, "they do not become slaves of the state; they remain slaves of God; government is never the Christian's master; he owes his allegiance only to God" (Arichea and Nida).

Verse 17 may be seen as a summary of the paragraph, and to give it proper balance perhaps it should be punctuated as containing two couplets: "Honor all men; love the brotherhood. Fear God; honor the king."

To "show proper respect" (lit., "honor," v. 17a) is to have regard for or value. "Love" (v. 17b) calls to mind 1:22. The "brotherhood" is a reference to the people of God, fellow believers. To "fear" God (v. 17c) is to have an attitude of awe, reverence, and worship. Only God is to be feared in this sense. The emperor ("king," v. 17d) is to be honored or respected (same word as that used at the beginning of the verse).

### *2. Duties of Servants (Slaves) to Their Masters (2:18–25)*

We come now to another part of the "seemly" behavior enjoined on the readers in verse 12. Having delineated the citizen-duties of Christians to the state, Peter next emphasizes the relation of Christian slaves to their masters.[6] "Slaves," the word employed in 2:18, translates a Greek word that is different from that ordinarily used in the epistles of Paul. The characteristic word of the latter is *doulos*, a bondslave (cf. v. 16, where the term occurs in Peter's epistle); the word employed here is *oiketēs*, house servants, that is, slaves who worked within the household. But too sharp a distinction should not be drawn between these two Greek words. Indeed, some interpreters

[6]That Peter, unlike Paul, says nothing about the duties of Christian masters may be an indication that few, if any, of his readers were slave owners.

(e.g., Arichea and Nida) think that slaves other than household slaves may be included in Peter's word. The slave, whether *doulos* or *oiketēs,* was the chattel of his master, whose power over the slave was almost absolute.

Two things probably come to the minds of most modern readers of this passage. First, the passage appears at first to be irrelevant to the twentieth century. But whatever may be said about the bearing of this section on twentieth-century life, we must first remember that Peter was writing primarily for Christians who were his contemporaries, and his words had immense relevancy for that day. First-century society, economically and politically, was in fact based on slavery. It has been estimated that there were as many as 60,000,000 slaves in the Empire. In many of the leading cities over half the population were slaves. Many of them were well educated and held responsible positions within their master's household. Then, from a practical point of view, we should keep in mind that if Peter could enjoin slaves, who had no rights, to be loyal to and work faithfully for their masters, how much more would he urge honest and faithful work upon Christian employees of our day, who enter voluntarily into their employment, who can bargain with their employers, and who can terminate their relationship to a company at any time.

A second problem about this passage (and others like it in the NT) that vexes many modern Christians is that the inspired writer did not condemn slavery. To every modern Christian the whole institution of slavery seems repulsive, and many are shocked to discover that the apostles did not even question slavery as such.[7] Several things may be said in response to this criticism of the apostolic writers. For one thing, though they did not in so many words condemn slavery, neither did they commend it. They simply accepted it as a fact of life in their society. Another thing: in their statements concerning the institution they sometimes attempted to regulate and modify it,

[7] Indeed, some commentators interpret 1 Corinthians 7:21 to teach that even if a Christian slave was offered freedom, he was to choose to remain a slave. The passage referred to is somewhat ambiguous and may be interpreted to mean that the Christian slave, if offered freedom, should accept it. See C. K. Barrett's Commentary on 1 Corinthians in *Harper's NT Commentaries.*

urging masters to treat their slaves with justice, kindness, and even brotherly love, and reminding them that their slaves had rights and that slave owners as well as slaves had a master in heaven (cf. Eph. 6:9; Col. 4:1). By such teachings the apostles called attention to principles that would eventually destroy slavery. Again, some think that the reason for the apostles' conservatism was the church's preoccupation with the thought of the imminent end of the age or perhaps their fear of dreadful retaliation if they encouraged social revolution. Kelly thinks the reason was the burning conviction of these early Christians that, through their fellowship with Christ, they had entered into a relationship of brotherhood with one another in which ordinary social distinctions, real enough in the daily round of life in the world, had lost all meaning (Gal. 3:28; 1 Cor. 12: 31; Col. 3:11; Phil. 8–18).

The primary duty urged upon slaves in this passage is submission, with emphasis on the duty of submission even to cruel and unjust masters (v. 18). This thought lead the apostle to discuss the sufferings of Christian slaves and to enjoin them to endure such sufferings patiently (vv. 19, 20). Finally, Peter reminded his readers that they were *called* to the patient bearing of trials, and he offered them the encouragement of the example of Christ, who also suffered innocently (vv. 21–25).

**a. The Command to Be Submissive (2:18).** Servants (household slaves and slaves in general) are to "submit . . . [themselves] to . . . [their] masters with all respect" (v. 18a). There is no finite verb in the Greek of verse 18, only a participle, that most interpreters understand as having imperatival force in this context.[8] The use of the participle—the root word is the same as that of the imperative verb in verse 13—shows that this unit, in Peter's thinking, sustained an intimate connection with the immediately preceding paragraph.[9] For the

[8]This use of the Greek participle, a rather frequent occurrence in 1 Peter, is generally thought today to reproduce a rabbinic Hebrew construction that employed participles to express rules of conduct (cf. Selwyn's essay in his commentary, pp. 387ff, and Daube's Appended Note in Selwyn, pp. 467–88).

[9]The close grammatical connection existing between verse 18 and verse 13 is an argument used by some to support the view that "every ordinance of man" (v. 13) refers not only to governmental authority but also to other institutions of human society that involve some measures of subjection.

meaning of the word, see the discussion of verse 13. The NEB interprets it here to mean "accept the authority of." The middle voice highlights the initiative of the slave in carrying out this duty.

"Masters" translates *despotais,* a term that is relatively rare in the NT. A strong word, it denotes absolute ownership of, and thus complete authority over, a person or thing. Its presence in the verse is an indication that the word "servants" does not include free persons. "Respect" (lit., "fear") may be understood in the sense of respect for the master or in the sense of reverence and awe for God, to whom all are ultimately responsible for the performance or non-performance of their daily round of duties. (We may reject outright the thought that "fear" refers to a cringing fear of the Master. This attitude is forbidden in 3:14.) It is difficult to decide between these two, for there is no way we can be sure which concept was in Peter's mind at the time of writing. Both are appropriate attitudes. I prefer the latter interpretation, feeling that it fits better verse 19's reference to being "conscious of God." Reverence for God should indeed govern all our conduct.

There are two kinds of masters: "the good and considerate" and "the harsh." But Peter does not make submission dependent on the character of the master. This is the slave's duty whatever the character and temperament of his master may be. In this context "good" probably connotes kindness (RSV), and the word translated "considerate" may be understood in the sense of "mild" or "fair." The literal meaning of "harsh" is "bent" or "crooked," and when used figuratively of people it has the sense of "perverse," "awkward to deal with" (Kelly).

**b. The Expansion of the Command (2:19–20).** Having acknowledged that there are kind and gentle masters as well as those that are perverse and cruel, Peter dwells now upon the relation of slaves to masters who are in the latter class. It was in this situation that the slave would be tempted to rebellion and self-assertiveness, but this situation also provided a unique occasion for the Christian slave to exemplify the enabling power of the gospel. Even when suffering cruel abuse, the Christian slave was to resist steadfastly the temptation to sullenness or disrespectful conduct. Bearing up under unjust punishment because of a consciousness of God is said to be "commendable." The Greek term (*charis*) is that that is usually translated "grace," but the word is used in many ways in the NT. Most often it speaks of God's favor shown to undeserving sinners. But here it obviously takes on a different meaning, though there is perhaps the suggestion that patient endurance of harsh treatment has about it the "quality of grace." Arichea and Nida, explaining that the term is obviously not used here with its "full theological meaning," conclude that it describes "a good action which is worthy of praise and approval." The NEB gives it a very general sense: "it is a fine thing." The idea is that patient endurance of undeserved suffering is an act that is pleasing to God.

"Because he is conscious of God" (v. 19; lit., "for conscience of God") is a phrase that gives much difficulty to interpreters. The Greek word for "conscious" (*syneidēsis*) appears also in 3:16, 21 and literally means "knowing—with." From this it comes to denote knowledge shared with one's self, that is, one's moral self-awareness (what we mean by "conscience"; cf. KJV or v. 19). The context in which it here appears suggests that we should interpret it as referring to the Christian slave's consciousness (or awareness) of God (understanding the genitive case of the Greek word for "God" to be what grammarians call "objective"). This interpretation is reflected in the RSV's "mindful of God," Moffatt's "sense of God," TCNT's "conscious of God's presence," and the NIV's "conscious of God." Mrs. Montgomery sees it as "a sense of duty" to God.

Verse 20 is an expansion upon the thought of verse 19 and serves to introduce the statement of verses 21–25 concerning the attitude of Christ under suffering. "But how is it to your credit if you receive a beating for doing wrong and endure it?"[10] The question is rhetorical, but the context clearly indicates that if an answer were given it would be "None!" If the punishment is deserved, praise for a proper response is out of place. The text does not indicate whether it is God or people bestowing the credit. Attention is directed not to who gives the credit, but who receives it. "Receive a beating" translates a Greek term used in

[10] A number of commentators observe that slaves sometimes boasted of ability to endure beatings without flinching. Peter's concern, though, is for something more than stoicism.

Mark 14:65 and Matt. 26:67 of the blows given to our Lord. The verb is a strong one, meaning "to strike with the fist," "to beat," or (more generally) "to treat roughly."

It is a different matter altogether if one endures suffering even when he has done what is right and good. This attitude, writes Peter, "is commendable [Gr., 'grace,' as in the first part of v. 19] before God" (v. 20b).

**c. The Great Incentive to Carrying Out the Command (2:21–25).** Verse 21a serves a double function. It caps the discussion of verses 19 and 20 and introduces the thought of that that follows.

The first incentive to submissive obedience, even when it involves suffering, is the desire for the approval of God (vv. 19–20; see discussion above). A second incentive was the nature of the Christian calling (v. 21a). The call referred to is God's saving call that issues in conversion. Elsewhere in this letter believers are said to be called out of darkness into God's marvelous light (2:9), called to inherit a blessing (3:9), and called to God's eternal glory (5:10). Here the idea is that Christians are called to patient endurance of undeserved suffering.

The third and greatest incentive to patient endurance of hardship is the example of Christ (vv. 21b–25). Peter describes the sufferings of Christ and shows that His attitude under those sufferings is an example to be followed by His people when they suffer innocently. But these verses go far beyond the idea of Christ as model for His people. They constitute a statement of great importance for our understanding of Peter's interpretation of Christ's death. At least six things stand out in the passage.

First, there is the implied thought that suffering was Christ's divinely appointed lot. Believers are called to endure suffering (v. 21a), but suffering is a part of our calling only because it was first a part of Christ's calling. This appears to be the connection between verses 21a and 21b (note "because"). During His earthly ministry He had taught His disciples that He (as the Christ) must suffer (Luke 24:25–27) and that all who would follow Him must be prepared to do the same (Mark 8:34; 10:38, 39).

Second, the sufferings of Christ were vicarious: He suffered "for you" ("for us," KJV), that is, on your behalf, for your benefit, to secure your redemption. (How Christ suffered for us is explained in v. 24.) It goes without saying, of course, that the sufferings of Christ's people did not have this character, but the reference to the vicarious aspect of Christ's sufferings does introduce a fresh and deeper motive for their imitation of Christ.

Third, Christ's sufferings were exemplary (vv. 21c–23). That is to say, there are aspects of His suffering that serve as "an example" or pattern for His people to follow. The Greek word for "example," a picturesque term found in the NT only here, is employed in classical Greek for a copy-piece to be traced or imitated by children learning to write. It has, to use Kelly's expression, "the air of the classroom clinging to it."

Thus the sufferings of Christ are left as a pattern or model "that you should follow in his steps" (v. 21c). "Follow" translates a compound word that means "to follow closely." The last word of the quotation ("steps") though always used figuratively in the NT, translates a term that signifies an actual footprint. In the plural, as here, it denotes the line of such footprints. Consequently, "to follow a man's footprints is to move in the direction he is going" (Kelly).

Peter's readers could not reproduce every aspect of Christ's sufferings, but verses 22 and 23 call attention to three qualities of that suffering that are patterns for His people. Verse 22 stresses the *innocence* of Christ. "He committed no sin, and no deceit was found in his mouth." These words, quoted from Isaiah 53:9, identify Christ with the Servant of the Lord whose agony the prophet had foreseen. It is significant that Peter, one of the disciples closest to Jesus during the earthly ministry, forthrightly affirms that Jesus was completely sinless, failing neither in deed (he "committed no sin") nor in word ("and no deceit was found in his mouth").

Verse 23a emphasizes *the patience and meekness* of Jesus, His unprotesting submission to maltreatment: "When they hurled their insults at him, he did not retaliate; when he suffered, he made no threats." These words, though not a quotation of the OT, may allude to Isaiah 53:7. More likely, Peter was drawing from his eye-witness knowledge of the Passion of Christ (cf. Mark 14:61, 65; 15:5, 17–20; Luke 23:9).

Verse 23b affirms Jesus' *trust in God*, suggesting that His confidence in the righteousness of God lay at the root of His patient endurance of insult and suffering. Rather than return abuse for abuse and threats for suffering, He "entrusted himself to him who judges justly." No object of "entrusted" is expressed in the Greek. The NIV follows KJV, ASV, NASB, and others in understanding the object to be "himself." Weymouth takes it to be "His cause," Goodspeed, "his case." The idea is that Christ was confident of vindication before God. Because He judges righteously, His verdicts are always just and fair.

Fourth, the sufferings of Jesus involved a bearing of "our sins in his body on the tree" (v. 24a). Earlier in the passage the vicarious nature of our Lord's sufferings was affirmed without elaboration ("for you," v. 21b). The statement now before us picks up that idea and amplifies it, explaining that He suffered "for us" in the sense that He bore (i.e., suffered punishment for) our sins on the cross. The "he himself" is emphatic. The thought is, "He and no other," "He alone." "Bore" renders a word that was a technical term of the sacrificial system, meaning "to offer," "to present." In the present passage it is understood by some to mean "bear the burden of," the suggestion being that Christ carried our sins as a burden (divinely laid upon Him) all through His earthly life and up to the cross. It seems better, however, to interpret the verb as meaning "bear (take) away." Christ bore our sins away by taking the blame for them, suffering the "curse" for them (cf. Gal. 3:13), enduring the punishment that was their due reward. He bore them in the sense that He was a sacrificial victim for them, His death making propitiation for them and removing them (cf. Isa. 53:12, where the Septuagint uses the same word).

It is worthy of note that in verse 24 Peter moves from the second person pronoun (used throughout this passage except in v. 24) to the first person: "our" sins. For one thing, it emphasizes that Christ's redemptive death has significance for all believers (including Peter), not just slaves. But perhaps it mainly was used confessionally. It was his way of uniting himself with his readers in acknowledging his participation in the benefits of Christ's death. "In his body" lays stress on the fact that Christ's redemptive deed was accomplished here on earth within the sphere and under the conditions of human life.

The word "tree" (Gr., *xulon;* lit., "wood") is a picturesque term for the cross. Other passages using this term are Acts 5:30; 10:39; 13:29; Gal. 3:13. In classical Greek it was used of the scaffold on which criminals were hung, and thus it had a connotation of criminality.

In verse 24b emphasis is placed on the purpose of Christ's death, which was that we, having abandoned our sins, might live for righteousness. The rendering of the Greek behind "might die to sins" is debated. The verb "might die" (Gr., *apogenomenoi*), occurring only here in the NT, can mean "die" and is so translated in the Arndt and Gingrich *Lexicon* and in many versions (KJV, ASV, RSV, TEV, et al.) The context, that sets "might . . . live" over against this word, lends strong support to this interpretation. However, there are interpreters who, while not denying that the idea of dying is probably in the background, prefer to understand the word to suggest abandoning or making a break with. Kelly, for instance, points out that the original and natural meaning of the verb is "to be put away from," "have no part in," "cease from." Accordingly, he renders the form in our text by the expression "having broken with" (cf. Moffatt). Perhaps, however, it is better to retain the idea of "dying" in translation, bearing in mind that in a context such as this a complete break with sin (i.e., its utter abandonment) is surely implied.

The positive purpose of Christ's death was that His people might "live for righteousness." The thought in "righteousness" is not imputed righteousness but practical righteousness, that is, righteous conduct, the doing of what is right.

Fifth, the sufferings of Christ bring healing (v. 24b). In "by his wounds you have been healed," a quotation from Isaiah 53:5, Peter returns to the second person pronoun. In doing so he emphasizes the special application of his teaching to suffering slaves. "Wounds," used only here in the New Testament, translates the word that speaks generally of "a bruise or a wound trickling with blood" (Arichea and Nida). More specifically, it was used of the cuts and bruises left on the flesh when a person was scourged. But again, the apostle points up the unique, vicarious nature of Christ's suffering. By His wounds (i.e., because He was wounded) "you have been healed." Theodoret's comment is apropos: "A new and strange method of healing; the doctor suffered the cost, and the sick received the healing" (quoted by Selwyn).

"Healed" suggests restoration to health from the wounds made by sin, that is, moral and spiritual healing. That this is the correct interpretation is indicated by the words that follow (v. 25).

Sixth, the sufferings of Christ are the means of bringing people to God: "For you were like sheep going astray, but now you have returned to the Shepherd and Overseer of your souls" (v. 25). "Going astray" here suggests the aimless wandering of sheep that have lost their way. The verbal is a compound construction (made up of a finite verb and a participle) emphasizing continuous action in the past (cf. NASB). It is a graphic description of the condition of Peter's first readers (and of all other people) in their unconverted condition.

Their present state is described in the words "but now you have returned to the Shepherd and Overseer of your souls" (v. 25b). "Have returned" translates an aorist passive indicative verb. Literally it reads, "but have now been brought back." The more literal rendering lays stress on the divine action in bringing wandering sinners to the Great Shepherd. The NIV rendering, grammatically just as legitimate, simply affirms the return without emphasizing the divine initiative. The main point, however, is clear. The readers are no longer astray from God, leading lives that lack in direction and purpose.

The reference to Christ as "Shepherd and Overseer" of His people was designed to encourage the readers. Whatever their trials and burdens, they had a trustworthy protector in Him. The two words are not to be kept entirely distinct; the latter probably amplifies the former by denoting a function of the Shepherd. "Shepherd" is the word translated "pastor" in Ephesians 4:11. The Greek for "Overseer" is *episcopos*, meaning literally "one who watches over." It might be translated here by "Guardian" or "Protector."

### 3. *Duties of Wives to Their Husbands (3:1–6)*

Having instructed citizens of their duties to government and slaves of their duties to masters, the apostle now addresses wives and urges upon them a loving submission to their husbands—even in instances where the latter are not believers. Two matters should be mentioned before proceeding with our interpretation of this passage. First, though Peter (in this passage) was not confining his remarks to wives with unbelieving husbands,[11] he does appear to have had them mainly in mind. The pagan husband would not only have a lack of sympathy for the faith of a Christian wife but might often be openly hostile to it.

A second thing to observe is that the much greater detail is given to the wife's duties (vv.1–6) than is devoted to the husband's duties (v. 7). This was due in part to the fact that women probably outnumbered men in the early Christian communities. Mainly, however, the greater detail given to the duties of wives was because the position of a Christian wife was ordinarily much more difficult than that of a Christian husband. Wives, therefore, needed more counsel and encouragement as to their conduct in the home.[12]

The major duty insisted upon is submission to the husband (v. 1), but other words of counsel are also given (vv. 2–4). The passage closes with a reference to "the holy women of the past," who are held up as models for the readers (vv. 5, 6). We may discuss the passage around four major concepts:

**a. Wives Are to Be Submissive to Their Husbands (3:1).** The command is given in verse 10: "Wives, in the same way, be submissive to your husbands." "In the same way," a phrase representing a single word in Greek, does not mean that the submission of the wife to her husband is just like the submission of a slave to his master. The Greek word was often used as a

[11] Note the phrase "that, even if any obey not the word," which suggests that the passage applies to all Christian wives—even those whose husbands are not Christians.

[12] The greater detail given to the duties of Christian wives is surely not to be interpreted as an indication that Peter was anti-feminist. The New Testament writings have in fact been "the greatest force for the liberation of women that history has known . . . , as may be verified by comparing their lot in countries influenced and uninfluenced by Christianity" (Polkinghorne, p. 592).

transition term to denote items in a series, much as we might use such words as "next." Here then, it denotes that the paragraph to follow is one in a series. (Observe the same construction in v. 7.)

For the meaning of "be submissive to," another participle in Greek (cf. 2:18), see the discussion at 2:13. Christian wives are to accept willingly the divinely ordained headship of the husband within the family, whether he is a Christian or not. Such submission, is not to be thought of as like that of a pagan wife to a pagan husband. In the Greek world a wife's status was little better than that of a slave. Peter is urging a distinctively Christian subordination of self, given not by compulsion or in resignation but voluntarily and gladly as a Christian duty. It goes without saying that the wife is not expected to act contrary to the will of God.

No inferiority of women—spiritual, moral, or intellectual—is implied. It is a subordination of function, involving woman's role as wife and mother within the intimate circle of the home. The NT consistently teaches that such wifely submission is not simply a matter of convention or social custom but a part of the plan of God in creation (cf. 1 Tim. 2:9–15). Verse 7 will make it plain that where both husband and wife are Christian, both sexes share equally in the blessedness of the new life.

The special reason given for the command is expressed in verse 1b: "so that, if any of them do not believe the word, they may be won over without words by the behavior of their wives." The wives addressed were identified with the Christian community, were concerned about the lostness of their husbands, and were apparently attempting to witness to them. "Do not believe" translates a single but very strong word in the Greek, perhaps implying open and active hostility to the gospel. Some think the word has a connotation of refusing to believe. Its literal meaning is "to be unpersuaded."

"The word" speaks of the word of the gospel, the message of truth about Christ and His salvation. The expression "without words" has reference to the wife's words of witness, concern, and appeal to her pagan husband.

Thc "winning" of the husband, which refers to his conversion to Christ, is an interesting concept. The NIV uses the expression "won over," but the Greek term has in it the idea of "to gain" (cf. Phil. 3:8, "that I may *gain* Christ"). In his becoming a Christian, the husband is gained by his wife, by the church, and for Christ. Kelly calls it "a stock missionary term for 'make a Christian'" and says it is "virtually equivalent to 'save.'" In 1 Corinthians 9:19–22 it is used by Paul in the sense of winning converts to Christ.

If pagan husbands were not to be reached and gained by the spoken witness of their wives (and others), then how? Peter answers: by their "behavior," that is, their Christian manner of life, especially their life in relation to others. (The word was a favorite with Peter, occurring six times in this letter and only seven times in the rest of the NT.) "What is implied here is that the wife gives her distinctive Christian witness to her husband, not by preaching at him, but by living before him, and particularly by being a good wife in relation to him" (Stibbs, p. 124).

**b. Wives Are to Live a Life of Purity and Reverence (3:22).** Peter holds out to wives the hope of gaining their husbands for Christ through their behavior, and apart from spoken words, because the husbands will see their "purity and reverence" (v. 2). The term "see" (cf. 2:12 for the same word) suggests close observation and thoughtful reflection. He takes note of her. All of this leads the husband to conclude that the truth of the gospel is evidenced in his wife's life.

Two qualities of the wife's behavior catch the husband's eye: her purity and her reverence. His attention to the gospel is won "through the eye rather than the ear" (Hiebert). "Purity" translates a term that has a wider connotation than sexual purity. Innocence, modesty, chasteness, freedom from admixture of evil—these all are contained in this word. Here it denotes irreproachable conduct. "Reverence" (lit., "fear") speaks not of cringing fear of the husband, but of an attitude of reverence for God. This should be the mainspring of life for every believer.

**c. Wives Are Not to Be Unduly Concerned with Outward Adornment, But Are to Cultivate Christian Character (3:3, 4).** The literature and art of the first two Christian centuries bear witness to the preoccupation of superficial women of the era with elaborate hairstyles, excessive make-up and jewelry, and ornate dress. Peter's statement draws a striking contrast between outward and inward beauty and urges Christian women to cultivate the latter. Verse 3 has been read as an outright prohibition of fixing the hair, wearing jewelry, etc. (cf. TEV), but this probably was not Peter's intended meaning. Several commentaries liken his words to the words of Jesus in John 6:27, "Do not work for food that spoils, but for food that endures to eternal life." We do not understand this to be a prohibition against working to earn our daily food. Rather, it points up the infinitely greater value of food that endures to eternal life. Similarly, Peter's words are to be taken as a caution against a distorted sense of values. The point is that inward beauty, which can be cultivated and attained by any Christian woman, is a thing of far greater value than outward adornment.

The braiding of hair, an art among Greek and Roman ladies, sometimes involved the intertwining of chains of gold or strings of pearls with the hair. Sometimes the elaborate hairstyles were secured by expensive combs and nets of gold. It was a process that consumed much time, and the end result was highly artificial and ostentatious. The "wearing of . . . fine clothes" is a reference to the wearing of ornate dresses. Ward thinks the expression refers to "the frequent changing of frocks" as a personal vanity.

Verse 4 describes the beauty that should be especially valued: that which is expressed in character, the "inner self" (lit., "the hidden person," "the heart"). The "inner self" is thought of not simply as the seat of emotions but as the center of one's being, that is, one's character and personality.

This inner loveliness is described as the unfading beauty that consists of a gentle and quiet disposition. The word for "gentle" may also have a connotation of humility and considerateness. "Quiet" denotes calmness, serenity, and tranquility—a spirit "that cannot be ruffled" (Luther). Such a spirit, disposition, or frame of mind, writes Peter, is in God's sight "of great worth," that is, "very precious." This is the ultimate test of conduct: Does it meet with divine approval?

**d. Christian Wives Are to See the "Holy Women of the Past" as Models for Their Conduct (3:5, 6).** This paragraph began with a statement of incentive to wifely submissiveness (the winning of unbelieving husbands); now it closes with another (the example of holy women of former ages). Peter appeals to the example of these devout women of the past to reinforce the argument he has set forth in the preceding verses. Three things are said of them in verse 5.

First, they were "holy." This means that, like all believers, they were called by and set apart for God, and so had a special relationship to Him. Second, they "put their hope in God." Third, they adorned themselves (NIV, made themselves "beautiful") with those traits of character that Peter has said all Christian wives should cultivate. That is to say, they exhibited a preference for the inward beauty that God approves. The reference to their being "submissive to their own husbands" seems to be mentioned as a special feature, perhaps the cardinal element, of this inward adornment; it is of course the attitude that was urged upon Christian wives at the very beginning of this passage.

In verse 6a Sarah is mentioned as especially exemplifying this attitude of domestic docility. She, the apostle writes, "obeyed Abraham and called him her master." The statement that she called Abraham her master refers to a remark she made when told that despite her barrenness and Abraham's advanced age, she would bear a son: "after I am worn out and my master is old, will I now have this pleasure?" (Gen. 18:12). The word translated "obeyed" essentially means to listen to, and then to carry out one's instructions or injunctions. In this context it denotes Sarah's wifely deference to her husband.

Christian wives show themselves to be Sarah's spiritual children if (or when) they do good and let nothing terrify them. "You are" translates an aorist tense that probably should be rendered "you became." If this rendering is followed, the reference is to the time of their conversion. The NIV and most other recent versions interpret the aorist as "timeless" and translate it by the English present. If this approach is taken, the idea is "you show yourselves to be."

The words "if ye do what is right and do not give way to fear" render two present participles. They have been interpreted by some as having conditional force (as in RSV, NIV, ASV); others have interpreted them as being causal or temporal (cf.

KJV). Either of these interpretations may be legitimate if one gives the verb "are" the sense of "show yourselves to be." But both, without considerable explanation, seem to suggest salvation by works. Best suggests that the two participles have imperative force; Hiebert and others think they are best interpreted as complementary, their action subsequent to the action of the aorist verb ("are" or "became," v. 6). In this interpretation, that is to be preferred, the participle denotes two qualities that are *evidences* of conversion. The doing "what is right" has, in this context, specific reference to the wife's dutiful regard for her husband. "Do not give way to fear" literally reads "not fearing any terror [or 'intimidation']." Hiebert understands that Christian wives "should not allow any event designed to terrify them to get a grip upon them," explaining that "External causes of fear might arise from the attitudes of society in general, the treatment received from hostile neighbors, or the threats and intimidations of an unbelieving husband." Moffatt translates it, "yield to no panic." We should see the phrase as mainly qualifying the leading injunction of the passage: "be submissive to your own husbands" (v. 1). It is an indirect reminder that the Christian wife's supreme duty is to obey God, and nothing is to be permitted to interfere with that—not even the wifely deference to the husband that the passage has enjoined.

*4. Duties of Husbands to Their Wives (3: 7)*

This verse, a corollary to the instructions just given to Christian wives, is a brief but comprehensive statement of duties that would prevent the husband's leadership from becoming oppressive and abusive. It assumes that both husband and wife are believers, referring to them as "joint-heirs of the grace of life" (ASV). Beare thinks the brevity of the counsel for husbands "reflects both the fact that they are not faced with the same tragic problems as the wives of hostile pagans, and also that men were much less numerous than women in these early communities."

On the phrase "in the same way" see discussion of verse 1. Here, as there, it translates a single Greek word that seems to be used to link this verse closely with the preceding discussion but at the same time to indicate that the apostle is moving to a new but related topic. Kelly sees this as a further development of the principle stated in 2:13. He points out that husbands, no less than wives, "owe a duty of respect to every human creature (ii. 13)." (See our discussion of 2:13 for Kelly's interpretation of that verse.) But since Peter has taught that husbands have a natural authority over their wives (cf. v. 1), it would be inexact, he thinks, to define the husband's respect for his wife as subordination. However, the principle of respect for every human creature requires that husbands "should exercise their authority with proper deference" (Kelly).

Two duties (both expressed by present participles, cf. 2:18; 3:1) are set before Christian husbands (v. 7a, b), and these are followed by a statement designed to encourage them in the performance of those duties (v. 7c).

**a. A Statement of the Husband's Duties.** (NASB, we think, reflects more accurately the sense of the Greek text of v. 7. The reader is urged to refer to it.) First, husbands are to "be considerate" as they "live with" their wives (v. 7a). The NIV, "be considerate as you live with your wives," is a free rendering of a construction that might more literally be translated, "dwell together according to knowledge as with a weaker vessel, the wifely one" (cf. Lenski's translation). "Continue to dwell together" (NIV, "live with") translates a present participle but it is generally recognized here as having imperatival force and as being parallel with the participles rendered "be submissive to" in 2:18 and 3:1. Kelly feels that the word has special reference to their sexual intercourse, but it is better to understand the term as covering the total marital relationship. The NEB therefore renders it, "conduct your married life."

"According to knowledge" (NIV, "be considerate") may mean that husbands are to live with their wives in accordance with their knowledge of God (and the gospel). On the other hand, it could denote knowledge of the wife: her nature, needs, and desires. Selwyn, therefore, takes it to mean that husbands are to exhibit practical understanding and tact. NIV's "be considerate" suggests the same idea. Lenski interprets "knowledge" to be "Scripture knowledge, over against pagan ignorance regarding the relation of husband and wife." Hiebert thinks the term suggests "an intelligent acceptance of [the wife]—as a weaker vessel."[13] Kelly defines "knowledge" as "Christian insight and tact," a conscience sensitive to God's will.

The second duty of husbands will be more clearly seen by referring to verse 7 in the NASB: "Live with your wives in an understanding way, as with a weaker vessel, since she is a woman; and grant her honor as a fellow heir of the grace of life." This version makes it clear that the first duty is to live with wives in an understanding way. The second is to "grant her honor as a fellow heir of the grace of life." "Honor" (NIV, "respect") includes courtesy and consideration. Goodspeed sees in it the idea of showing deference to. This duty is somewhat subordinate to the first duty, explaining how a husband lives with his wife "according to knowledge."

"Wives," which is not the usual word so translated in the NT, is an adjective meaning "feminine." Used here with the article, it has the force of a noun and is virtually equivalent (according to Kelly) to "the female sex" (cf. Reiche, "female element"). Arndt and Gingrich, however, say the word is here a periphrasis for "woman" or "wife" (cf. NASB). Lenski gives it adjectival force in his translation ("wifely"). (See reference to Lenski, above.)

Kelly explains that the point to be taken is that "in all their relations but particularly their sexual relations with their wives, Christian husbands should not assert their strength arbitrarily and make selfish demands, but should respect their partners' scruples."

Two reasons are given for carrying out these two duties. One is the fact that the woman is "the weaker partner [lit., 'vessel';]" and therefore deserves chivalrous consideration. The word for "weaker" here denotes physical weakness, there being "no innuendo of moral or intellectual inferiority" (Kelly). The husband is physically stronger in that he is more muscular.

The meaning of "partner" ("vessel") is disputed. The word originally signified a "jar," "dish," or "instrument" that someone makes use of. In the NT it is sometimes used of people (Acts 9:15; 2 Tim. 2:21; cf. 1 Thess. 4:4, where it is debated whether

---

[13] Hiebert's interpretation reflects that he construes "weaker vessel" with the first appeal of verse 7. See the translation given in the preceding verse.

it refers to one's wife or to one's own body). Selwyn interprets it here to mean "body" in the sense of "person." Arichea and Nida caution that we must not take the reference to woman as the weaker vessel to mean that she is simply a tool or vessel for men to use. The language implies that both husband and wife are vessels (i.e., instruments for God to use).

The other reason for carrying out these duties is that the wife is "a fellow heir [co-sharer] of the grace of life." The general sense is that in Christ she has spiritual standing and privileges equal to those of her husband. The "grace of life" may be interpreted to mean grace "which is (consists of) life"[14] or the grace "which bestows life" or the grace "which is for life."[15]

**b. The Incentive for Fulfilling These Duties.** Verse 7c, an infinitival construction expressing a negative purpose, relates to both of the duties that have been set before Christian husbands. The TEV takes the liberty of rendering it as an independent sentence and clearly brings out the meaning: "Do this so that nothing will interfere with your prayers." Implicit in this statement is the principle that our relations with God are profoundly affected by our relations with other people. This is especially so in the intimacy of home life. "Hinder" translates a Greek term that literally means "to cut in," "to interrupt," and thus to hinder. In ancient times it was used of cutting up a road to impede the progress of an advancing army. "Prayers" translates a word that denotes generally any worshipful approach to God. The plain truth of this text is that God will not hear the prayers of a man who bullies and abuses his wife. Kelly points out that 1 Corinthians 7:1–7 is "an illuminating commentary" on the passage.

Johnstone writes that while this clause might well be a motive to the carrying out of any duty, "it has a specialty of force in its application here; for violation of the law of love, especially towards those who in God's providence are nearest to and most dependent on us, has a quite peculiarly chilling and deadening power, and is as a mist which certainly hides the face of God."

---

[14] This interpretation takes "life" to be a genitive of identity (cf. "city of Dallas").

[15] This interpretation takes "life" to be an objective genitive.

Perhaps we should not leave this verse without remarking that it takes for granted that Christians will habitually engage in prayer. "The heirs of life," writes Leighton, "cannot live without prayer: none of them is dumb; they all speak."

### C. Appeals to Christians Generally (3:8–12)[16]

Following the introductory statement of 2:11, 12, everything in this unit up to this point has been addressed to various special classes in the churches. The present paragraph is not addressed to any specific group but contains admonitions for all believers regardless of their social or marital status. It appears on the surface to be a kind of summary of all that has preceded in this unit (cf. NEB, "To sum up"; NAB, "In summary"), but it really is more than that. It concludes the unit (cf. TEV, "To conclude"; TCNT, "Lastly") and serves to make the transition to a new line of thought that begins at 3:13.

Selwyn writes that the Greek term that introduces this paragraph "always seems to introduce a fresh paragraph and not simply to summarize what has gone before." Hiebert sees this paragraph as gathering up the detailed duties of the different groups listed in the earlier part of this unit and linking them together "in a general statement portraying the essentials of Christian character." Verse 8 appears to be advice for believers as they relate to one another within the Christian community; verse 9, advice for believers as they react to their pagan neighbors—mankind at large. (One cannot insist on this, however.) Verses 10–12 close the paragraph with a citation of OT Scriptures that reinforces the apostle's appeal for his readers to abstain from retaliation.

#### *1. Christians in Relation to Other Christians (3:8)*

Five adjectives, all denoting virtues that enhance fellowship within the Christian community, describe the attitudes that Christians should have toward one another. "Live in harmony,"

---

[16] There is considerable difference of opinion among scholars as to the proper way of dividing the material of 3:8ff. Some see 3:8–22 as at least loosely bound together into a single unit, having perhaps three subdivisions (8–12; 13–17; 18–22). We are following those who view the present passage as concluding the unit begun at 2:11.

suggests being united in spirit, aim, and purpose; minding the same things; having common interests (cf. Rom. 15:5; Phil. 2:2). "Be sympathetic," translates a Greek word (*sympatheis* ) that literally suggests suffering with others and denotes fellow-feeling, that is, "sharing in the feelings of others, whether those feelings be of joy or of sorrow" (Arichea and Nida). "Loving as brothers" denotes the special love that binds together believers in Christ. It translates *philadelphoi* and suggests that Christians are to love *because they are brothers*, not just because they may find each other to be lovable. They belong to the same family, have a common spiritual parentage (cf. 1:22). "Compassionate" means that believers are to be sensitive to the needs of others. The word speaks of feeling and affection. Throughout the NT, as well as the Septuagint, it regularly is used of the deepest human emotions, especially love and compassion. It has been called "a peculiarly biblical virtue" (Cranfield). Of the five adjectives used in this verse, only this one occurs elsewhere in the NT. The word for "humble" in ancient extra-biblical writings was almost always used in a bad sense: "base," "ignoble," "mean."[17] The word appears only here in the NT, though a similar word meaning "humility" occurs several times. Philippians 2:3 represents humility as that attitude in which one esteems other people more highly than oneself.

*2. Christians in Relation to Unbelievers (3:9)*

The words of verse 9 speak of an attitude Christians are to show toward all people, whether believers or unbelievers. But in the present context it seems likely that they were primarily intended to set forth the response that Christians were to make to harsh treatment that they received from their pagan neighbors. The heart of it is that they were to avoid a retaliatory spirit: "do not repay evil with evil, or insult with insult." "Evil" refers to malicious deeds; "insult" has to do with abusive language.

Instead of stooping to the level of their enemies, Christians were to give back "blessing." This word, a participle in Greek, literally means to speak well of, that is, to praise. But in this context it has the connotation of prayer and intercession for,

[17] Selwyn comments that "the Christian use of the word is one of the plainest examples of the transvaluation of values achieved by Christianity."

invoking God's blessing upon. It may include the idea of showing kindness to, that is, returning good words for insult, and good deeds for malicious deeds.

To encourage this response in his readers, Peter adds: "because to this you were called so that you may inherit a blessing" (v. 9b). It is not clear what is meant by "to this" (Gr., *eis touto).*The words may look back to the immediately preceding words ("with blessing") or they may look forward (the inheriting of blessing). Some see it as looking both ways. Moffatt, for example, expresses it thus: "For this is your vocation, to bless and to inherit a blessing." Leighton interprets similarly: "called to blessing as our inheritance, and to blessing as our duty," explaining that the words "to this" relate to both.

### 3. *These Appeals Enforced by Scripture (3:10–12)*

Peter frequently supports his arguments by citing Scripture, and that is the purpose of verses 10–12. The passage brought forth is the Septuagint rendering of Psalm 34:12–16, only slightly modified as it is interpreted in light of the gospel. It is intended in a general way to enforce all the exhortations of verses 8 and 9, but this particular Scripture was perhaps especially suggested by the last part of verse 9 (which refers to the Christian's inheriting a blessing). The substance of the quotation is that believers are to live in love and righteousness and peace, for this is the way to the highest enjoyment of life (10, 11) and it pleases God (12). Hiebert quotes E. Y. Mullins as calling this passage "an ancient recipe for a happy life."

"Whoever would (better, 'desires to') love life and see good days" is an instance of Hebrew parallelism, the two expressions (loving life and seeing good days) denoting the same thing. It was not length of life but its quality that concerned the psalmist. Both he and Peter were thinking "of a life and of days that are full of rich fruit" (Lenski).

Johnstone thinks that in this passage "life" is obviously in the first instance, life on earth, "but under the light of the gospel the mind passes directly and unhesitatingly . . . to think also and chiefly of the full, glorious, endless life of heaven." Similarly, Kelly, for instance, feels that Peter has greatly deepened the sense of the passage, "giving the key words a strongly eschatological colouring." For him, therefore, "life" and "good days" stand for eternal life, the "salvation ready to be revealed in the last times" (1:5). We think it better to restrict the meaning to life on earth.

Peter's prescription for one who would love (have) life and see good days is given in verses 10b–11. The last half of verse 10 has to do with speech; verse 11, with deeds and action. Turning away from evil (v. 11a) perhaps is to be seen as instruction on how to behave under provocation and threat of harm. Doing "good" here likely means practicing kindness. To "seek peace" (v. 11b), is to make it a matter of diligent search.

Verse 12 gives the motivation for what has just been said. For the Lord's "eyes" to be on the righteous is for Him to watch over them, guard and protect them. "Those who do evil," in the original setting of the Psalm, refers to unbelievers, the wicked. Some interpreters think that although the term obviously includes nonbelievers, the context requires us to see here a more general reference. Their conclusion is that the reference in the present passage is broad enough to include Christians who succumb to wickedness, returning evil for evil, etc. Our preference is to interpret "those who do evil" as referring to unbelievers.

**For Further Study**

1. Make a list of the specific groups to which Peter speaks in 1 Peter 2:11–3:12. What directive or command does he give to each group?

2. In Matthew 22:15–21 and in Romans 13:1–7 the New Testament gives directions to Christians concerning their relationship to the government. Compare and contrast each of these sections with that in 1 Peter 2:13–17.

3. In Ephesians 6:5–8, Paul gives advice to Christian slaves in their relationships to their earthly masters. Compare and contrast Paul's advice with that of Peter in 1 Peter 2:18–25.

4. Does Peter's description of husbands in 1 Peter 3:1 suggest the likelihood that most of them are Christians or non-Christians? What is the condition of husbands as set forth in Ephesians 5:25–31?

# Chapter 4

## Obligations of Christians as a Persecuted People

(1 Peter 3:13–5:11)

To this point the sufferings of the readers, which were the occasion for the writing of this letter, have been mentioned almost incidentally; now these sufferings loom large in all that the apostle says. Kelly therefore writes that at this point we reach "the main section of the letter." Lenski comments that the real purpose for which the epistle was written "has now been reached, namely to enlighten, comfort, and strengthen the readers in suffering and trial."

As is true of the rest of the letter, the present unit, though containing weighty theological teaching, assumes hortatory character. In this instance the appeals are all related in some way to the sufferings and trials[1] to which the readers were being subjected or that were at least an imminent danger for them.

It should be borne in mind that the apostle is not discussing sufferings in general, but sufferings incurred for righteousness' sake. What was in mind was not those sufferings that are the common lot of humanity but the sufferings that are incurred because one is a Christian.

Perhaps the best approach to this unit is to understand 3:13–4:19 as giving general counsel to those under persecution and to see 5:1–11 as containing a series of special appeals to various groups within the Christian community.

[1]It is debated whether these sufferings were inflicted by the pagan neighbors of the Christians or were officially imposed by the government. Peter does not explicitly tell us, but the arguments for the former are the more convincing.

## A. General Counsel for Those under Persecution (3:13–4:19)

A number of strands of thought are interwoven through this section. The first, having to do with the attitude one should cultivate as he faces persecution, stresses the confidence with which the righteous can meet their persecutors and endure their suffering (3:13–17). Next, holding up the great example which is found in the sufferings and subsequent triumph of Christ, the apostle shows that the basis of the believer's confidence is the victory of Christ in and through His sufferings. This fact offers strong encouragement to suffering saints, for if they share in their Lord's passion, they will share also in His triumph (3:18–22). This is followed by an appeal to use the time that remains to honor God (4:1–6) and to remember the approaching end and the moral and spiritual demands this places upon the Christian (4:7–11). Finally, in light of the inevitability of sufferings, the readers are urged to endure them with submission, joy, and dignity and to entrust their souls to the loving care of their God (4:12–19).

### *1. Cultivate a Proper Attitude with Reference to Suffering (3:13–17)*[2]

It is fitting that this section (3:13–4:19), all of which has to do with persecution, should begin with a statement informing the readers what their frame of mind should be as they face and endure sufferings for righteousness' sake. The teaching of the passage may be summed up under four leading ideas:

**a. Christians Are to Remember That If They Are Zealous for That Which Is Good, They Cannot Be Really Harmed. (3:13–14a).** But in the event that suffering for the sake of righteousness should come, they are to see it as a privilege of Christian discipleship and count themselves religiously fortunate.

The paragraph begins with a rhetorical question: "Who is going to harm you if you are eager to do good?" (v. 13). The expected answer is "Nobody!" "Harm," that may denote any

[2]We have made a major break between verses 12 and 13, but one should observe that a very close connection exists between these two paragraphs. The Greek text of verse 13 begins with a single connective, meaning "and" (omitted by NIV ).

kind of injury or mistreatment, means (in this context) "really harm" (i.e., affect their faith adversely or perhaps inflict permanent harm). The thought then is not that they will, by a good life, escape all abuse or hurt but that regardless of what the enemies of the gospel may do to them they cannot injure them in the ultimate sense.[3]

"Eager to do good" speaks of a wholehearted devotion to, an absolute passion for, what is good. To be zealous for something is to desire it so strongly that the attaining of it becomes a passion, and one strives for it with all his heart.

"But even if ye should suffer for what is right . . ." (v. 14) translates an optative construction, a usage quite rare in the Greek of New Testament times. Ordinarily, the optative in a context such as this would suggest that suffering for righteousness' sake is possible but highly unlikely. But since the apostle has mentioned more than once that his readers are indeed suffering (cf. 2:12; 2:19), this interpretation of the optative in our text would leave the impression that they are suffering for wrongdoing. It is most improbable that this was Peter's intended meaning. Arichea and Nida offer a better interpretation. They think Peter perhaps realized that "what he said in verse 13 could be misunderstood as exempting Christians from any kind of suffering, and he immediately adds that suffering is indeed a possibility [the force of the optative], and suffering for doing right is something that Christians should count as a privilege." When believers are wholeheartedly devoted to the good, they are beyond the reach of "harm" but not beyond the reach of suffering.

The conclusion to the conditional clause with which verse 14 begins is expressed in the words, "you are blessed." Suffering for righteousness' sake, is then a privilege of Christian discipleship that brings much reward (cf. Matt. 5:10, 11; 1 Peter 4:14). The Greek employs the one word, "blessed" (or "happy;" Gr., *makarioi*), the same word with which each of the Beatitudes of Jesus begins. It has the connotation of a "distinctive religious joy" (Hauch, TDNT).

---

[3]Some take the meaning to be, "Who will wish to do you any harm?" This, however, seems to be a less likely interpretation.

**b. Christians Are to Meet Their Sufferings with Courage, Letting the Fear of God Drive Out of Their Hearts the Fear of Man (3:14b–15).** In saying, "Do not fear what they fear," the apostle may have been urging his readers not to fall away by fearing (i.e., giving religious reverence to, worshiping) the gods that their persecutors feared (i.e., gave religious reverence to, worshiped). They were, on the contrary, to "set apart Christ as Lord"—that is, they were to revere Christ, acknowledging Him alone as Lord.

The words "do not fear what they fear" are capable of another meaning, namely, do not be afraid of your persecutors. This is the interpretation to be preferred and is expressed by the NASB: "Do not fear their intimidation."

The Greek of "Do not be frightened" employs the verb used by Jesus in John 14:1, "Let not your heart be troubled." Here it conveys the sense of disturbed, terrified, or distressed. "Don't be alarmed by their threats" seems to express the meaning. Instead of being frightened by men, the readers are to "set apart Christ as Lord." This rendering construes "Lord" as a predicate. It may, however, be the direct object, the word "Christ" being in apposition with it. The rendering then will be "sanctify the Lord Christ in your hearts." The former construction is preferable.

"Set apart" does not here mean "to make holy," but "to acknowledge as holy," "to reverence," "to honor." "In your hearts" shows that this reverence accorded to Christ is to come from the center of one's being.

This inward reverence for Christ as Lord will express itself outwardly by a constant readiness "to give an answer to every one who asks you to give the reason for the hope that you have" (15b).[4] "Answer" translates the Greek *apologia,* the basic meaning of which is "defense." What Peter enjoins then is not a nebulous explanation meant mainly to appease the foes of the gospel, but rather, a frank defense of Christianity. The Christian must always be ready "to testify, to correct ignorance about Christ, to spread the gospel light, to win others for Christ, to justify his own hope, and . . . silence evil speakers" (Lenski).

[4]We are looking upon these words as an expression and explanation of the statement "sanctify . . . Christ, etc."

It is debated whether Peter was thinking of police interrogation or of a less formal inquiry put forth by hostile individuals. An argument for the former is that *apologia* (defense, answer) often had the technical sense of a legal defense against a charge, and the word for "reason" (Gr., *logon,* a rational and intelligent account) could have a judicial connotation. On the other hand, those who see here an allusion to a less formal, unofficial inquiry point to "the extreme generality" of the word "always" and the phrase "everyone who asks," contending that "the latter at any rate conjures up something much more ordinary and everyday than court cases can have been" (Kelly, p. 143). We conclude, with Kelly, that the reference is probably general and comprehensive, not limited to questions asked in court but not excluding them either.

The "hope" referred to is the "living hope" of 1:3 and the hope "in God" mentioned in 1:21 and 3:5.

The last phrase of verse 15 is a caution: The readers are to answer their opponents "with gentleness and respect." The former word (meaning humility, or courtesy) suggests that there is to be no arrogance or pride but a becoming gentleness of spirit that might commend the gospel to those of a suspicious mind. The latter word may denote either an attitude toward God (reverence, awe) or an attitude toward the inquisitors (respect).

**c. In the Midst of Their Sufferings Christians Are to Maintain a Good Conscience and Always Exhibit to the World a Good Manner of Life (3:16).** The word for "conscience" was used earlier in 2:19. There, however, the sense (as required by the context) was consciousness or awareness of God (see discussion of 2:19). Here it denotes the awareness of the quality of one's actions—whether they are right or wrong. A "clear" conscience is an awareness of being free from guilt, of having nothing to hide.

The latter part of verse 16 teaches that when Christians live in this manner there is hope that the result will be that those who vilify their good conduct in Christ will come to feel shame for their slander. The word translated "speak maliciously" (*katalaleisthe*) means to speak evil of, defame, or slander. The Greek word for "slander" (*epēreazō*), used only here in the New Testament, is stronger and describes a threat or a verbal abuse.

The good "conscience" is inward, subjective, unseen. The good "behavior" is outward and visible—something even the enemies of the gospel could observe. "In Christ" suggests that the believer's union with Christ is the source of the excellence of Christian behavior. Such a life is possible only because one is in vital union with Christ.

**d. Christians Are to Meet Their Sufferings with Awareness That Such Sufferings Are a Part of the Providence of God (3:17).** "It is better, if it is God's will, to suffer for doing good than for doing evil." In essence the apostle is appealing for an attitude of submission to the will of God. An underlying thought in the statement is that the readers would not be experiencing suffering were it not willed by God. That will, whether as purposive or permissive, covers every facet of human life. It is possible then to do good and still suffer. In such cases, suffering is no disgrace for the Christian. God, in spite of that suffering and through it, is working out a providential purpose (Rom. 8:28–30). The believer may not always be able to discern that purpose, but he can safely trust the loving God who permits the suffering to come.

### *2. Look to Christ, Whose Vicarious Death and Triumphant Resurrection Are the Basis for the Christian's Confidence and Encouragement in Suffering (3:18–4:6)*

How this passage fits into thc context is a matter that has generated considerable debate. (See Dalton, pp. 103ff.) Even greater debate has focused on the meaning of the passage. It is without question the most difficult unit in 1 Peter and one of the most difficult in the entire Bible.

It is rather generally agreed that 3:18–4:6 constitutes a unit and that it has two clearly defined parts, one a statement of doctrine (3:18–22) and the other an exhortation based on that statement (4:1–6). Expressed otherwise, 3:18–22 expounds Christ's suffering and affirms His victory over evil; 4:1–6 shows how His people share in that victory.

**a. The Meaning of 3:18–22** The import of 3:18–22 is that Christians suffering for their faith are to draw encouragement from the fact that Christ has suffered and died, and by His death and resurrection has won a stupendous victory over the forces of evil—a victory in which, by virtue of their union with Christ, believers share. Dalton's summary statement is:

> The line of thought is clear enough: The Christian, even in His suffering, has the victory over his pagan persecutors (3:13–17). The basis of this victory is to be found in the suffering of Christ, His death and glorious resurrection.

A superficial reading might lead one to think that Peter "lost his way" in the development of his thought, that he began at verse 18 with the intention of holding up the sufferings of Christ as an example, but went off on a tangent and never got back to the topic with which the text begins. A more careful reading shows that the apostle is setting forth something far more profound than the exemplary character of Christ's sufferings. His purpose (of which he never lost sight) was to show that Christ, in spite of a cruel death at the hands of wicked men, has won a great victory over all the powers of evil. Believers, by union with Him, are destined ultimately to share His triumph.

"For," with which verse 18 begins, points up that Peter introduced this passage to show his afflicted readers the basis for the encouragement that he has given them in verses 13–17.[5] This, as Kelly puts it, "is nothing less than the victory which Christ has won, by his death, resurrection and ascension, over the forces of evil; the fruits of which Christians share."

Our discussion, which must be kept relatively brief, will focus on four matters of major significance: the suffering/death of Christ and His subsequent resurrection (v. 18); the preaching of Christ to the spirits in prison (vv. 19–20a); Christian baptism (vv. 20b–21); and the triumph and enthronement of Christ (v. 22). From a structural point of view verses 19–21 are almost parenthetical, for the thought with which verse 18 closes ("made alive by the Spirit") is repeated and expanded in verse 22.

[5] A careful reading of the passage strongly suggests that this initial clause does not refer exclusively to the preceding verse, "as if the writer were referring his readers (as he did in the similarly worded sentence in ii. 21) to Christ as the pattern of innocent suffering; here there can be no question of Christ as an example, since His act was unique and redemptive" (Kelly). "For" then looks back to and seeks to justify all that was said in 3:13–17: when unjustly abused, the readers can count themselves blessed (3:14), for they, as believers, participate in the victory Christ has won over the powers of evil.

*(1) The Suffering/Death of Christ (3:18).* The principal statement of verse 18 is that "Christ died."[6] Five things are said about this event that succinctly sum up the significance of what Christ did for us. First, He suffered/died "for sins" (lit., "concerning sins"; cf. Heb. 5:3; 10:26; 1 John 2:2). The idea is that He suffered and died "in connection with" sins. What that connection was we learn from the context, that makes it clear that it was not Christ's own sins but ours that Peter had in mind.

Second, Christ suffered/died "once for all." This phrase (a single word in Greek) is not to be mistaken for "once upon a time." Its meaning is that Christ's redemptive deed was efficacious, and therefore does not need to be repeated.

Third, Christ suffered/died, "the righteous for the unrighteous." The idea is that Christ the righteous one died for the unrighteous (TEV, "a good man for bad men"). This phrase teaches both the innocence of the Savior and the vicarious nature of what He did, ideas that have been expounded earlier in 2:21–24.

Fourth, Christ suffered/died "to bring you[7] to God." The Greek verb for "bring" is used in only two other passages in the New Testament (Luke 9:41; Acts 16:20). The related noun form, used more frequently, denotes access, the leading or bringing of

---

[6] KJV, ASV, Phillips and others have "suffered" (Gr., *epathen*), a reading with strong attestation and preferred by the third edition of the UBS and the 26th edition of the Nestle-Aland Greek texts. "Died" (Gr., *epethanen*) is supported by the great majority of manuscripts and ancient versions. On textual grounds alone, then, the claims of this reading are overwhelming. Most recent versions prefer it (cf. RSV, NEB, NASB, TEV, NIV, Berkeley, Weymouth, and TCNT). On the other hand, the sense of the passage appears to lend support to "suffered" as the correct reading. Advocates of this view argue that the relationship of verse 18 to verses 13 through 17 requires "suffered," for in verses 13 through 17, not death but suffering is the theme. Furthermore, to say that "Christ" also *died* seems to imply that the Asian Christians were being killed, but of this there is no evidence in the letter.

It is not a matter of great importance, for the essential meaning of the text is not seriously affected. The Greek word for "suffered" is commonly used for death when applied to Christ (TCNT, 5:913, 917). Selwyn observes that the Greek word for "suffered" was used in literary Greek for dying, and it is agreed by all that whatever reading one follows here—"suffered" or "died"—the reference is to Christ's death.

[7] Some think there is a better manuscript support for reading "us" (*Gr., hēmas*) in this place than for reading "you" (Gr., *hymas*). The latter is the reading followed by Goodspeed, NAB, TEV, NIV, etc. The former reading is preferred by KJV, ASV, Moffatt, RSV, NEB, JB, Berkeley, etc.

someone into the presence of another. Paul used it of the way to God, opened for us by Christ (Rom. 5:2; Eph. 2:18; 3:12). In bringing us to God Christ brought us into a right relationship with God, a relationship that had been broken by sin.

Fifth, Christ's suffering involved violent death and was followed by resurrection (v. 18d). "He was put to death in the body but made alive by the Spirit." Three problems confront the interpreter in dealing with this sentence. These relate to: (a) the connection of verse 18d with the earlier part of verse 18, (b) the meaning of "put to death" and "made alive," and (c) the meaning of "flesh" and "spirit." Let us look briefly at each of these.

(a) The connection of verse 18d with the earlier part of verse 18. "Put to death" and "made alive" are participles in the Greek text, but the NIV and a number of other versions (e.g., JB, GNB, TEV) render them by finite verbs and make them part of a new sentence not grammatically connected with the earlier part of the verse. However, Greek texts generally separate these words from the earlier portion of verse 18 only by a comma and use a full stop at the end of verse 18 (cf. NASB, Berkeley, and with slight modification, Goodspeed). The latter punctuation is to be preferred because it shows more clearly the close relation of "put to death, etc." with the immediately preceding statements.

What that relationship is, is not clear. "Put to death . . . alive" may be loosely connected with the statement "Christ suffered/died." Viewed in this manner, the two phrases resume the thought of Christ's suffering and expand upon it: "For Christ also suffered . . . , being put to death in the flesh, but made alive, etc."

(b) The meaning of "put to death" and "made alive." The Greek term behind "put to death" suggests the violence of Christ's death. Selwyn observes that in the gospels this is "the invariable connotation" of the Greek term and concludes that the violence of Christ's death was probably in Peter's mind when the present passage was written.

"Made alive," a "glorious antithesis" to the preceding declaration of death (Hiebert), is best understood as a reference to the resurrection of Christ. Best affirms that the word "normally refers to the resurrection in the NT . . . and that is its reference here." (In at least six other passages the Greek verb here employed refers to the resurrection of the dead [John 5:21; Rom. 4:17; 8:11; 1 Cor. 15:22, 36, 45].)

(c) The meaning of "flesh" and "spirit." The NIV (following KJV, Berkeley, and others) capitalizes "Spirit," and in so doing interprets the word to be a reference to the Holy Spirit: "put to death in the body but made alive through the Spirit." This interpretation, though quite possibly correct (and preferred by a host of interpreters), seems to obscure the parallelism of "flesh" and "spirit."

The ASV, RSV, and NEB use lowercase for "spirit" and thus preserve the antithesis of the Greek text, where "flesh" and "spirit" exhibit the same case construction and are obviously set one over against the other (*thanatōtheis men sarki* [flesh] *zōopoiētheis de pneumati* [spirit][8]). The ASV and RSV render these words quite literally: "put to death in the flesh, but made alive in the spirit." Kelly differs only slightly, translating "flesh" and "spirit" as datives of reference: "put to death *with reference to* the flesh . . . made alive *with reference to the spirit*" (italics ours). The contrast of flesh and spirit is not between the body of Christ and the activity of the Holy Spirit upon that body (as is suggested by NIV). Nor is the contrast between two complementary parts of Christ: "flesh," the outward person, i.e., His body; "spirit," the inner person, i.e., His soul. Kelly explains that both terms (i.e., flesh and spirit) designate

> . . . the whole Christ regarded from different standpoints. By *flesh* is meant Christ in His human sphere of existence, considered as a man among men. By *spirit* is meant Christ in His heavenly, spiritual [resurrected] sphere of existence, considered as divine spirit; and this does not exclude His bodily nature, since as risen from the dead it [his body] is glorified. The datives are datives of reference, and the creedal excerpt is affirming the paradox that, regarded as man, Christ was done to death, but, regarded as eternal spirit, that same Christ in the fullness of His being, His body of course included, has been restored to life by God's power. Indeed, it is as thus risen and glorified that He "brings us to God."

[8]Observe the contrasts: *Thanatōtheis* (put to death) . . . *zōopoiētheis* (made alive); *men* (on the one hand) . . . *de* (but on the other hand); *sarki* (in [with reference to] flesh) . . . *pneumati* (in [or with reference to] spirit).

A similar use of "flesh" and "spirit" occurs in Romans 1:3, 4, where Christ is said to have been "born of the seed of David according to the flesh, . . . declared to be the Son of God with power, according to the spirit of holiness, by the resurrection of the dead" (ASV). See also 1 Timothy 3:16: "He was manifested in the flesh,/Justified in the spirit" (ASV). Here "flesh" and "spirit" mark respectively Christ's earthly and exalted states—in R. T. France's words, the "natural human sphere of existence and the "eternal spiritual state of existence."[9]

*(2) Preaching to the Spirits in Prison (3:19–20a).*

This short passage, without question, presents the most perplexing exegetical problems of the entire epistle—perhaps of the whole New Testament.

The first problem concerns the connection and meaning of the prepositional phrase "through whom" ("in which," ASV, RSV; *en hō*, Gr.). It is generally agreed that "spirit" (the last word of v. 18) is the antecedent of the relative pronoun ("whom" or "which") at the beginning of v. 1.[19] "Through whom" (NIV) is the proper rendering if one understands "Spirit" (v. 18) as referring to the Holy Spirit. The thought then is: through the agency of the same Spirit that raised Christ, He (Christ) went and preached to the spirits in prison.

On the other hand, if "spirit" (v. 18) is understood as referring to Christ in His heavenly sphere of existence, a more fitting translation of verse 19 is: "in which (spirit) He went and preached to the spirits in prison." Dalton understands this to

[9]R. T. France, "Exegesis in Practice: Two Samples," *New Testament Interpretation* (ed. I. H. Marshall: p. 267). Cf. Wayne Grudem, who feels that France correctly interprets the contrast between "flesh" and "spirit," but thinks he "overly restricts the 'eternal, spiritual sphere' to mean only the resurrected state of Christ. The 'flesh-spirit' contrast of v. 18," he explains, "is between spheres of activity, not exactly between the two things mentioned in those spheres in v. 18, the pre- and post-resurrection states of Christ" ("Christ Preaching Through Noah . . . ," *Trinity Journal*.

[10]Selwyn understands the relative to have a more general reference and to mean something like "in which state" or "in which circumstance" or "better and more broadly, 'in which process', *in the course of which,* referring to Christ's passion and resurrection generally" (p. 197). This interpretation makes the prepositional phrase ("in which") the equivalent of a conjunction meaning "when." Reiche (*The Disobedient Spirits and Christian Baptism,*" pp. 110f) interprets the phrase to mean "on which occasion."

mean "in which [resurrected state] He went, etc." In support of this view he writes:

> once we take *pneumati* as "in the sphere of the spirit," then we should take *en hō* as "in this sphere," "under this influence," or even "as one now made alive in the spirit." In other words, the person who does the preaching in 3:19 is the risen Lord. (p. 140)

Grudem, on the other hand, takes the phrase to mean "in which realm, namely the spiritual realm," explaining that it does not necessarily mean "in the resurrected body."

"Also" is not to be interpreted to mean that Christ preached to the spirits in prison as well as to other (unnamed ) spirits. It rather implies that in addition to an activity in the spirit already named (being made alive: resurrection), there is yet another pertinent aspect of that activity, namely, His preaching to the spirits in prison.

As we look at the entire statement of verse 19, a whole cluster of questions clamors for answers: Who are the spirits in prison? In what sense are they "in prison"? When, how, and for what purpose did Christ preach to them? What was His message? And how does all of this fit in with the context? In answer to these questions four principal views emerge. No one of them is completely satisfactory, for each of them leaves many unanswered questions; and each view may be variously modified by its respective advocates. Limitations of space require that the four views be only briefly stated.

(a) The first view affirms that the "spirits" are the souls of people who perished in the Flood. The preaching was *by the pre-incarnate Christ through Noah* (i.e., the Spirit of Christ preached through the patriarch) to Noah's disobedient contemporaries. The preaching was done on the earth while these people were living on the earth—indeed, *while they were disobedient*. Its purpose was to call them to repentance. Peter refers to the hearers of the message as "spirits in prison" because at the time he wrote these words they had been dead for centuries and were disembodied spirits under confinement and awaiting the judgment of God. (Alternatively, they are called "spirits in prison" because when they were alive on earth they were imprisoned in sin and ignorance.) This is the view suggested by the KJV and the NIV, both of which use the proper noun "Spirit" (v. 18) and supply the preposition "in" with "flesh" (v. 18) and "by" or "through" with "Spirit" (v. 18). Many of the older commentators favor this interpretation. (See for example N. M. Williams' treatment of the passage in *An American Commentary* [ed. by Alvah Hovey].) A key feature of this interpretation is its understanding of the participial construction rendered by the NIV as an attributive modifier ("who disobeyed long ago"), More recently Wayne Grudem has given convincing evidence that this construction should be translated not as an attributive modifier but as adverbial: "when they formerly disobeyed." Against this view it may be argued that the context points to a preaching subsequent to Christ's death and resurrection. Grudem ably answers this and other objections to the view.

(b) The second view of the passage also affirms that the "spirits" are the souls of the people who perished in the Flood. But the preaching was not through Noah *but by Christ in person in the period between Christ's death and His resurrection,* millennia after these people had died. This view has been advocated in a variety of forms. Some interpreters think the proclamation was a mere announcement of the completion of Christ's redemptive work of His triumph, and of the doom of the "spirits in prison"; others (among them, with varying modifications, are Bigg, Cranfield, Reiche, and Hunter) think it was an offer of salvation (a "second chance"). (If it was an offer of salvation, two questions must be answered: [a] Why was the offer made to this one generation of sinners only and to no one else? [b] How is such an offer, after this life is over, to be reconciled with the whole tenor of Scripture, that is consistently opposed to such a view?)

Those who adhere to this general interpretation of the passage often draw far-reaching but unscriptural conclusions from it. Beyschlag, for example, writes in his *New Testament Theology* as follows:

> From all the obscurities of this remarkable utterance the bright thought stands out that the mercy of God revealed in Christ and Christ's death is not limited to the world of the

> living, but reaches beyond it into the quiet of that other world of the departed, and is made manifest in it by Christ Himself. (vol. 1, p. 416)

Salmond observes that this interpretation is surrounded by

> difficulties more numerous and more serious than its advocates are accustomed to confess. It is not simply that it has little to support it elsewhere, or that it runs singularly athwart the general teaching of scripture . . . . It is at fault in a number of things, contextual and grammatical. (*Christian Doctrine of Immortality*)

(c) The third view (and perhaps the most widely accepted today) affirms that the "spirits" are fallen angels[11] who are "kept in darkness, bound with everlasting chains for judgment on the great Day" (Jude 6; cf. 2 Peter 2:4). It is urged that the term "spirits" is never used in Scripture of human beings without the addition of qualifying words to make this clear (Heb. 1:7; 12:23). In further support of this view most of its advocates argue that Jewish and early Christian tradition identified the "sons of God" of Genesis 6:2 with fallen angels. The preaching was *by Christ in person,* some placing it in the interval between Christ's death and resurrection, others at the time of His ascension. The substance of the proclamation, though not stated by Peter, is thought to be Christ's victory and the fallen angels' doom (cf. Col. 2:15 and v. 22 of the passage under consideration. See Jude, NEB; Dalton, p. 173).

J. N. D. Kelly, a proponent of this view, states that

> there is a growing conviction among scholars that, if the obscurity of the passage is to be cleared up and its relevance appreciated, the key must be sought in the myth of the sin and condemnation of the rebellious angels of Gen. vi. 1–4, which fascinated the imagination of late Jewish apocryphal writers . . . [The text] which is most illuminating is I Enoch, a compilation which has exercised great influence on the NT . . . and which relates with picturesque detail how the revered Enoch . . . was sent by God to announce their doom to the fallen angels.

[11]Some exegetes (e.g. Reicke) maintain that both fallen angels and human souls are denoted by Peter's term.

As for the place where the preaching to the imprisoned spirits occurred, Dalton, Kelly, and others think that the context points not to the nether world but to the upper regions. Kelly supports this contention with three arguments:

> First, it is natural to regard Christ's journey as taking place after His being **made alive in the spirit**; and if these words denote His resurrection, the journey must be His ascension. Secondly, while the verb translated **went** . . . could conceivably be used of descending into the nether world, it is nowhere so used in the NT, and such a verb as . . . "go down" . . . would be more suitable. Thirdly, the present verse can hardly be dissociated from 22, where precisely the same word (*poreutheis*) undeniably denotes His ascension (cf. Acts i. 10f.).

The substance of the proclamation was a "triumphant announcement" that the power of these wicked spirits had been broken. Two practical lessons were conveyed to Peter's readers by all of this: The first was that their unbelieving neighbors who were badgering and bullying them were merely reproducing the rebellious characteristics of the demonic powers whose agents they were and that they were surely destined to share their doom. Second, since Christ by His death and resurrection had triumphed gloriously over the spiritual hosts of wickedness (Eph. 1:20–22; Col. 2:15), believers were destined just as surely to participate in Christ's victory developed in verses 20–22.

Among the advocates of this third interpretation, in addition to Dalton and Kelly (already cited) are Selwyn, Stibbs, Blum, France, and Hiebert.

d. The fourth view of the passage is that the imprisoned spirits were people of the apostolic age living in the "prison house of sin."

The preaching was a proclamation by Christ to these people *through Peter and his fellow apostles* (cf. Isa. 42:5–7; 49:8, 9; 61:1). Of this sinful race the antediluvians to whom Noah preached were notorious examples. The reference to Noah is explained as follows: The result of his preaching for 120 years was the saving of "only a few people, eight in all," while the preaching of our Lord following His resurrection and ascension had resulted in the remarkable conversion of three thousand souls in one day. Some advocates of this view suggest that there is a "suppressed apodosis" that makes the passage intelligible and points the contrast. The difference of result between Noah's preaching (expressed in the passage) and the preaching of Christ through the apostles (the "suppressed apodosis") is thus explained by the accession of spiritual power that accrued to Christ by His resurrection from the dead. This view has been advocated by a relatively small number of scholars, notably John Brown.

In this view the scene of the preaching is earth, not hades (the nether world) and not the heavenly regions. The time of the preaching is the apostles' day, after the resurrection and ascension of Christ, not the day of Noah and not the period between Christ's death and resurrection. The preaching therefore was not that of the pre-incarnate Christ through Noah or of Christ while His body lay in the tomb, but of the resurrected and ascended Christ through His apostles.

In this interpretation Peter's purpose was to show his readers that in their sufferings they were following in the footsteps of their master and might expect to share in His victory. The reference to the antediluvians serves as a foil to set off more distinctly the power with which Christ has been endued (since His death and resurrection).

Of all these theories, the second, it seems to us, is the weakest. All in all, the first is to be preferred. Understood in this manner, the passage serves (1) to encourage the readers to give a bold witness just as Noah did, (2) to assure them that they, though few in number (like Noah and his family), will surely be save, and (3) to remind them of the certainty of the divine judgment on their enemies and of Christ's ultimate triumph over all the forces of evil (cf. Grudem).

*(3) Christian Baptism (3:20b–21).* The water by (or through) which Noah and his family were saved suggested to Peter the water of baptism. "This water [of the Flood] symbolizes baptism that now saves you also" (v. 21a). This is the NIV's free rendering of a Greek construction that literally reads "which [water] in the counterpart [antitype], baptism, now saves you." Verse 21 therefore teaches that the water of the Flood has its counterpart—the idea is that of similarity or

correspondence—in the water of baptism. To state it otherwise, the Christian's experience in baptism is then seen as corresponding to (prefigured by) the experience of Noah and his family in reference to the Flood. The water of the Flood wiped away the antediluvian world and made possible a fresh beginning. Similarly, baptism pictures the believer's break with his past life and his entrance upon new life in Christ.

As water "saved"[12] Noah, so baptism is now saving you, Peter tells his readers. The "now" is to be understood as simply denoting "the time of the New Dispensation" (Cranfield). The use of the present tense "saves" (*sōzei*) is in keeping with the fact that the salvation begun in the new birth (1:3–5) has not yet been completed. It is a process that is going on and will be consummated at the end of the age.

In what sense can it be said that baptism "saves"? Such a statement seems to run counter to the general teaching of the New Testament (Matt. 3:6–8; 28:19, 20; Acts 2:41; 8:12, 30–33; 9:17, 18; 10:43-48; 16:14, 15, 29–34). We must therefore interpret it in a manner that does not contradict passages that state the way of salvation in unambiguous language. A. T. Robertson affirms that the saving by baptism that Peter mentions is symbolic, not actual. There appears to be therefore a twofold symbolism here, the Flood symbolizing baptism and baptism symbolizing salvation. Rienecker/Rogers state that "baptism is the occasion and sign of transition from an old way of life to another that is marked by a new ethic."

It is true that in the New Testament baptism and the experience of salvation are sometimes represented as intimately bound up together (e.g., Acts 2:38). Perhaps this is because in the apostolic age baptism appears to have followed immediately one's acceptance of Christ. Indeed, baptism was seen as the confession of one's faith, the rite whereby one openly identified himself with the Christian community and pictured one's union with Christ in death and resurrection (Rom. 6:3–8). The rite did

[12]The more literal sense of the passage is that Noah and his family "were brought safely through" the flood waters. That is to say, the ark, not the water, was that which saved them. Yet, as Hiebert observes, "the picture contains the paradoxical truth that the flood waters that brought death to the wicked were the very means of . . . their deliverance [for Noah and his family]; the water buoyed up the ark and brought Noah and his family safely through to the new world."

not effect the union; it only pictured it. The apostles doubtless did not envision an unbaptized Christian, and they assumed that the outward ceremony and the inward reality went together.

Lest his readers should misunderstand the reference to baptism as "saving," Peter added two explanatory statements: (a) baptism does not actually remove "dirt from the body" (lit., it is not "the putting off of the filth of the flesh") (v. 21b). The literal rendering of the Greek leaves room for interpreting the words as referring literally to the removal of dirt from the body or metaphorically to the removal of spiritual or ritual defilement. Here Peter is denying the baptismal remission of sin. (b) Baptism is "the pledge of a good conscience toward God." The idea is that in baptism one makes a pledge to God out of a good conscience. The Greek word for pledge (*eperōtēma*) is used only here in the New Testament. Derived from *eperōtaō,* it basically means "a question," "an interrogation," "an inquiry in" (cf. ASV). Moulton and Milligan have shown that in the papyri the noun *eperōtēma* was sometimes employed of the question and answer process used in establishing a formal or legal contract. The word was therefore a suitable one for the act of Christian baptism, where questions were asked of the candidate, and these were met by the candidate's responses. Baptism, therefore, is represented as the believer's response to the work of God in his heart.

"Of a good conscience" may mean either that the pledge proceeds out of (i.e., is given by) a good conscience, or it may mean that the pledge is a pledge to maintain a good conscience.

A "good" conscience is one cleansed by the blood of Christ and assured of acceptance with God. Baptism then is the believer's pledge (or answer) to the work of God in his heart.

*(4) The Triumph and Enthronement of Christ (3:22).* He "has gone into heaven and is at God's right hand—with angels, authorities and powers in submission to him." "Gone into heaven" is a reference to the ascension and enthronement of Christ,[13] who forty days after His resurrection ascended to heaven to sit at the Father's right hand (the position of highest privilege, honor, and authority) (Ps. 110:1; Acts 2:34–36; Phil.

[13]The resurrection and the ascension/enthronement are to be seen as two phases of one great act.

2:5–11; Heb. 1:3; 12:2). There He ministers in behalf of His people as High Priest (Heb. 4:14–16; 7:25) and Advocate (1 John 1:9–2:2).

The main purpose of Peter's assertion was to emphasize the complete victory that Christ had achieved over all "angels, authorities and powers." The reference in these last words is to all ranks of spiritual beings, though Peter may have had especially in mind Satan and the evil hosts associated with him (cf. Eph. 1:21; 6:12; Col. 2:15). The three different terms seem to designate different groups or ranks of these superhuman powers. Lenski contends that the reference is to good (unfallen) angels. However, the all-inclusiveness of Peter's language, and other passages such as Ephesians 6:12 and (especially) Colossians 2:14–15 make the reference to evil (fallen) angels more likely. Peter's first readers would have considered these evil, superhuman beings to be the real powers behind the persecutions being meted out to them by unbelievers. They would therefore find great encouragement in the assertion that "angels, authorities and powers" had been brought into subjection to Christ (v. 22). Indeed, Christ's universal sovereignty can and should be a source of enormous assurance to all afflicted believers.

Some of the practical lessons pointed up by this perplexing passage are the following: (a) the enormous significance of Christ's redemptive work—more far-reaching than any of us can imagine; (b) the need for a courageous witness to a hostile world (after the example of Noah); (c) the importance of Christian baptism and the breadth of meaning conveyed by its symbolism; (d) the reality and power of the world of evil spirits; (e) the magnitude of Christ's triumph and the extent of His sovereignty; and (e) the encouragement that we can draw from realizing that we share in the victory of our risen, reigning Lord.

**b. The Meaning of 4:1–6.** As was pointed out above, 3:18–4:6 is to be seen as a single literary unit containing two subdivisions. The first subdivision (3:18–22) is mainly didactic and doctrinal, the latter (4:1–6) is hortatory and practical. The former thus constitutes the basis on which is built the more practical appeal contained in 4:1–6. Dalton understands the principal thrust of 3:18–22 to be Christ's victory over evil; of 4:1-6, the share of believers in this victory (p. 238).

The paragraph under consideration begins with the inferential conjunction "Therefore" (4:1), which shows that what follows flows logically from the assertions of 3:18–22. It is especially linked with 3:18a, which speaks of the sufferings of Christ. All of 4:1–6 is in essence an appeal to the readers to make Christ's sufferings a practical force in their lives, by drawing strength and encouragement from them. The main difficulties are in verses 1 and 6, the intervening verses being relatively free of interpretive problems.

The passage falls quite naturally into three parts: (1) an urgent appeal for the readers to arm themselves with the same attitude that Christ had in His earthly life, the point being that such an attitude is necessary equipment in dealing with suffering for righteousness (vv. 1–2), (2) incentives for carrying out the injunction of the first two verses (vv. 3–4), and (3) encouragement (vv. 5–6).

*(1) The Appeal (4:1–2).* In these verses some understand the apostle to be teaching essentially the same thing that Paul teaches in Romans 6:1–14. However, Peter is not referring to being dead to sin in the Pauline sense.

Peter speaks again of the suffering of Christ "in his body" (v. 1a; lit., "in his flesh"; cf. 3;18), calls upon his readers to arm (equip) themselves "with the same attitude" that Christ had (v. 1b), reminds them that their suffering for Christ advances their progress in holiness (v. 1c), and shows that as a result of their experience with Christ they are no longer to live the rest of their earthly lives for the fulfilling of "evil human desires" (lit., "the rest of your time in the flesh to the lusts of men"), but for the doing of the will of God (v. 2).

Verse 1. "Therefore" (KJV, "For as much as") shows that Peter is about to draw an inference from the fact of Christ's sufferings. "Since Christ suffered in his body" (lit., " . . . in the flesh") alludes to the statement in 3:18 that "Christ died" and that He "was put to death in the body" (lit., " . . . with reference to flesh"). The suffering mentioned in 4:1a may include Christ's total experience in His earthly life, but the term primarily refers to His redemptive death.

Some interpret "Arm yourselves also with the same attitude" as Peter's equivalent of Paul's "count yourselves dead to sin" (Rom. 6:11), but, as stated above, the two apostles are not saying exactly the same thing. Calvin comments that Peter's words intimate "that we are really and effectually supplied with invincible weapons to subdue the flesh, if we partake as we ought of the efficacy of Christ's death" (p. 121). "Arm" means to equip or arm with the appropriate tool or weapon. The tense of the verb (aorist) suggests action to be undertaken decisively, with a sense of urgency. "Attitude" translates a Greek word that quite literally means "what is in the mind" (hence, RSV's "thought"). Here, "attitude," or "mind-set," or "disposition" best expresses the meaning. For Christians to have the same attitude that Christ had toward sin and suffering is for them to have such abhorrence of sin that they would willingly suffer for righteousness.

"Because[14] he who has suffered in his body [lit., flesh] is done with sin" is somewhat parenthetical and has been variously interpreted. Calvin, Beare, Dalton, and others see it as a proverbial expression related to Roman 6:7 ("for anyone who has died has been freed" [lit., justified from sin]). Kelly takes the statement of our passage to be about Christ and the finality of His work against sin. Others (Dalton, e.g.) apply it to both Christ and the Christian. It is best to understand the reference to be to the believer and his suffering.

The word "suffered" in itself does not necessarily mean that death had actually taken place; it may simply mean that one has effectively passed through the experience of suffering, an experience now viewed as terminated. "In his body" (flesh) points to actual physical suffering, not figurative suffering. The context, however, "makes it clear that not just any physical suffering is in view; it is suffering that has been endured for the cause of righteousness as a believer" (Hiebert). Patient endurance of such suffering does indeed have moral value. As Leighton remarks, "Affliction sweetly and humbly earned doth

[14]The word translated "Because" (*hoti*) may mean "that." If this meaning is accepted, the words that follow give the content of the mind the readers were to have. See Moffatt's translation and the discussions in Dalton and Brown.

purify and disengage the heart from sin, weans it from the world and the common ways of it." The verb ("is done with")

> carries a note of triumph; he has effectively broken with a life dominated by sin. It need not mean that he no longer commits any act of sin, but that his old life dominated by the power of sin has been terminated. . . . He who in loyalty to Christ and in his power has steadfastly endured persecution rather than join in the practices of the pagan world has demonstrated that the pursuit of sin in his life has ended. (Hiebert)[15]

Verse 2 delineates the purpose for which the readers were to arm themselves with Christ's attitude toward sin and suffering: "that ye no longer should live the rest of your time in the flesh to the lusts of men, but to the will of God" (ASV). These words are grammatically related to the command to "arm yourselves," not to the phrase that immediately precedes ("is done with sin"). The NIV, by beginning a new sentence with verse 2, obscures this connection.

"As a result" is a free rendering of a Greek construction (*eis to* with an infinitive) that literally reads "to the end that, etc." No subject pronoun is expressed in the Greek text (cf. NASB, RSV). Conceivably one could supply "he" (NIV, KJV, NEB, et al.), "we," or "you" (Weymouth, Moffatt, GNB; "ye," ASV). It seems best to insert "you," since this makes the connection with the leading verb ("arm yourselves") more clear.

The purpose[16] Peter sets before his readers for arming themselves is twofold. The first is negative: that they should not live the rest of their earthly lives "for evil human desires" (lit., "the rest of your time in the flesh to the lusts of men"). The "rest of" their earthly life looks to the future, reminding them that the time remaining was at best brief. Living "to the lusts of men" (ASV) is expressed more clearly by NIV's living "for evil human desires." God's people are not to live merely to satisfy human appetites.

The second purpose of arming themselves is positive: "but rather for the will of God"—that is they should live their lives for the doing of God's will. TCNT has *guided* by the will of God;

[15]A detailed discussion of 4:1 may be found in Dalton, pp. 239–57.

[16]The Greek construction could express result. This is the idea brought out in the NIV.

Norley, "in *doing* God's will"; Williams, *"in accordance with God's will"*; TEV, *"controlled* by God's will" [all italics mine]). The conjunction "but" (Gr., *alla*) marks a sharp contrast. Thus two very different lifestyles are set before us in verse 2: one is devoted to satisfying evil human desires; the other, to the doing of the will of God. There is no middle ground. Arming oneself with the mind (attitude) of Christ imparts power to break with the former and to carry out the latter.

*(2) The Incentives (4:3–4).* Peter motivates his readers to arm themselves with the mind of Christ by reminding them of the radical change that has taken place in their lives (pagan ways have been abandoned and now belong to the past, v. 3), of the degradation of pagan life (unfit for the people of God, vv. 3b, 4a), and of the abuse heaped upon them by their former pagan associates (v. 4b). Although they had once shared in the vile and despicable sins that were a part of pagan life, all of that had now been put decisively behind them. They had "spent enough time in the past doing what pagans choose to do—living in debauchery, lust, drunkenness, orgies, carousing, and detestable idolatry" (v. 3). "What pagans choose to do" expresses faithfully the idea of the Greek, but it somewhat obscures the marked contrast between doing "the will of God" (Gr., *thelēmati theou,* v. 2) and following "the counsel [will] of the gentiles" (*to boulēma tōn ethnōn*).[17]

The catalog of vices has to do with excesses of sex, drink, and wild parties. In the Greek text all six terms used for these evils are in the plural form, pointing up the many manifestations of these sins. The first two words in the catalog speak of sexual sins. "Debauchery" suggests unbridled lustful excesses, conduct that shocks public decency. "Lusts" are illicit desires. "Drunkenness," "orgies," and "carousing" all relate to the intemperate use of alcohol. "Drunkenness" renders a word that literally suggests "overflowings of wine" (*oinophlugiais*). It means habitual drunkenness and depicts the person so described as "soaked to overflowing with wine" (Hiebert). "Orgies" translates a word (*kōmois;* from *keimai,* to lie down) that denoted festal gatherings or merrymakings, such as those in

[17]This phrase, incidentally, gives support to the view that the first readers of this letter were Gentiles.

honor of a god, particularly Bacchus. "Carousing" translates a word (*potois*) the verb form of which (*pinō*) means "to drink." Thus it denotes a "drinking carousal."

The word "detestable," used to describe idolatry, quite literally suggests "not allowed" or "unlawful." But since idolatry was commonly practiced and not banned by the laws of the day, Peter must not have meant that the idolatry he described was illegal. Selwyn thinks the Greek word here has nothing to do with lawfulness, but expresses the idea of being exceedingly evil. Lenski argues for retaining the sense of "unlawful," contending that Peter was writing to Christians from the *Christian* standpoint. NEB'S "forbidden" perhaps expresses the same thought.

The fourth verse expands upon the statement of verse 3, describing the reaction of the readers' pagan neighbors to the new lifestyle of the Christians. "They think it strange that you do not plunge with them into the same flood of dissipation, and they heap abuse on you." The first part of the verse speaks of astonishment and perplexity. "Plunge" translates a word that literally means "run together." The idea is that of rushing to associate with the wicked behavior of their pagan neighbors. "Flood" is a felicitous rendering of a word that literally means an "overflowing." "Dissipation" translates a term (*asōtias*) that describes "the character of an abandoned man" (Robertson, p. 123). Its root is the same as the word for the "wild" (KJV, "riotous") life of the Prodigal (Luke 15:13).

The last part of verse 4 speaks of the bitter resentment of the pagans, causing them to heap verbal abuse upon the Christians. There is nothing in the Greek for "on you"; indeed, only one Greek word lies behind the NIV's "and they heap abuse on you." The word is a participle (*blasphēmountes*) that may mean either "slandering" ("abusing") or "blaspheming." The absence of an object in the Greek makes it permissible to adopt either meaning—that is, either abusing believers or blaspheming God.

*(3) Encouragement (4:5–6).*The mention of pagan blasphemy and slander turned Peter's thoughts toward the approaching day of reckoning, the prospect of which was seen as an encouragement to believers subjected to the abuse of an unbelieving society. They could face misrepresentation and

slander with calm confidence and courage, knowing that their detractors would some day "give account to him who is ready to judge the living and the dead" (v. 5). It is implied that they will receive the sentence that they deserve. It is not clear here whether the Judge is the Father or the Son. However, since Christ has been the principal subject of the discussion from 3:18 onwards, it is probable that "him" refers to Christ. God the Father is often represented in Scripture as Judge (cf. 1 Peter 1:17; 2:23), but in John 5:22 we are taught that the Father "has entrusted all judgment to the Son"; and in Acts 17:31 we are told that God "will judge the world with justice by the man [Christ] he has appointed."

That Christ stands "ready to judge" suggests that He may proceed to judge at any moment.

"Living and dead" embraces all the human race, "living" referring to all of those alive on the earth when the end comes, and "dead" denoting all of those who will have already died.

The mention of Christ as vindicator of His people (v. 5) leads Peter to add a further consideration designed to encourage his readers. This has to do with the purpose of the preaching of the gospel. "For this is the reason the gospel was preached even to those who are now dead, so that they might be judged according to men in regard to the body, but live according to God in regard to the spirit" (v. 6).[18]

"For," the conjunction with which the verse begins, is explanatory and connects verse 6 with what has preceded—especially verse 5. "This is the reason" translates two Greek words (*eis touto*) that literally mean "to this end" (or, "for this purpose"). The "end" or "purpose" or "reason" for the preaching of the gospel is defined in the words that follow: "so that they might be judged, etc." That is to say, the reason "the gospel was preached [*euēngēlisthē*] even to those who are now dead" was "that they might be judged according to men in regard to the body [lit., 'in the flesh'], but live according to God in regard to the spirit." The Greek of the latter half of verse 6 contains two

[18] Masterman writes that this verse "has been described as the most difficult text in the Bible." Kelly calls it "a very obscure statement which has perplexed commentators." An excellent history of its interpretation is given in Dalton's work, pp. 42–54.

balanced clauses (set off by the Greek particles *men* ["on the one hand"] and *de* ["on the other hand"]) in which there are three contrasts: judged/live, flesh/spirit, and men/God. It is rather widely held that the word "judged" is concessive in force, the meaning being "so that, though judged, etc., they might live, etc." (cf. Goodspeed, RSV, NEB). The main statement of the purpose of the gospel's being preached is in the words "that they might . . . live according to God, etc."

"The gospel was preached" translates a single Greek word (*euēngelisthē,* from which we get the word "evangelize"). The term is passive in form, and no subject is stated in Greek. Kelly prefers to render it "he [Christ] was preached." The tense of the verb is aorist (simple past), suggesting that the reference is to a definite historical event. "The dead" have been variously identified (see Dalton, pp. 42–54): (a) the spiritually dead (cf. Eph. 2:1; Col. 2:13) John Brown and others; (b) the righteous dead of the OT era;[19] c) all the dead who departed this life before Christ died and who never had the opportunity of hearing the gospel while they were alive on earth (Beare, Best, and others). Proponents of this view generally connect the statement of 4:6 with the thought of 3:19. That is to say, the gospel was preached to "the dead" by Christ at the same time that He made proclamation to the imprisoned spirits. The fourth view, (d), sees a reference to departed Christians, that is, believers to whom the gospel was preached and by whom it was received before they died (Moffatt, Selwyn, Dalton, Kelly, Hiebert, and others). "The dead," therefore, are not people who were dead when the gospel was preached to them, but people who were dead at the time Peter wrote these words. They heard and believed the gospel while they were still alive, and then they subsequently died.

The first interpretation (a) is highly improbable. "Dead" obviously has a literal meaning in the immediately preceding verse, and to give it a different connotation in verse 6 would require overwhelming reasons. Furthermore, a reference to the spiritually dead would seem to require a present tense verb (i.e.,

[19]The argument is that though strictly speaking the OT saints did not need conversion when Christ came into the world and died, it was appropriate that they should hear the gospel.

"the gospel *is being preached* to the spiritually dead") rather than the aorist (past tense) "was preached." The argument involved in the second (b) interpretation seems to be arbitrary and irrelevant. In regard to the third (c) interpretation it should be pointed out that there is no hint in the text that 3:19 and 4:6 refer to the same event. In 3:19 Christ is described as making a proclamation. Here (4:6) the verb is passive, and it is most unlikely that it means "the gospel was preached by Christ." The fourth (d) interpretation is much to be preferred because it is in keeping with the general tenor of Scripture, it does justice to the immediate context, and it is appropriate to the needs of the readers. We know that in the apostolic period the deaths of believers caused considerable anxiety and heart-searching (cf. 1 Thess. 4:13 ff). This might have been especially true in instances where believers were martyred. Peter's words therefore serve to give strong encouragement to his readers. The fact that their Christian loved ones and friends

> had died like other men might raise the question of whether their new faith had gained them anything. In the eyes of their opponents, they seemed to have gained nothing; though they claimed to have received a new life, they died like other mortals. Peter assured them that though they had died, they would fully share in the life brought by the Savior. (Hiebert p. 251)

Peter teaches that the benefits of the gospel reach beyond the grave. Indeed, from the human point of view ("according to men") departed believers were "judged . . . in regard to the body" (i.e., experienced physical death, which as the penalty of sin is common to all mankind), but from the divine point of view ("according to God") the life imparted to them in and through Christ at the time of conversion does not end at death but endures forever.

"Judged . . . in regard to the body" marks the body (lit., "flesh") as the sphere in which the "judgment" took place. This, then, is a reference to the believer's death. Some, however, understand it as a reference to the judging of Christians as hostile pagans (cf. 4:2–4). "Body" (lit., "flesh") and "spirit" are "the two spheres of existence. They stand for life within its physical limitations, and life in its spiritual dimension"

(Mounce). See the discussion of "flesh" and "spirit" given in connection with 3:18.

"Judged" is an aorist tense in Greek, denoting a definite, once for all occurrence. "Live" is a present tense verb, bringing out the continuity of the life received in Christ.

### 3. *Live in Awareness of the Approaching End (4:7–11)*

This paragraph continues Peter's counsel for Christians who were suffering for their faith. The reference to the final judgment (v. 5) and the eschatological thought of living eternally in regard to the spirit (v. 6), led naturally to the discussion of living life with an awareness that "The end of all things is near" (v. 7a).

Our discussion will revolve around the two leading ideas in the paragraph: (a) the affirmation of the impending "end of all things" (v. 7a), and (b) the duties incumbent on believers in view of the approaching end (vv. 7b–11).

**a. The Affirmation of the Nearness of the End of All Things (4:7a).** In Greek the word for "all things," placed first in the sentence for emphasis, is to be interpreted in its most comprehensive sense. It refers not to the dissolution of the Jewish nation (John Brown) but to the end of the age. That this is its meaning is confirmed by the reference to the final judgment in the immediately preceding verses and the close grammatical connection that exists between those verses and the statement under consideration.

About this bold assertion, which is the lead sentence of the paragraph under study, we may make two observations: First, it tells us that this world will not go on forever. As Paul put it, "For this world in its present form is passing away" (1 Cor. 7:31). One day it will come to an end. The Bible elsewhere associates this end of the age with the coming of Christ in glory (1 Cor. 15:23–28; Phil. 3:20–21; 2 Thess. 1:5–10).

Second, it tells us that the end "is near." The Greek term (*engiken*), that means "to approach," "to draw near," is in the perfect tense and represents the end as having drawn near and being now in a position to break in. The idea is that the end is impending or imminent. Peter's words echo a conviction that was universal in the early church (cf. Rom. 13:12; 1 Cor. 7:29;

Heb. 10:25; 1 John 2:18), but in 1 Peter this conviction is particularly intense and vivid (cf. 1 Peter 1:4, 8–12, 20; 4:17).

Nineteen centuries have passed, and still the end has not arrived. Was Peter mistaken? We think not. The affirmation of the nearness of the end—its being "at hand"—is not to be interpreted as meaning that Peter thought it would occur in a matter of days or weeks or months or even a few years. (If that is what he meant, Peter was mistaken.) We must remember that no dates were revealed to the apostles relative to the time of the end (cf. Matt. 24:36; Acts 1:8). They were cautioned to be always expectant and ready, and so are we. And we must remember that God does not reckon time from our limited perspective; with Him a thousand years are as a single day (2 Peter 3:8–9).

The end is at hand in the sense that we are already in the last days. The Incarnation of God in Christ was the climax of the ages, and there is a true sense in which everybody who has lived since that momentous event has lived in the last days (cf. Acts 2:16f; Heb. 1:1f; 1 Peter 1:20).

This assertion of the impending end must be seen in its context. From this we can see that it is intended to give encouragement to God's people in their trials and troubles and to serve as a strong incentive to live faithfully for God while there is time. Indeed, as Jesus said, "Night is coming, when no one can work" (John 9:4).

**b. Duties Incumbent on Believers in View of the Impending End (4:7b–11).** A characteristic feature of 1 Peter is the manner in which the author sets forth doctrinal truth and then makes practical appeals on the basis of that truth. The present passage is an instance of that. Verse 7a has stated a great truth; now (vv. 7b–11) the writer will draw out lessons for living based on that statement. This is the significance of "Therefore," (v. 7b), a word that points back to the immediately preceding statement and draws an inference from it. In general the idea is that awareness of the proximity of the end should make us careful about the ordinary duties of the Christian life.

Four duties are especially enjoined:[20] (1) Live a life of

[20]Two things should be observed about verses 7b–11. First, the ideas stated in our outline are not as separate and distinct as our treatment might suggest. There are only two imperative verbs in the entire unit, and these are in verse 7.

discipline and prayer (v. 7b). There are three key expressions here: "be clear-minded," "self-controlled," and "pray." The first two are aorist imperatives, the tense giving to each of the verbs a connotation of urgency and decisiveness. The last is actually a noun in the Greek. All of them have to do with the disciplined and well-ordered life and may be seen as summing up the cautions and instructions of 4:1–6. The first expression translates a Greek word the basic meaning of which is "be of sound mind." It was sometimes used of mental health, as in Mark 5:15 and Luke 8:35, where we are told of a demoniac whom Jesus restored to "his right mind." In the present passage the word is used in the sense of being sensible and serious, of keeping one's head, keeping one's mental and moral balance, not giving way to worldliness or panic or fanaticism. The second word, that was used in 1:13 and appears again in 5:8, primarily denotes abstention from alcohol, but in the New Testament it is used more generally of self-control and clarity of mind. Mainly it speaks here of that sobriety of judgment that enables one to see things in proper perspective—more specifically, in light of the impending end of the age.

Perhaps we should not make rigid distinctions in the meanings of these two verbs. F. W. Beare comments that both "suggest a disciplined life, with all the faculties under control and the energies unimpaired by any excess."

How these three terms—"clear minded," "self-controlled," and "pray"—are related to one another in our text is open to question. Most versions, however, couple the first two words together and relate both to prayer. Some of the versions seem to connect "pray" only with the second word ("self-controlled"). For example, in ASV the clause reads, "be ye therefore of sound mind, and be sober unto prayer." Moffatt appears to see the three terms as coordinate, each being independent of the others: "Steady then, keep cool and pray."[21]

---

In the NIV they are rendered "be clear-minded and self-controlled." The commands to "love," "offer hospitality," "use" spiritual gifts, etc. either render Greek participles or express an idea implied in the context. These words derive their imperative force from their relation to the two imperative verbs of verse 7a. Second, all that follows the command to love may be seen as various manifestations of love.

[21]It should be pointed out that the word rendered "pray" in NIV and in

(2) Love one another intensely (v. 8). Along with clear-mindedness, self-control, and prayer, Peter presses upon his readers the duty to "love each other deeply." The NIV rendering loses some of the vigor of the original. The Greek word for "deeply," used only here in the NT, is an adjective built on a root that has a connotation of "stretching out," or "straining." Xenophon used the cognate verb to describe a horse at full gallop. The related adverb is used in 1 Peter 1:22, where it is translated by such words as "earnestly" (TCNT), "fervently" (KJV), "intensely" (Goodspeed), "with all your strength" (NEB).

"Above all" shows that love is of primary importance (cf. 1 Cor. 13; Gal. 5:13–14). Indeed, love may be seen as the controlling idea in the remainder of this paragraph.

The duty of mutual love is enforced by words loosely quoted from Proverbs 10:12: "because love covers a multitude of sins." This must not be interpreted to mean that our love atones for ("makes up for") sins—whether our own or someone else's. The general sense probably is that love will cause us to forgive again and again. In the OT, to "cover" sometimes means to "forgive" (cf. Ps. 32:1; 85:2).

(3) Practice hospitality (v. 9). Hospitality appears to be introduced at this point not only as a conclusion from the nearness of the end but also as "one of the duties of love" (Calvin). No finite verb appears in the Greek text of the verse, the verbal idea being expressed by an adjective meaning "hospitable" (lit., "friendly to strangers"). The KJV renders it "Use hospitality"; RSV, "Practice hospitality"; NIV, "offer hospitality."

One must remember that respectable inns were almost nonexistent in the Roman world; hence the need for Christians to open their homes to one another. This also accounts for the frequency with which the NT enjoins Christians to practice hospitality (cf. Rom. 12:13; 16:1f; 1 Tim. 3:2; Titus 1:8; Heb. 13:2; 3 John 3–5). Best thinks Peter's words were also intended to encourage believers to open their homes for the use of local house-churches in worship and fellowship.

Such hospitality was to be extended "without grumbling"

---

Moffatt's version is not a verb in Greek. The ASV, quoted above, gives a more literal rendering.

(i.e., ungrudgingly), counsel doubtless given because Peter realized that hospitality is subject to abuse by guests lacking sensitivity. Extending hospitality indiscriminately might, in fact, be quite dangerous. Peter's choice of words therefore indicates that he recognized the difficulty of carrying out his command. Positively, "without grumbling" means "with gladness."

(4) Use individual gifts to serve one another (vv. 10–11). A further conclusion from the nearness of the end—and another manifestation of love—concerns the faithful use of one's gift(s). "Each one should use whatever spiritual gift he has received to serve others" (v. 10a). Peter's statement assumes that each believer has some God-given endowment for service. The "gifts" of our text, therefore, are not the special privilege of only a select number of God's people.

Four things are to be observed: First, though NIV places a period at the end of verse 9, the most widely used Greek texts separate the two verses by only a comma. Thus, there is a very close connection between the thought of verse 9 and that of verse 10. Second, "gift" translates the term *charisma*, that is built on the Greek word for "grace." The gifts therefore are grace-gifts. That is to say, they are a free bounty from God, not a reward for merit. Furthermore, as "grace-gifts" they are to be distinguished from natural endowments and should be understood as special capacities for service graciously bestowed by God on His people. Third, Peter's words clearly teach that one's gifts are not a private luxury to be hoarded but equipment to be used for the benefit of other people.

Fourth, these divine endowments are in fact a sacred trust from God, as is clearly expressed in the more literal translation of verse 10b: "as good stewards of the manifold grace of God" (ASV, NASB). A "steward" was one (usually a trusted slave), to whom the management of an estate was committed. He was not the owner, only the administrator (cf. Luke 16:1–4). A "good" steward was one who was true to the trust put in him, one who faithfully carried out his duties. This notion is brought out in the NIV rendering: "faithfully administering God's grace in its various forms." The context suggests that "grace" (Gr., *charis*), that in the New Testament generally denotes God's undeserved favor), may stand for the gifts (*charismata*) that He graciously bestows on us.[22]

"Various" translates a word that literally means "many-colored." It suggests both richness and great variety, along with "an undertone of the harmonious beauty which is exhibited in the union of the different gifts" (Beare). The divinity of gifts exists so that Christ's body (the church) will lack nothing that it needs for ministry.

Verse 10 sets forth principles relative to gifts; verse 11a, b expands upon the thought by singling out gifts of speech and action (service) as examples. First, speech: "If anyone speaks, he should do it as one speaking the very words[23] of God" (v. 11a). That is, what he says when professing to speak for God is to be a true communication from God. The reference is not to ordinary conversation primarily but to preaching and prophecy and perhaps even to tongues. As for service (action), it should be done "with [lit., 'out of'] the strength God provides"; that is, in dependence on His enablement. "Serves" may perhaps be interpreted as embracing all types of Christian work (e.g., caring for the sick, hospitality, almsgiving) except that having to do with speaking (mentioned in the first part of the verse). "Provides" translates a Greek term (*chorēgei*) that originally meant "to lead a chorus," then "to defray the expenses of providing a chorus" for public festivals. Its meaning was extended, as here, to the idea of providing for needs generally, often with the sense of an abundant or lavish supply. The thought is that God meets all our needs (here, strength for service) with unlimited liberality.

Verse 11c gives the motive and/or goal of all that we do for God: it is "that in all things God may be praised [lit., glorified] through Jesus Christ." These words probably should be construed with the whole of verse 11, not (as NIV) with just the immediately preceding words. Indeed, Beare feels that "in all things" gathers up everything said in the entire paragraph (vv. 7–11). The clause ("so that, etc.") is understood by him as a kind

[22]It should be remembered, as noted above, that the Greek words for "grace" and "gift" are built on the same root.

[23]The Greek term is used especially of divine utterances.

of "all-embracing imperative": "In all things, let God be glorified."

The paragraph closes with a doxology: "To him [God] be the glory and the power for ever and ever. Amen." The NIV, in supplying the verb "be," interprets Peter's words as a prayer. It would be just as proper to interpret it as an indicative and more in keeping with the pattern of other fully stated doxologies in the NT to supply "is"/"are" or "belong"/"belongs" and understand the utterance to be a statement of fact (cf. ASV, RSV, NASB, GNB, and others). Glory (splendor) and power (might, sovereignty) do indeed *belong* to God. They are inherently His.

*4. See Suffering in Proper Perspective; Understand Its Place and Its Meaning in the Christian Life (4:12–19)*

Many scholars (e.g., Beare and Cranfield) think the material from this point in the text (4:12) to the end has no vital connection with what has gone before. They argue that this unit seems to reflect a different situation from that seen in the earlier part of the letter. That part of 1 Peter (1:3–4:11) is thought by some to be a baptismal sermon (i.e., a part of general baptismal instruction); the references to suffering are said to be more or less hypothetical). The material beginning at 4:12 is thought to be either a letter (i.e., a separate distinct document) or an appendix occasioned by the ordeal of suffering confronting the readers. Selwyn, Kelly, and others oppose such a dissection of 1 Peter and argue convincingly for its unity. With this latter position we are in full agreement.

Trials hold a large place in this letter. Near its beginning Peter called attention to the readers' suffering "grief in all kinds of trials" (1:6), and beginning in 2:18, he urged slaves, who were a part of the Christian fellowship, to bear up under the pain of unjust suffering because of their consciousness of God. From 3:13 onward suffering and trial have been the dominant theme. Indeed, Peter intimates that things will get worse before they get better (4:12).

**a. Verses 12–13 Call upon the Readers Not to Be Astonished by the Severe Sufferings Coming upon Them. They Are Reminded That They Are Linked in Fellowship with Christ and His Sufferings, and in That They Are to Rejoice.** The severity of the trials being experienced by the recipients of this letter is suggested by the word translated "painful trial." This is a defensible but less than satisfying rendering of the Greek. The more literal reading of the ASV ("fiery trial") is to be preferred. Selwyn lists three meanings of the term "fiery": (a) a burning, (b) exposure to the action of fire (as in baking or boiling), and (c) testing by fire (as in the purifying of metals). He thinks there can be little doubt that the last meaning is the proper one here: "a process of refining by fire is going on amongst them for their testing." The Greek word (*pyrōsis*) is built on a root meaning "fire." In this passage Arndt and Gingrich translate it "fiery ordeal." In the only other New Testament passage where the word occurs it refers to the burning of Rome (Rev. 18:9).

Peter mentioned that the fiery trial was coming upon them for the purpose of testing ("to prove you," ASV), making manifest the reality or unreality of the readers' faith. The more literal rendering of the ASV points out that Peter wanted his readers to see that God was permitting them to suffer for a purpose, that purpose being the refining of their faith and the overall discipline of their life.

Instead of being bewildered or resentful they should rather rejoice,[24] being aware that in the measure in which (to the degree that; Gk., *katho*) their sufferings are a participation in Christ's sufferings they should rejoice in them. The larger context leads us to conclude that the ground for rejoicing is not in the sufferings themselves but in the fellowship with Christ that they make possible. The last clause of verse 13 is to be construed with the command to "rejoice" (v.13a) and may be interpreted as expressing the purpose ("in order that . . . ") or the contemplated result ("so that . . . ") of fulfilling that command. The latter is the more probable meaning and is expressed by the NIV: "So that you may be overjoyed when [at Christ's coming] his glory is revealed" (cf. Rom. 8:17f; Phil. 3:10f; 2 Tim. 2:11f). The thought is that the present joy of suffering Christians prepares them to experience an even more rapturous joy when, in eternity, they find themselves sharing in Christ's glory. The more they suffer for Christ, the greater their

[24]The word in Greek is a present tense imperative, suggesting a continuous attitude and activity.

ground for rejoicing will be. "Overjoyed" is an attempt to bring out the meaning of a combination of two words in the Greek that have to do with joy. One, the more common term, is used for "rejoice" in the first part of verse 13; the other, an especially strong word added for emphasis, conveys the idea of exultation (cf. 1:6, 8). The revelation of Christ's glory refers to the consummation when Christ's glory will be manifest, and every knee shall bow in recognition of His majestic sovereignty.

**b. Verses 14–16 Encourage the Readers Not to See Their Suffering for Christ's Sake as a Misfortune or as Something to Be Ashamed of, but as a Privilege for Which to Be Grateful to God.** In being "insulted [reviled or abused][25] because of [lit., in] the name of Christ" they are truly blessed. The reason for this is that "the spirit of glory and of God rests" upon them (v. 14). That is to say, believers suffering "because of the name of Christ" are already participating in the divine glory. The NIV rendering, which follows the KJV and others, represents one interpretation of an unusual Greek construction: *to tēs doxēs kai to tou theou pneuma*, "the of-the-glory and the of-God Spirit." A word must be understood before "of the glory." Selwyn sees a reference to the Shekinah[26] and translates it "the Presence of the Glory, yea, the Spirit of God" (cf. TCNT). The first phrase in this translation refers to the Shekinah; the second is the more precise definition and explanation. The NIV reading reflects the view that is preferred by most interpreters. The sense is "the Spirit of glory, which is also the Spirit of God."

In verses 15 and 16 Peter interjects a qualification,[27] reminding his readers that there is a difference between suffering deservedly for wrongdoing and suffering innocently for the name of Christ. The readers must make sure that their sufferings are of the latter kind. "If you suffer, it should not be as a murderer or thief or any other kind of criminal, or even as a

---

[25]Kelly points out that the Greek verb and its cognates often are associated in the New Testament "with the indignities and maltreatment which Christ had to endure."

[26]"Shekinah" (not found in the Bible) was used by the rabbis of the physical manifestation of the divine majesty. "Glory" (*doxa*) is used for the Shekinah in Rom. 9:4 and perhaps James 2:1.

[27]At the beginning of verse 15, the Greek text uses a conjunction (*gar*, "for") at the beginning of verse 15 that has no equivalent in the NIV.

meddler" (v.15). The Greek text individualizes this injunction, its literal reading being "let not *any* of you suffer as a murderer, etc." The twofold use of "as" shows that the list falls into two divisions, the first three ("murderer," "thief," "any other kind of criminal") forming one group, the fourth word ("meddler") designating a separate category. "Murderer" and "thief" are specific, "any other kind of criminal" (one word in Greek, "evildoer") is general. The Greek word for meddler, used only here in the New Testament, is interpreted in a variety of ways: "one who covets what belongs to another" (Calvin), "concealer of stolen goods," or "one who meddles in things that do not concern him" (i.e., "a busybody"; cf. KJV). The meddling[28] that Peter had in mind could have been any one of several things, but whatever it was the apostle considered it to be disreputable.

It would be shameful for a Christian to suffer as a murderer, etc., but "if you suffer as a Christian [i.e., simply because you are a follower of Christ, not because you are guilty of any wrongdoing], do not be ashamed, but praise God that you bear that name" (v. 16). This is one of only three occurrences of the word "Christian" in the Bible (cf. Acts 11:26 and 26:28). It is generally thought that it was first used by non-Christians as a nickname for Christians, and that it probably was a term of contempt (cf. Acts 26:28).

The NIV's "praise God that you bear that name" is an interpretive rendering of a construction that literally reads, "let him praise [honor, magnify] God in that name." The precise meaning of the last phrase ("in that name") is debated. The "name" is generally understood to be the name "Christian," that occurs in the first part of the verse. The general idea is that Peter's readers were suffering in the cause of Christ because they were identified with Him, and were like Him. Therefore they were not to be ashamed of those sufferings, but were to praise God for the privilege of bearing His name and suffering in His cause.

---

[28]The Greek word (*allotriepiskopos*) may be literally rendered, "a supervisor of things belonging to another (person)," "a bishop over other men's matters," or "an observer of other people's affairs." TEV aptly renders it, "trying to manage other people's business."

**c. Verses 17–18 Another Reason Why Christians Should Accept Their Sufferings without Complaint. They Are a Part of the Process of God's Judgment of the World.** In that process now is the time or "appropriate season" for Christians to experience disciplinary judgment, for in the divine order of things judgment begins with the family (lit., "house, household") of God.[29]

The passage is in three parts. The first (v. 17a) makes an assertion; the second draws an inference (v. 17b); and the third enforces this with a quotation of Proverbs 11:31 (Septuagint). Space permits comment only on the assertion: "For it is time for judgment to begin with the family of God" (v. 17a). The point is that a kind of preliminary judgment is already occurring. Since that is so, the final doom of the disobedient is sure to follow soon—and with unimaginable fury. The recipients of this letter were to find encouragement in knowing that God was at work in their sufferings.

Verses 17 and 18 are full of practical lessons for all. First, they teach that judgment (chastening discipline) begins in time with the family of God. As presented in this passage, the judgment experienced by Christians is not punishment for sin but a necessary purifying process. Second, the sufferings of Christians (their present judgment) are a harbinger of the coming judgment of the world. If judgment begins with God's own house, it certainly will not stop there. Third, the passage teaches that judgment will fall with terrifying vengeance on those who refuse to believe in Christ. The language is without elaboration because the writer's main objective was to encourage believers to stand firm under trial. It does suggest, however, that the judgment becomes more devastating as it goes on. Fourth, the passage teaches the seriousness with which the

[29]Calvin speaks of being afflicted for the name of Christ as a "necessity" that "awaits the whole Church of God." Christians, he explains, are not only subject to "the common miseries of men," but are especially subject to chastisement" by the hand of God. Then, with more submission, ought persecutions for Christ to be endured. For except we desire to be blotted out from the number of the faithful, we must submit our backs to the scourges of God." Similarly, John Brown writes that God's disciplinary judgment falls upon His people "as a proof of their membership in His family, and a pledge of their escape from the end of those whom the last judgment shall find disobedient to the Gospel."

Christian life should be lived. Even "the righteous" (the believer) is saved with difficulty. (The allusion is to the severe trials Christians must endure.) Peter's purpose was not to raise doubts about the salvation of true believers, but, as Best observes, to emphasize "the greatness of God's effort in saving them." The mention of the doom of the wicked is intended to stiffen the resolution of all who read this letter. It is also a warning that apostatizing in order to avoid the hardship of the Christian life is folly.

**d. Verse 19 Rounds Out the Paragraph by Indicating That Christians Are to See Their Sufferings as an Occasion for Committing Themselves to the Faithful Creator—for Protection and Safekeeping.** "So then" points up that Peter is about to draw a conclusion to a logical deduction from the preceding discussion. To "suffer according to God's will" means that the suffering under discussion is a part of God's will (plan). It is providentially ordered (cf. 1:6; 2:15; 3:17; 5:6). This is so in two senses: (a) God's permissive will is involved in letting the enemies of the gospel persecute His people. They could do nothing unless they were allowed by God. (b) God's purposive will is also involved. Christians' sufferings are used to bring them into larger conformity to Christ (cf. Rom. 8:28ff). "Commit" translates a banking term used of making a deposit, or of entrusting something valuable to someone for safekeeping. The same word is found in 2 Timothy 1:12. "Faithful" calls attention to the reliability of God. He can be trusted.

### B. Special Counsel for Elders, for Young Men, and for the Whole Christian Community (5:1–11)

We need to remember that at this point Peter was still thinking of his readers as a people enduring the stress of persecution (cf. comments at 3:13). In the preceding section (3:13–4:19) he has offered them counsel of a general nature, encouraging them to cultivate a proper attitude with reference to suffering (3:13–17); to look to the experience of Christ, who through suffering triumphed over all the forces of evil and holds out to us the promise of sharing in His victory (3:18–4:6); and to live with an awareness that the end of all things is at hand (4:7–11). The section closed somewhat as it began, with an appeal for the readers to see their suffering in proper perspective—that is, to understand its place and meaning in the Christian life and to let bewilderment give place to joy and trust in God (4:12–19).

In the passage now before us Peter offers special counsel for the pastoral leaders of the churches (5:1–4) and for the younger men (believers) in the churches (5:5a). These units are followed by concluding appeals for the whole Christian community (5:5b–11).

### *1. Counsel for Elders (5:1–4)*

The Greek text of verse 1 begins with a word (*oun*) that has no equivalent in the NIV. An inferential conjunction that may be rendered "therefore" or "so," it functions here to show that what follows is counsel that grows out of the discussion in the preceding verses. It is generally agreed that "elders" (v.1) has here an official connotation and refers to pastoral leadership in the churches (cf. v. 5a, where the same Greek word is used in the nonofficial sense of "older men"). This term had its roots in Jewish synagogue life and appears to have been used interchangeably with "bishop" (overseer) and "pastor" (shepherd).[30]

We cannot be sure of all of the duties of the elders as set forth in verses 2–4, but the phraseology suggests that they included the ministries of provision and protection ("Be shepherds"), leadership and supervision ("overseers"). All of this was to be carried out in an attitude of humble service and care ("not lording it over").

Peter appeals to the elders in his capacity as a "fellow elder, a witness of Christ's sufferings and one who will share in the glory to be revealed" (v.1). His terms point up his desire to identify with his readers and to give added appeal for their obedience. By use of the expression "fellow elder" the apostle not only assures the elders that he had responsibilities similar to

[30] For "elders" see Acts 14:23; 15:2; 16:4; James 5:14. For the use of "elder" and "bishop" interchangeably see Acts 20:17, 28; Titus 1:5, 7. The word "pastor" appears as a title for a church officer (function) only in Eph. 4:11; however, the verbal form of the word is found in Acts 20:28 ("Be shepherds"); and in the passage under study (5:2, "Be shepherds"), where it is a charge to the "elders."

theirs but that he also had a fellow-feeling for them in their bearing of ministerial burdens.[31]

Lexicons give two definitions of the word "witness." Those who advocate the meaning "one who testifies" sometimes point out that Peter was not actually present at the crucifixion and thus could hardly have described himself as an eyewitness of our Lord's passion. Those who advocate the meaning "eye witness" may argue that though the Gospels do not tell us that Peter was present at the crucifixion, it is quite possible that he was among "those who knew him [Jesus]" and who "stood at a distance, watching these things" (Luke 23:49). With Alford, Selwyn, Stibbs, Cranfield, Hiebert, and others we prefer to interpret it in the sense of "eyewitness."

The "glory to be revealed" is reference to the final and complete unveiling of Christ's glory at His Second Coming.

There is only one command given to the elders: "Be shepherds of God's flock" (v. 2a). The verb is built on the same root as the word for "pastor" (Eph. 4:11; cf. Heb. 13:20, where the same word is used of Christ, and 1 Peter 5:4, where a compound form is used of Christ). "Shepherd" embraces the ideas of guiding, feeding, protecting, and so forth—things involved in the work of a shepherd in reference to his flock.

This one command is amplified in verses 2b–3 by three Greek participles. These are rendered respectively "serving as overseers," "not lording it over," and "being examples."

Verse 4 holds out the promise of reward for elders who serve faithfully: "And when the Chief Shepherd appears, you will receive the crown of glory that will never fade away." The Chief Shepherd is Christ. The word for "crown" (Gr., *stephanos*) was used for the perishable wreath that was given to athletes who were victorious in the games and to citizens who distinguished themselves in public service. Christ, because He suffered death, was crowned with glory and honor (Heb. 2:9). His faithful undershepherds may expect to share that glory. That their crown "will never fade away" means it will last forever.

[31]Since the word plays down Peter's apostolic status, some feel that its use here is an argument for the Petrine authorship of the book. A forger would hardly have done this.

This puts it in sharp contrast with the much-coveted but perishable wreaths given to victors in athletic games.

### *2. Counsel for Younger Believers (5:5a)*

"In the same way" renders a transition word denoting a new turn in the discussion or perhaps an additional item in a series of appeals (cf. 3:1 and 7). Alford renders it "in your turn" (p. 383).

"Young men" is a single word in Greek, meaning simply "younger." In this word and in the word for "those who are older" (translated "elders" in v. 1) the reference is clearly to age, not to office. Peter, writing in the first century, was doubtless thinking of young "men" and older "men," but the broader principle of the subordination of all younger persons to those who are older is imbedded in his words.[32] In this context to "be submissive to" means to show deference to, to respect, to revere. There is no notion of obedience to ecclesiastical authority. The form of the verb suggests a voluntary submission.

### *3. Counsel for the Entire Christian Community (5:5b–11)*

The pervading thought of the passage has to do with suffering and steadfastness. Specifically, Peter calls for humility toward one another and toward God (vv. 5b–7) and for self-control and spiritual alertness (vv. 8–9). The unit continues with an assuring promise of God's gracious help in times of distress (v. 10) and closes with a doxology (v. 11). All Christians who suffer innocently may find needed help and encouragement in this passage, but it was especially addressed to persons suffering for their faith.

**a. Be Humble, Recognizing God's Sovereign Control and Never-Failing Care (5:5b–7).** Verse 5b, containing appeal for humility in reference to fellow Christians, employs picturesque language: "Clothe yourselves with humility." The imagery is that of a slave tying on an apron and preparing to serve. The verb translated "clothe yourselves" (*enkomboomai*) was built on

[32] Kelly writes that in ancient times "the division of society into older people and younger . . . was just as much taken for granted as the division into men and women, free men and slaves, etc." The word for "younger," though masculine in form, was commonly used of both men and women.

the root of a word (*enkombōma*) that denoted the apron or overall that the slave tied over his sleeveless vest to work. The wearing of such an apron set the slave apart from the free man. Some think that there is an allusion to our Lord's girding Himself with a towel in preparation for washing the disciples' feet on the night of His arrest (see John 13:4).

"Humility" is the opposite of arrogance and conceit. The wearing of humility as a garment should not be interpreted to mean that humility is to be put on as matter of outward show; it is rather to be worn as the garment of the spirit, as a characteristic attitude that expresses itself in practical action toward others.

The reason for, or incentive to such humility (stated in a quotation from the Septuagint reading of Prov. 3:34) is found in an attitude of God: He "opposes the proud but gives grace to the humble." "Opposes" translates a verb that literally means "sets himself against," the imagery being that of an army lined up against an enemy. The Almighty, as it were, declares war on the proud! The "proud" are those who are arrogant and haughty, persons lacking the humility for which Peter appeals. All those who thus elevate themselves "shall have God for their enemy," and He will "lay them low." (Calvin). The humble receive markedly different treatment from God. To them He gives "grace," that is, He bestows His favor upon them, and they find acceptance in His sight.

Verse 6 urges suffering Christians to humble themselves "under God's mighty hand," the motive being "that he may lift you up in due time" (i.e., the time of the End). The suggestion here is that humility is not just an attitude toward other people, but is essentially an attitude that acknowledges and submits to the sovereignty of God. It is a call not for passive resignation but for voluntary acceptance of the circumstances that were theirs under the permissive will of God. In doing this, they will find themselves ultimately vindicated. "God's mighty hand," a bold but frequently used figure in the Old Testament (cf. Exod. 3:19; 6:1; 13:3), conveys the thought of God's power exercised in reference to His people, whether for deliverance or for discipline. The implication of Peter's statement is twofold: (a) God is in control of all that happens and (b) He wants His people to trust Him and submit humbly to His control.

Verse 7 shows one way of doing the latter: "Cast all your anxiety on Him" (cf. Matt. 6:25–32; Ps. 55:22; 1 Peter 4:19). The NIV rendering (as well as that of most other modern versions) employs an imperative verb, and by doing so implies that this verse is an additional and separate command. The Greek, however, uses a participle, not an imperative. The participle is to be construed with the command of verse 6 ("Humble yourselves, etc."). That is to say, it is to be understood as explaining that imperative verb. Kelly gives the sense: "the true Christian attitude is not negative self abandonment or resignation, but involves as the expression of one's self humbling the positive entrusting of one's self and one's troubles to God."

"All your anxiety" includes "all the readers' individual cares and concerns, whether due to memories of the past, pressures of the present, or fears concerning the future" (Hiebert). The Greek for "all anxiety" is such that it means something like "the whole of" your anxiety.

Peter's readers were encouraged to throw all their worries upon the Lord by the reminder that God "cares for" His people (v. 7b). Hiebert rightly observes, "All that creates anxiety for us, whether momentous or trivial, is a matter of concern to Him."[33]

**b. Be Controlled and Alert, Remembering the Vicious and Constant Activity of the Devil (5:8–9).** Recognition of God's sovereignty and His fatherly care does not negate our responsibility. Nor does it justify indulgence and carelessness. Our duty is clear: "Be self-controlled and alert." The NEB better catches the ringing force of the Greek: "Awake! be on the alert!" (There is no conjunction between the two Greek verbs.) The first word ("Be self-controlled") suggests being free from every form of mental and spiritual drunkenness. Positively it means to be well-balanced, self-controlled (Bauer, Arndt, and Gingrich). (For further discussion see comments on 1:13 and 4:7.) The second

[33] Beare's comment is worthy of note: "The conception of God as concerned with the affliction of man is the peculiar treasure of Judaic and Christian faith; Greek philosophy at its highest could formulate a doctrine of His perfect goodness, but could not even imagine in Him an active concern for mankind."

word ("be . . . alert") literally means to be awake or to keep awake; figuratively it means to be on the alert, be watchful (Bauer, Arndt, and Gingrich).

The reason for vigilance is stated in verse 8b: "Your enemy the devil prowls around like a roaring lion looking for someone to devour." The identity of this enemy is shown in the next term, "the devil." This word is used in the Septuagint for the Hebrew "Satan" and means "slanderer." The description of the devil as one who "prowls around like a roaring lion, etc." points up his vicious nature ("a roaming [ravenous] lion"), his restless activity ("prowls around"), his malignant intention ("looking for someone to devour [lit., 'to gulp down']").

The believer's proper action in regard to the devil is not to flee but to "Resist him, standing firm in the faith, etc." (v. 9; cf. James 4:7). The word for "resist" is a military term (lit., "stand against"). (In v. 5 the same word is used of God's resisting the proud.) An aorist imperative, it denotes that the action is to be undertaken decisively, with a sense of urgency. The sense is, "Take your stand against." It calls for an act of will, for taking a solid stand against the vicious enemy of God and His people. The armor needed to withstand the devil is described in Ephesians 6:10–18.

Our "standing firm in the faith" as we resist the assaults of Satan will assure our victory. Standing firm translates a single word, that in a physical sense was used to describes something solid and firm like a foundation. Used here, the word denotes an attitude of firmness or unyieldingness. "In the faith" is understood by some to speak of faith subjectively (trust, confidence in God). However, it seems better to take "faith" in its objective sense—that is, as the true gospel. The NIV reflects this interpretation.

As an encouragement to his reader's firm resistance to the devil Peter adds, "because you know that your brothers throughout the world are undergoing the same kind of sufferings" (v. 9b). The sense is,

> Do not give way under the attacks of the devil. Remember that you do not stand alone in your struggle against him; the same kinds of sufferings you are experiencing are being accomplished in other Christians elsewhere in the world.

They, like you, are in the world and like you, must expect such trials. They are, in fact, an inseparable part of life as long as believers are in the world.

"Your brothers" translates an uncommon term ("brotherhood") that emphasizes the oneness and solidarity of believers. "Undergoing" renders a word about which there has been considerable debate. Alford thinks that much of the discussion has been unnecessary, concluding that the word has "its usual N.T. meaning of 'accomplish'; 'complete.'"

**c. Draw Strength from the Promise of God's Help and the Assurance of Ultimate Perfection (5:10–11).** Verse 10 is rendered as a prayer in the KJV and NKJV ("but may the God of all grace . . . perfect, establish, etc.," NKJV). Almost all recent translations follow a Greek text that uses future tense verbs in the verse and they accordingly interpret the verse as a promise rather than as a prayer ("And the God of all grace . . . will himself restore you, etc.," NIV). Our enemy may be (as v. 8 has taught) powerful, determined, and vicious, but we have One on our side who is more than a match for him.

The apostle reminded his readers that they did not stand alone against the devil. Their brothers throughout the world were enduring the same suffering. Here he seems to say, "Whether you apprehend that or not, one thing is sure: the God of all grace has called you to His eternal glory and is working in and for you to make you strong."

Three things are said about God in verse 10, each designed to give comfort and encouragement to the reader. First, He is "the God of all grace" (cf. 2 Cor. 1:3, "God of all comfort"). This means that He is the source of all spiritual help, that He is sufficient for every need that His people may have. "All" grace may also point to the variety of His grace (cf. 4:10, "God's grace in its various forms"). Second, He "called you into his eternal glory in Christ." The verb "called" puts stress on the sovereign action of God. This call came to the readers when they heard and received the gospel. "Glory" sums up all the good that God has in store for His people in the age to come. It is essentially the Christian's sharing in God's eternal glory. The eternality of glory is in sharp contrast with the "little while" of the readers' sufferings (v. 10c; cf. 1:6, "for a little while you may have had to suffer grief"). "In Christ" is construed by some with "called" (e.g., Bengel, Kelly, Hiebert); by others (e.g., Bigg, Wand) with "glory." Third, God "will himself restore you and make you strong, firm and steadfast." "Himself" is emphatic; He and no other will do this.

It is a matter of debate whether there are three or four verbs in the great promise (cf. ASV and RSV that follow a text using three verbs; KJV, NKJV, and NIV that follow a text using four verbs). One's decision on this matter will not appreciably affect the sense. Whether three words or four, together they promise the strength, courage, and hope that the readers need for facing their troubles. "Restore" (Gr., *katartisei*) suggests the thought of a fitting together or of ordering and arranging properly. Here it may mean to put in proper order or to perfect. Selwyn explains that the Greek word means "to make whole," pointing out that it is used elsewhere "of making good" that which is weak (Ezra 4:12, Septuagint), torn (Matt. 4:21), or defective (1 Thess. 3:10), and of "perfecting" that which is in course of preparation (Luke 6:40; Heb. 13:21). He concludes that re-establishment rather than perfection (completion) is the main idea here. Alford, Hart, Hiebert and others feel that "to bring to completion" (perfect) is the idea here. Perhaps we should not define the word with rigidity, but rather understand in it the ideas of mending, restoring, equipping, and perfecting. "Make strong" (Gr., *stērixei*) was used in a literal sense of the stabilizing of something by providing a support so that it would not totter. The essential meaning is that God will give a firm footing to His beleaguered people, will establish them so that they cannot be shaken. The Greek word that NIV translates "Make . . . firm" (Gr., *sthenōsei*) has not been found anywhere else in biblical or in secular Greek (Kelly). It means to strengthen or make strong. In our own strength we are sure to fail, but the promise here is that God will impart to us the strength necessary for all our trials. The meaning of the word that NIV translates "Make . . . steadfast" (Gr., *themeliōsei*)[33] is to found or to lay the foundation of. Figuratively, it means to establish, to set upon a firm foundation

[33] Some manuscripts have no equivalent for this word. However, the majority of the manuscripts contain the word. Kelly comments that "its insertion is hard to explain if we assume that it was originally absent."

or to strengthen. The idea of setting upon a firm foundation seems to be what is expressed here.

The *doxology* calls attention to the mighty power of God that guarantees the fulfillment of the preceding promises: "To him be the power[34] for ever and ever. Amen." Perhaps it would be better to translate, "To Him *belongs* the power, etc." or "His *is* the power, etc." Selwyn sees the doxology as "affording an additional reason for faith and fortitude: power belongs to God, now and to eternity."

**For Further Study**

1. Baptism is an issue over which the opinions of Christians differ. Use a topical Bible or concordance to discover other New Testament passages that discuss the subject of baptism. List your own personal convictions after study.

2. In 1 Peter 4:3 Peter describes the past life of his readers. Make a list of the habits and traits from which God had delivered them. Make a similar list of habits and attitudes for which you would like God's personal help or strength.

3. In 1 Peter 4:10–11 Peter discusses the subject of spiritual gifts. The New Testament discusses this same subject in Romans 12:3–8, 1 Corinthians 12, and Ephesians 4:7–12. Study these other passages to learn the varieties of gifts and the purpose of gifts.

4. Another passage in the New Testament that discusses the topic of suffering is James 1:2–4. Compare and contrast the emphasis of this passage with that of 1 Peter 4:12–19. J. I. Packer has a chapter in his book *Knowing God* entitled "The Adequacy of God." Read its content for further information about the attitude of Christians and suffering.

5. Use a topical Bible or a concordance to discover other passages in which the temptations of Satan are described. What do these passages indicate about the areas of life in which Satan tempts?

---

[34] Manuscript support for the addition of the words "and the glory" (KJV) is weak.

# Chapter 5

# Conclusion

(1 Peter 5:12–14)

Peter has now completed the body of his letter. Four matters are briefly presented in the closing verses: a summary description of his letter (v. 12), the final greetings (v. 13), a request (v. 14a), and the benediction (v. 14b).

### A. A Summary Description of the Letter (5:12)

This verse tells us at least three important things about 1 Peter. First, it was written "with the help of Silas" (lit., "by [i.e., through] Silvanus"),[1] a man mentioned by name nine times in Acts. The statement here could mean that: (a) Silas was the bearer of the letter to its readers; (b) Silas, as amanuensis, wrote under the general direction of Peter. The second view is preferable. Understanding this view helps to explain the difference in the style of Greek in 1 Peter and that found in 2 Peter, where no reference is made to Silas's help in writing.

Second, the letter takes the form of encouragement and testimony. The word "encouraging" covers the ethical instructions of the letter as well as the appeals to bear suffering with fortitude and hope. "Testifying," that Kelly describes as "a strong verb that implies that [Peter's] testimony carries weight," suggests confirmation and reliability. Peter was saying that his entire letter was an earnest testimony to confirm that the message of salvation received by his readers was, in spite of all

[1]"Silas" is the Greek form and "Silvanus" the Latinized form of a Hebrew name. There is no valid reason for disputing the identification of the "Silas" of Acts 15:40 with "Silvanus."

the suffering that had subsequently befallen them, the true (authentic) grace of God.

Third, the letter concerns "the grace of God," in which the readers are urged to stand fast. In light of this verse Griffith Thomas concludes that three themes run through 1 Peter: God's grace, Peter's testimony, and the believer's duty.

**B. The Final Greetings (5:13)**

First, there is a greeting from the chosen "lady" in Babylon. "She who is in Babylon" has evoked considerable discussion. The words are understood by some to refer to something (perhaps, a church) personified as a female; by others, to an actual, female person. If the reference is to a person, she could only have been Peter's wife (cf. 1 Cor. 9:5). Alford argues for this interpretation. Kelly thinks this interpretation "is in the highest degree improbable; the writer surely would have named her or indicated her identity by some less roundabout phrase." The majority of interpreters prefer the former view, contending that the reference is to a sister congregation located in Babylon and elect (chosen) like the readers (cf. 2 John 13). The Greek word for "church," though not used here, is feminine.

"In Babylon" suggests that Peter was in this place when he wrote his letter. Three views as to the identity of Babylon have been put forth: (a) that it was Babylon in Mesopotamia, (b) that it was Babylon in Egypt,[2] and (c) that "Babylon" was a cryptic name for Rome. Most scholars think it is improbable that either of the first two interpretations is correct and, taking note of the fact that in both Jewish and Christian circles of the first century "Babylon" was increasingly used as a symbolic name for Rome, opt for the third view. In support of this is early tradition that speaks of Peter's being in Rome, and the lack of evidence that Peter was ever in Mesopotamia or Egypt.

Second, there is a greeting from Mark. It is generally agreed that "Mark" is John Mark, the author of the second gospel. Peter calls him his "son," apparently using the word in a figurative or

[2]This Babylon was in general decline in the first century, and the Jews living there had been forced to abandon it in Claudius's reign (A.D. 41–54). Strabo and Josephus mention a military outpost in Egypt called "Babylon." The headquarters of a Roman legion, it was located near Old Cairo.

spiritual sense (cf. Paul's use of the same word of Timothy, 1 Tim. 1:2). In the early days of the Christian movement Mark was a part of the Christian community in Jerusalem, and Peter had been a familiar visitor in his home (cf. Acts 12:12–17).

### C. A Request (5:14a)

The "holy kiss" (as Paul puts it, Rom. 16:16; 1 Cor. 16:20; 2 Cor. 13:12; 1 Thess. 5:26) was an established custom of greeting in early Christian history. There is difference of opinion about the origin of the custom. Kelly writes that it was "entirely Christian in origin, without precedent in the synagogue." Others hold that the custom was already established before it was taken up by the Christians (cf. Hiebert). Beginning as a pure expression of brotherly affection, it later became subject to abuse. Early church councils found it necessary to regulate the practice, and by the end of the thirteenth century kissing as ritual had almost entirely disappeared.

### D. The Benediction (5:14b)

The letter is concluded with a benediction: "Peace to all of you who are in Christ." This is a fitting close to a letter written to people living in the midst of turmoil and suffering.

# Introduction to 2 Peter

This letter has had rough treatment at the hands of Christians down through the centuries, and many questioned its very inclusion in the Canon. "At the Reformation it was regarded as second-class Scripture by Luther, rejected by Erasmus, and regarded with hesitancy by Calvin" (Green). Despite these difficulties the church did accept it and recognized the accuracy of its claim to apostolic authorship and authoritative content.

**A. Authorship**

The writer of 2 Peter intends to be seen as the apostle Peter (1:1, 14, 16–18; 3:1, 15). A popular theory, however, is to see that the letter is a pseudepigraph, a writing published after Peter's death to honor him and to say what he might have said in a situation of difficulty. This idea has raised ethical problems in the minds of many who see a resort to deceit and trickery as unworthy of one who claimed to be a committed Christian. The external evidence for authorship is not conclusive, for "no book in the Canon is so poorly attested among the Fathers, yet no excluded book has nearly such weight of backing as 2 Peter" (Green). There is little early evidence in favor of the authenticity of 2 Peter, but in the third and fourth centuries there is evidence that it had a growing acceptance.[1] Guthrie notes that there is no evidence that the writing was ever rejected as spurious despite the hesitancy about its reception (*New Testa-*

[1]Bigg's commentary provides the best collection of patristic references designed to support Petrine authorship.

*ment Introduction,* III, 142). Those who are reluctant to accept Petrine authorship of the epistle often point to its dependence on Jude, but Guthrie indicates that it is not entirely certain that Peter copied Jude (*New Testament Introduction,* III, 147). Some also note the reference to Paul in 3:15 as indicating a time when a collection of Pauline writings had been made (a time most certainly later than Peter's lifetime), but Peter may be referring only to those writings of Paul known at the time of his writing of 2 Peter.

Green, in deciding for Petrine authorship of the writing, points out that those who hold to the view of a pseudepigraphical author have not succeeded in showing how the author could avoid ethical compromise with Christian conviction. He also indicates that he is impressed by the similarities between 1 and 2 Peter in both vocabulary and doctrine, and to some extent, with the Petrine speeches of Acts.

## B. The Occasion and Date of 2 Peter

With Peter as the author, the book would seem most likely to have been written from Rome shortly before Peter's death (1:15). Peter had apparently worked among these readers and was giving them exhortations that he would have delivered personally if he were present (1:16). He realizes that his own work is nearly concluded, for he refers to his passing as if it were near (1:14). The letter also has the attitude of urgency that suggests that there was a definite threat from the infiltration of false teachers who would appear on the scene (2:1). However, the frequent use of a future tense in describing these false teachers (2:2, 3) suggests that the writing is to have a preventive effect when the heretics appear on the scene. Peter intends to strengthen his readers in faith and moral commitment so that they will be able to resist the ungodliness of those who will threaten their spiritual life.

The date of 2 Peter would be toward the end of Peter's life, before A.D. 68. It seems most likely to see it as written not too long after 1 Peter, but there is no specific reference in the writing that allows us to place the time of writing clearly.

### C. The Recipients of 2 Peter

In 1 Peter the specific provinces in which the recipients live are mentioned (1 Peter 1:1). In 2 Peter no specific destination is clearly mentioned, but Peter's references suggest that he wrote the letter to a specific community and not merely as a general circular letter (1:12–15; 3:1, 14). Some see the reference to a second letter in 3:1 as a clear suggestion that the writer had penned 1 Peter. If this is true, then the author is seen as writing a second letter to those mentioned in 1 Peter 1:1. However, the interpretation of 3:1 (q.v.) does not demand that the reference be to 1 Peter, for there may be an allusion to a writing of Peter now lost. The absence in 2 Peter of specific quotations from the Old Testament (when many are found in 1 Peter) may appear to suggest that the recipients were more Gentile than Jewish, but 2 Peter does contain many references to Old Testament events (2:5, 6, 7, 15).

Since there is no information by which to draw a firm conclusion, it is better to leave the destination an open option although it is possible to see it as written to the same group that received 1 Peter. The destination of the writing is not a factor in its interpretation.

### D. False Teaching in 2 Peter and Jude

The descriptions of the false teachers in 2 Peter 2 are quite closely paralleled by Jude's reference to them in verses 4–19. In 2 Peter the problem of heresy is introduced only gradually, but there is some preparation for the discussion of 2 Peter 2 in the first chapter. Jude, by way of contrast, leaps into a denunciation of the heretics almost from the beginning.

Both Peter and Jude suggest that the lives and teachings of the heretics deny the lordship of Jesus (2 Peter 2:1; Jude 4). They defiled the Christian practice of the love-feast, practiced immorality themselves, and infected others with their wickedness (2 Peter 2:10, 12–14; Jude 4, 12). The heretics were crafty in their speech and played with their words in such a way as to curry favor with those who could benefit them economically (2 Peter 2:3, 14; Jude 16). They appear to have posed as either visionaries or prophets in support of their claims (2 Peter

2:1; Jude 8). They are also self-willed and prone to set up divisions that reflect their own view of confident superiority (2 Peter 2:2, 10, 18; Jude 19). The false teachers denounced by Peter deny the Parousia of Christ (3:1–4), but Jude does not mention this tendency. In describing the false teachers Jude frequently uses a present tense to describe them (vv. 8, 12, 16), and one might suppose that the problems with the false teachers had already arisen. Peter appears to write with more of a preventive purpose, and his use of the future tense (2:2, 3) might indicate this. Jude also makes reference to apocryphal material in enforcing his points (vv. 9, 14), but Peter does not refer to this.

Many of these traits—arrogance, divisiveness, extreme wickedness—later made up the troublesome doctrines of Gnosticism. A movement with some of these traits was already present in Corinth as early as the fifties (1 Cor. 6:12–20). These false teachers display a general antinomian tendency, but they need not be pushed into the second century, for such practices as pride and immorality were also first-century occurrences.

In noting the similarities between Jude and 2 Peter it is possible to feel that Peter copied Jude, Jude copied Peter, or that both are dependent upon a common source. There is such extensive agreement between Jude and 2 Peter that some common linkage is almost certain. Almost the whole of Jude 4–19 has some similarity to material in 2 Peter 2. Those who favor the dependence of Jude on Peter point to the use of the future tense in predicting the false teachers in 2 Peter 2 compared with the present in Jude. Also, some note that an apostle as prominent as Peter would not likely take material from the obscure Jude. Those who feel that Peter copied Jude point to the freshness of Jude's style and the probability that the longer letter of 2 Peter would copy the shorter document of Jude. The difference in language, ideas, and order between Jude and 2 Peter is pointed out by those who see a common source for both writings. Green inclines to the latter view and feels that the source might have been a document that denounced false doctrines of an antinomian variety and pointed out the doom awaiting the false teachers (p. 54).

## For Further Study

1. Read the articles on "The Second Epistle of Peter," "Judas (A Brother of the Lord)," and "The Epistle of Jude" in the *Zondervan Pictorial Encyclopedia of the Bible.*

2. Read 2 Peter and Jude in several modern versions of the Bible. A good version to use is the New International Version, published by Zondervan. Notice repeated words, phrases, and ideas. After several readings make a personal outline of both letters.

3. Read carefully 2 Peter 2 and Jude 5–19. List the similarities in references to events and personalities in both writings.

4. Use commentaries to determine the source of Paul's words in the following passages: Acts 17:28; 1 Corinthians 10:4; 2 Timothy 3:8. Notice the similarities between Paul's references and the references of Jude to apocryphal writings in Jude 9 and Jude 14, 15.

## Outline of 2 Peter

I. Introduction
II. Overview and Salutation (1:1,2)
III. Provisions for Spiritual Growth (1:3–21)
  A. The Call and Election of the Christian (1:3–11)
  B. The Testament of Peter (1:12–15)
  C. The Power and Glory of Christ (1:16–18)
  D. The Divine Message of Scripture (1:19–21)
IV. Danger Ahead—False Teaching (2:1–22)
  A. A Self-centered Emphasis on Immorality and Greed (2:1–3)
  B. A Certainty of Judgment for Those Following False Teaching (2:4–10a)
  C. Insolent Attitudes toward Divine Commands (2:10b–11)
  D. The Arrogance, Lust, and Greed Due to Spiritual Ignorance (2:12–16)
  E. The Emptiness and Spiritual Slavery from Following Their Teachings (2:17–19)
  F. The Ultimate Separation from God (2:20–22)

V. A Reminder of Divine Hope (3:1–13)
 A. The Promise of the Lord's Return (3:1–4)
 B. The Proof of the Lord's Return (3:5–10)
 C. The Application of the Lord's Return (3:11–13)
VI. Closing Admonitions (3:14–18)

# Chapter 1

## Overview and Salutation
(2 Peter 1:1, 2)

The Book of 1 Peter is written to Christians facing persecution, and Peter seeks to fill his readers with hope in the light of their difficulty. In 2 Peter the readers are facing false teaching that bears some resemblance to Gnosticism, and here the emphasis of Peter is placed on the true knowledge of God.

Peter begins his second letter with a salutation resembling that of 1 Peter. In 1:3–21 he outlines God's provisions for the spiritual growth of His people. He discusses the call and election of God's people (vv. 3–11), and he presents their election as an incentive for individual effort in demonstrating traits of godliness. In verses 12–15 Peter suggests that he will provide a reminder of God's promises that may be available to encourage his readers even after his death. As another provision for spiritual growth he cites the power and glory of Christ in verses 16–18, and then he refers to the divine message of Scripture in verses 19–21. The prophecies of Scripture are viewed as instruction given to aid the readers in spiritual preparation for the future.

The grave danger of false teaching is mentioned in 2:1–22. Peter warns of the immorality and greed of these false teachers in verses 1–3, and he warns of the certain judgment of God on those who walk in their paths (vv. 4–10a). He points out the insolent attitudes of the false teachers toward divine commands in verses 10b, 11, and he focuses on the arrogance, lust, and self-indulgence of the heretics in verses 12–16. Despite the fact that they promise liberty and power to their followers, the false teachers entice their followers into spiritual slavery (vv. 17–19). The actions of these false teachers demonstrated their true character, for they were returning to the style of life that they preferred, an indication of their lostness (vv. 20–22).

In 3:1–13 Peter reminds his readers of the divine hope that a belief in Christ's return inspires. Some of the false teachers were denying the promise of the Lord's return (vv. 1–4), and Peter uses history (vv. 5–7), Scripture (v. 8), the character of God (v. 9), and a specific promise of Christ (v. 10) to prove the fact of the Lord's coming. A fervent belief in the return of the Lord is an incentive for godly living (vv. 11–13).

In 3:14–16 Peter refers to the writings of Paul as further evidence that the patient waiting of God is leading toward salvation for His people. The conclusion in 3:17, 18 calls upon the readers to develop in their experience of grace and the personal knowledge of God.

**Salutation (1:1, 2)**

The opening of 2 Peter follows the commonly used letter form in New Testament times of "A (the writer) to B (the recipients)" with a greeting included. As a Christian writer Peter included an extended theological description of himself and his readers. He also includes in the greeting of verse 2 a specifically Christian wish for his recipients. He omits mention of a geographical location.

In verse 1 the spelling in the Greek text for "Simon" is actually "Simeon," a form used with the name of the apostle elsewhere only in Acts 15:14. This is a Hebrew spelling of Peter's name and may serve as an indication of the authenticity of the writing. In speaking of himself as a "servant and apostle" Peter blends personal humility with an awareness of apostolic authority.

The "faith" described by the apostle is used in the sense of a trust that brings a personal salvation. The faith of Peter's readers is described as equally precious with that of the apostles. The "receiving" of this faith is described with a word (Gr., *langchanō*) that means "to obtain by lot," and it served as a reminder that the saving experience of the Christians was a gift of God's grace. We should not press the interpretation of the word to suggest that God randomly gave salvation to some but not to others.

The term "righteousness" explains the reason for the equality of privilege between apostles and later generations. Here it speaks of the absolute fairness of Jesus by which both the apostles and later generations have an equality of opportunity and status.

The last phrase of verse 1 finds Jesus being described as both "God and . . . Savior."[1] The absence of the Greek article before "Savior" is a point in favor of this interpretation, and elsewhere in the letter the writer uses a similarly constructed phrase, "our Lord and Savior Jesus Christ," when there is no doubt that the entire phrase points to Jesus Christ (1:11; 3:18). Even though the term "God" (Gr., *theos*) is not commonly used in the New Testament to refer to the Son, there are a number of texts where "God" does apply to Jesus (John 1:1; 20:28; Heb. 1:8). In other instances in 2 Peter where the word "Savior" appears it is clearly a reference to Jesus (1:11; 2:20; 3:2, 18). Peter is taking the term "Savior," an Old Testament name for Jehovah, and is boldly applying it to Jesus. He had also referred to the saving work of Jesus in his sermon preached at Pentecost (Acts 2:21). In the Hellenistic world and the later Roman world, rulers were honored as "Saviors," and "it is probable that a title used by pagans to set forth the impious pretensions of kings and emperors is here being deliberately claimed for Christ" (Cranfield).

In verse 2 Peter wishes grace and peace to his readers. He had earlier greeted the readers of 1 Peter with a similar wish (1 Peter 1:2). Grace is the loving favor that God shows to sinners and that He has shown fully in Jesus Christ. Peace includes all the material and spiritual blessings given to man by God. It is the condition of being right with God along with all the blessedness that that brings (Rom. 5:1–5).

Peter was writing to people who claimed to know Christ but

[1]The issue of interpretation is whether Peter is distinguishing God and Christ or is calling Jesus God. Alford feels that he is distinguishing God and Christ and cites the obvious distinction in verse 2 in favor of this. Another commentator joining with him is Huther who adds that the close conjunction between "God" and "Savior" points to their oneness. In these verses the terms "God" and "Savior" appear to refer to Jesus Christ.

who were being tempted to revert to the practice of disobedience. His emphasis on "knowledge" in verse 2 is a reminder that the correct knowledge of Christ will produce grace and peace plus full commitment and holiness. "Knowledge" is not merely an exercise of the intellect (Phil. 3:8, 10), but it refers to a personal experience with Jesus Christ.

In 2 Peter two different words for "knowledge" are used. Here Peter uses the word *epignōsis*, a term translated as "full knowledge" by Williams (also used by Peter in 1:3, 8; 2:20). The other term, *gnōsis*, is translated "knowledge" by Williams (also used by Peter in 1:5, 6; 3:18). Bigg distinguishes between the terms with the observation that *gnōsis* "appears to denote good sense, understanding, practical wisdom." He adds that *epignōsis* refers to the knowledge of Christ and is used by Plutarch to describe scientific knowledge in such a field as music. Lenski adds that *epignōsis* "is a true, clear, full knowledge that is personally embraced and has the strongest effect on the personal religious life."

The object of this knowledge is "God and . . . Jesus our Lord." Most translations (e.g., "with God and with Jesus our Lord," Berkeley [MLB]) see both the Father and the Son as the objects of knowledge. No difference should be seen between this type of knowledge and that of Jesus Christ alone (cf. 2 Peter 3:18). In a true sense it is Jesus alone who is the object of the knowledge of the Christian.

**For Further Study**

1. Read "Second Epistle of Peter" in the *Zondervan Pictorial Encyclopedia of the Bible.*

2. Read again the salutation of the letter of 1 Peter. Observe the differences between the salutations of this epistle and 1 Peter in such areas as the name of the writer, the location of the recipients, and the greeting given to them.

# Chapter 2

## Provisions for Spiritual Growth

(2 Peter 1:3–21)

Peter was eager to contribute to the spiritual growth of his readers. Their commitment was not to be barren and sterile but alive and maturing. He indicated four sources of potential power for spiritual development in his readers. First, he mentioned the divine power of God that had resulted in their calling and election. His recipients had become the heirs of special promises that could lead them to experience the very glory of God. They were to make diligent effort to add to their lives every needful spiritual trait. Second, he mentioned his own witness. Peter felt that he would not live long, and he determined to leave with his Christian friends a reminder of the promises of God that would aid their growth. Whether these were oral or written, Peter saw them as a source of help for struggling Christians. Third, he cites the power and glory of Christ as seen in the Transfiguration. This power, now available for the Christian, was no clever fable but a reality of which Peter had been an eyewitness. Finally, Peter mentioned the divine message of Scripture. This message was a source of warning and instruction for Peter's readers, for it had its source in God Himself.

### A. The Call and Election of the Christian (1:3–11)

Peter assumes the calling and election of his readers. This position provided for them many spiritual privileges (vv. 3, 4). On the basis of these privileges they are to demonstrate the character that is the product of faith (vv. 5–7). Further, they are to be fruitful in their knowledge of Jesus Christ (vv. 8, 9), and they are to keep constantly before them the goal of godliness (vv. 10, 11).

### *1. The Privileges of God's People (1:3, 4)*

Many writers view verses 3, 4 as linked in thought with the salutation (e.g., Bigg, Kelly) so that Peter is seen as explaining that grace and peace are multiplied in knowing Jesus because God has given us all that we need. Cranfield more properly suggests that the verses are "connected, not with what precedes them, but with what follows: they give the ground for the exhortation contained in vv. 5–7."[1]

In verse 3, Peter makes their divine call a basis for an appeal for godly living. "It is not entirely certain whether Jesus or the Father is conceived of as issuing the call and offering the divine power . . . . But Jesus is the last person mentioned, and the *glory and virtue* [NIV goodness] are more appropriate to Him than the Father. In either case, the point is that the One who calls, enables" (Green).[2] "Life" is the new divine life that is the property of all believers in Christ. "Godliness" is more related to practical conduct rather than mere devotional service to God. The word "given" will "always carry a certain regal sense describing an act of large-handed generosity" (Strachan). "Knowledge" is again a knowledge of Christ, a reference to basic Christian knowledge gained at conversion. The "us" is a reference to Christians in general and not merely to the apostles. Thus, Peter is saying that all Christians are the object of the call that he has described. Evidence for this is seen in the fact that verse 10 takes up the idea of the call of Christians in general based upon the mention of the idea in verse 3.

Peter concludes his statement of the Christian's calling by indicating the agency of Jesus in this calling. Christians are called by the moral excellence and personal impact of Jesus.

[1]Bauckham says that "the connection with v 2 is largely stylistic, whereas the connection with vv 5–7 is fundamental to the flow of argument."

[2]Kelly feels that "his divine power" is a reference to God because of the statement in Romans 8:32 that with Christ God will freely give us all things. He sees the one who has "called us" as a reference to Christ because it is more natural to see Christ as the object of the Christian's knowledge. The reference to "glory" seems to be a reminder of the glory of Christ seen at the Transfiguration.

The moral excellence or "goodness" (Gr., *aretē*) of Christ is a reference to qualities demonstrated in concrete deeds. It is not merely a static quality. The "glory" (Gr., *doxa*) of Christ is that demonstration of the divine character that causes the love and worship of men. These twin traits become the means of attracting outsiders to the Savior.[3]

In verse 3 Peter has indicated that Christ has given us all that is useful in salvation and holiness by the knowledge of Christ. In verse 4 he summarizes again the nature of this gift and attaches a condition for experiencing its reality.

The "through these" of verse 4 refers back to the "glory and goodness" of verse 3. The saving intervention of Christ in His Incarnation has bestowed on all Christians His precious and magnificent promises. As later explained in 3:13, these promises must surely include the return of Christ, the establishment of a new heaven and earth, and an entrance into Christ's kingdom. The use of a Greek perfect tense for "given" suggests that these promises are firmly guaranteed.

The appearance of "so that" (Gr., *hina*) in verse 4 may show the purpose of giving the promises, or it may explain the content of the promises.[4] Either option makes excellent sense in the context, but it seems most suitable to see the *hina* clause as explaining that the content of the promises of God includes a participation in the divine nature (cf. the usage of "that" [*hina*] in John 13:34 and 1 John 5:3).

Peter's use of the phrase, "participate in the divine nature," finds him employing language that had much similarity with Greek philosophical and religious thought. He was doubtless deliberately using terms to which his readers could relate, but he filled the terms with a distinctively Christian understanding. He is not saying that man is absorbed into the deity, for that

[3]The text with "glory and goodness" is uncertain, for some manuscripts read "through (Gr., *dia*) glory and goodness" rather than "by his own (Gr., *idia*) glory and goodness." Green asserts that a copyist could easily have mistaken "through" for "by his own," and he feels that it is proper to view the nouns and their modifiers as an instrumental, "by" and not "to" (KJV).

[4]W. H. Griffith Thomas and Bigg take the former option and note that the purpose of giving the promises is to make people partakers of the divine nature. Lenski and Bauckham feel that the clause following the *hina* is in apposition with "promises," and they view this as a more natural way of seeing the connection of the clause with the foregoing words.

would ultimately nullify the possibility of a personal encounter between the individual and God. He is speaking of a real union with Christ with much the same meaning as conveyed in John 1:12, Romans 8:9, and Galatians 2:20. This idea of a deep spiritual union with Christ has also been conveyed in 1 Peter 4:13 and 5:1 by describing the readers' participation in Christ's sufferings and glory. Peter meant that by their spiritual commitment to Christ his readers had become true sharers in Christ personally. This relationship would be deepened by the fulfillment of these promises in eternity.

Peter's last phrase in verse 4 speaks of an escape from "the corruption . . . caused by evil desires" and adds a condition for partaking of the divine nature.[5] Thomas views the phrase as indicating the prerequisite for participating in the divine nature. The corruption is a moral corruption (cf. 2:12), and Christians will escape this corruption by their wilful putting away of all wickedness and hypocrisy in their lives (1 Peter 2:1).

In verse 4 Peter has reminded his readers that because of the promise of their ultimate fellowship in eternity with Christ, they will be sharers of a deep spiritual union with Christ. To share in this ultimate glory, they must now firmly renounce sin. The promises of future glory thus become an incentive to present godliness.

### *2. The Products of Faith (1:5–7)*

In view of their new birth, their receipt of precious promises, and the divine power of Christ, Christians must expend diligent effort. Peter concluded verse 4 with an emphasis on the promises available to Christians and with an appeal to avoid the negative influence of corruption. He now urges his readers to demonstrate positive effort. There are specific moral traits to be added to their lifestyle. The NEB catches the spirit of Peter's appeal by translating, "With all this in view, you should try your hardest to supplement your faith." Building upon "faith" as the foundational rung of the ladder, Peter urges his

[5]Kelly feels that the phrase shows a reason why Peter's readers can expect to share in the divine nature—because they have escaped the corruption of the world. He says that "the aorist participle points to a definitive act, and so there is probably an allusion to their baptism and their renunciation of sin."

Christian friends to manifest more deeply seven additional qualities of Christian character.

Peter recognizes that Christian character is not the product of human effort alone. He understands that sharing in Christ's nature provides a divine incentive to godliness. Human effort is necessary, but alone it is inadequate. Human commitment must take its place alongside what God has done.

Peter's word, "add to," suggests generous and costly participation.[6] The Christian must enthusiastically participate with God in producing a Christian life that will honor Him.

The foundation stone for building this Christian character is faith, an initial acceptance of God's love as offered in the gospel. Bauckham describes it as "the specifically Christian "faith" in the gospel which is the basis of all Christian life."

The first trait to be added to "faith" is "goodness" ("moral excellence," NASB; "resolution," Moffatt). Bigg indicates that the word refers to "right conduct under discipline." By this trait good habits are established, and fleshly desires are dissipated.

Possessing this "goodness" leads to "knowledge," a reference to the intellectual part of human personality. Most commentators distinguish "knowledge" here (Gr., *gnōsis*) from the "knowledge" (Gr., *epignōsis*) of verses 2 and 3 by identifying this as practical wisdom. Bauckham sees it as "the wisdom and discernment which the Christian needs for a virtuous life and which is progressively acquired." Kelly sees it as a "discernment of God's will and purpose."

A third trait to be developed is "self-control" ("temperance," KJV; "self-restraint," Alford). This trait is to be demonstrated in every aspect of life. In Greek moral philosophy it referred to controlling the passions instead of being controlled by them. For the Christian "self-control is submission to the control of the indwelling Christ" (Green). In selecting this word Peter was making a jab at the licentiousness of the heretics (2:2; 3:3), who followed their own lusts and felt that maturity showed

[6]Green indicates that "add" (Gr., epichorēgeō) was drawn from Athenian drama festivals, in which a rich generous donor, known as the *chorēgos*, joined with the writer and the state in providing for expenses in a production. This man paid the expenses of the chorus, and he tried to outdo other donors in providing lavish equipment and training for the choruses.

itself in an absence of restraint. For Peter godliness meant submission to divine commands, not freedom from them.

A fourth trait to be developed is "perseverance" (Gr., *hypomonē*; "steadfastness," Moffatt; "patient endurance," Williams). This is a trait by which a man bears up under persecution or adversity. This is "the temper of mind which is unmoved by difficulty and distress, and which can withstand the two Satanic agencies of opposition from the world without and enticement from the flesh within" (Green). It is not to be compared to a Stoic trait of accepting all that happens as from a blind fate, but it involves a faith in God's promises and an experience of His power. It sees all that happens as produced by the wise and loving hand of the Father (cf. James 1:2–4).

The fifth trait discussed by Peter is "godliness" ("piety," TCNT; "devotion to God," Phillips). Godliness is a right feeling and behavior toward God, "a very practical awareness of God in every aspect of life" (Green). This trait in a Christian would stand in contrast with the heretics who deny "even the sovereign Lord who bought them" (2:1).

Such godliness must not be solitary and morose, but it must include "brotherly kindness" ("love to the brethren," Weymouth; "a spirit of brotherhood," Goodspeed). This was an affection in the Christian family for fellow-believers, brothers and sisters in the faith. It would demand kindness, generosity, and courtesy for those in the household of faith.

The seventh and crowning trait of Peter's ladder of faith is "love," ("Christian love," Moffat; "universal love," Williams). This term (Gr., *agapē*) was used in the New Testament to denote the attitude that God has demonstrated to us and that He wants us to demonstrate to Him and to others. Green points out that "in friendship (*philia*) the partners seek mutual solace; in sexual love (*erōs*) mutual satisfaction. In both cases these feelings are aroused because of what the loved one is." With *agapē*, love is evoked because of what God is, not because of what we are. This love has its origin in the agent, not in the object. It can be seen as a wilful desire for the highest good of the loved one, a desire that demonstrates itself in sacrificial action for that person (1 John 3:17). Only when Christians show this quality of love do they demonstrate that they are Christ's disciples (John 13:34, 35).

By outlining this ladder of faith Peter has demonstrated that partaking of the divine nature does not grant an exemption from ethical claims on the Christian. Sharing in this nature makes ethical growth and moral commitment a possibility.

*3. An Appeal to Fruitfulness (1:8, 9)*

The positive reason for having the graces mentioned in verses 5–7 is given in verse 8, and the negative reason appears in verse 9. Peter wants his readers to be strengthened with a genuine knowledge of Christ so that they might resist the invasion of error that is on the horizon.

To make a positive contribution to the lives of Christians, these traits must grow and increase. The phrase, "if you possess" (Gr., *humīn huparchonta*), utilizes a verb that denotes "property which one really possesses and which is therefore fully at one's disposal" (Kelly). The foregoing traits must really be in the lives of Peter's readers. Further, these traits must "abound" (Gr., *pleonazonta*). They must be ever increasing in their influence.

The result of having accessible traits of godliness that are always maturing is that the Christian readers are kept "from being ineffective and unproductive." This phrase—literally it means "they make you neither idle nor unfruitful"—uses a figure of speech known as litotes, affirming an idea by denying its opposite. The idea is that the readers become useful and productive. The two adjectives are nearly synonymous, but "ineffective" (Gr., *argos*) describes faith without works in James 2:20, and "unproductive" (Gr., *akarpos*) uses the metaphor of fruit in reference to good works or ethical traits (cf. Titus 3:14). Translators render "ineffective" as "useless" (NEB) or "barren" (KJV) and "unproductive" as "unfruitful" (KJV) or "barren" (NEB).

The term "knowledge" (Gr., *epignōsis*) is again (cf. its earlier use in vv. 2, 3) used in reference to the personal knowledge of Jesus Christ gained in conversion. Peter is saying that a developing Christian character will render a Christian active and fruitful with reference to knowing Jesus Christ, the root from whom all moral progress proceeds. Here the idea is not so much that having the Christian virtues leads to a fuller knowledge of Christ as it is that the knowledge of Christ provides everything necessary for the godly life. The knowledge of Christ produces virtues of firm Christian character that provide an effective, fruitful experience.

The absence of these traits affords a negative contribution to the lives of Peter's Christian friends. The opening phrase of verse 9, "if anyone does not have them, he is . . . blind," introduces a conditional statement. Peter's readers may not lack the traits that Peter has just described, but if they do, they are blind. To be "blind" suggests to be without sight. This condition is far more serious than that of the other word, "nearsighted" ("shortsighted," TCNT). This second word (Gr., *muōpazō*) may also suggest to "blink" or to "shut the eyes." Peter may be suggesting that a man is blind because he has blinked or deliberately closed his eyes to the light. This person will be more easily attracted by the nearness of the things of earth than by the more distant verities of heaven.

A person who is this "blind" is one who has "forgotten that he has been cleansed from his past sins." The forgiveness that a believer receives at his conversion and demonstrates in baptism marks a decisive break with the old life of sin (Col. 3:1–3). This conversion should serve as the beginning of a virtuous life. The Christian who fails to grow and mature forgets the joyful delight of his conversion and may relapse into his pre-conversion sins. The spiritual condition described here is the total lack of assurance of salvation. A believer who fails to grow and develop will forget the high cost of his redemption and his initial joy in receiving it. These solemn words become an incentive to push the Christian on to the attainment of maturity.

### *4. The Goal of Godliness (1:10, 11)*

The "therefore" of verse 10 refers back to the whole of the preceding paragraph in verses 3–9. In the light of God's wonderful gifts that lead to an increased knowledge of Christ, Peter's Christian friends must exert themselves. Peter introduces this goal of godly living by issuing a command and then outlining two results that are derived from following that command.

The command is that Peter's readers are to "be all the more eager to make your calling and election sure." Peter's statement here concerning "calling and election" penetrates to the heart of the paradox of election and free will. The calling and election of an individual to salvation are secure in the counsels of God. However, they are insecure unless they are demonstrated by a holy life. Peter is not suggesting that one must work in order to attain his election, but he clearly states that individual behavior is the proof or disproof of true election. Peter's subject in this command is not the securing of salvation but the development of assurance about it. His command is necessary because his readers were in danger of being led astray under the influence of teachers who believed that immorality would not incur divine judgment. The infinitive "make" is in the Greek middle voice, and this signifies the urgency of the cooperation of the human will in the process. Note the similarity of ideas in Paul's words in Philippians 2:12, 13.

The first result from following this command is that the readers will never fall. Peter is not referring to the stumbling into sin that can characterize each believer at times (James 3:2), but he means that a Christian will be delivered from a "disastrous coming to grief" (Green). The idea is similar to the "fall beyond recovery" in Romans 11:11 and is captured in spirit by the NEB translation: "If you behave so you will never come to grief." The imagery for "falling" is "drawn from the surefootedness of a horse" (Green). The idea again is that a Christian must be making steady progress in his Christian growth. If he does, he will not stumble but will make surefooted progress. Such progress will be a source of assurance for the individual, but it will also protect him from the ruin brought about by sin.

The second result from obeying Peter's command is a glorious entrance into the eternal kingdom of Jesus (v. 11). The imagery used is that of a spiritual pilgrim on a long journey. The splendor of his destination incites him to the attainment of the goal of his journey. The verb for "receive a . . . welcome" is the same word translated as "add" (Gr., *epichorēgeō*) in verse 5 (q.v.). The word does not so much emphasize the importance of human participation in the process of salvation as it indicates "the lavish provision made by the divine generosity" (Bauckham). Green adds that the idea of entry into the kingdom may be related to an honor given to a victor in the Olympic Games. "His home city, in her joy and pride in his success, would welcome him back not through the usual gate, but through a part of the wall specially broken down to afford him entrance" (Green).

Peter describes the kingdom to which the pilgrim is moving with three emphases. First, it is an eternal kingdom. It pertains to the life of the coming age. In Christ the life of the coming age has invaded the present age (Luke 11:20). The final things have been started, and they will be consummated. This consummation will mean eternal life for the people of God, but it will mean eternal punishment for God's enemies (Matt. 25:46). Second, the entry that Peter describes is seen as future. Christians, to some extent, already share in the divine nature (v. 4). They already experience the righteousness, peace, and joy of the kingdom of God (Rom. 14:17). However, there is still a future element to the hope of the Christian, and each believer, like Abraham, is to press on toward that city made only by God (Heb. 11:10). Third, this kingdom belongs to "our Lord and Savior Jesus Christ." Reference to the kingdom as Christ's rather than God's is not very common in early Christian writings (Matt. 6:33; 13:41; for contrast see Eph. 5:5). The phrase, "kingdom of Christ," is not to be distinguished from the kingdom of God. The kingdom is called Christ's kingdom in that it is entered by relationship to Him (Mark 10:21, 24) and will produce harmonious relationships between Christ and His people. This kingdom that belongs to Christ is not simply another name for "heaven," but it is the "cosmic reign of God in righteousness in the new heaven and new earth" (3:13; Bauckham).

These words conclude Peter's first paragraphs and constitute a moving appeal not to allow an arid intellectualism or an antinomian compromise to dilute Christianity. This passage does agree with several in the New Testament that indicate that the degrees of happiness in heaven are dependent on the faithfulness with which we have built a foundation of character and service upon the foundation of Christ (Luke 12:47, 48; 1 Cor. 3:10–15). The Christian is encouraged to live in the light of the privileges already given to him. He must also look ahead to the final judgment and seek to live in the light of that event.

## B. The Testament of Peter (1:12–15)

In this section Peter indicates his intention of leaving a testament to remind his readers of the things that he has taught them. His use of a future tense ("will always remind") suggests that composing this testament was a future activity and did not refer to this letter. Peter viewed this testament as a provision for the spiritual growth of his friends in that it would prevent their spiritual forgetfulness.

In this section Peter discusses the future use of such a testament (v. 12), the present need for it (v. 13), and the pressing demand for it (vv. 14, 15).

### *1. Future Use of a Testament (1:12)*

The "so" refers back to the glorious entry into Christ's eternal kingdom. On the basis of this future hope, Peter reminds his readers of the promises of verses 4–8 and teaches them the high moral character and strenuous moral effort that must characterize those seeking eternal life. These are the truths designated by "these things" in verse 12. It is not so much that these are traits that merit eternal life as it is that possession of these traits will characterize the seeker after eternal life.

Peter presents an unusual grammatical form to describe his determination to remind the readers of spiritual truth.[7]

Its meaning is that Peter desires always to be ready to remind his readers of the need for spiritual progress. He had demonstrated that readiness in the past and stood ready in the present and future. Peter's readers needed this reminder in their present circumstances when God's grace was being used as a cloak for immorality (2:19) and the knowledge of God was claimed as a substitute for obedience (cf. 1 John 2:4). Peter's

[7]The structure includes a form of "I mean to" (Gr., *mellēso*), the future tense of a verb normally completed with an infinitive. Zerwick views the expression as the use of the two verbs (periphrastic idea) to form a future. Strachan feels that it is not merely a periphrastic future but expresses the writer's determination to be prepared at any time the necessity arises—past, present, future.

word for "remind" is intended to stir up the memory to recall what may have been forgotten.

Peter intends to remind his readers of principles and teachings that they might lay aside despite his conviction that they "are well grounded in the truth that has already reached" (NEB) them. To describe them as "established" suggested that they were "well-grounded in the Christian faith, instructed in it, firmly committed to it, and therefore not likely to be easily misled by false teaching" (Bauckham). The "truth" was that in which they had been taught. Peter is convinced that they have a good grasp of such truth as has reached them.

One need not view Peter as devious to feel that he uses good psychology in thus commending his readers. The fact was that they faced a terrible onslaught against their faith from false teachers, but Peter sends them into this battle with a word of commendation for their firm grounding. The testament that Peter was promising to his readers would certainly provide for the future a reminder of God's gracious provisions just as Peter had labored in the past to help them to understand.

### *2. Present Need of a Testament (1:13)*

Peter considered his reminders of God's appeals to be right because such an action would help his readers and would also be a fulfillment of his duty as an apostle. Peter's use of "tent of this body" is a reference to his human body as a temporary dwelling place for this life. The metaphor of a tent used in reference to the body of this life accords well with the idea of life as a pilgrimage. Kelly notes that the imagery of the body as a tent "is probably drawn from the life of nomads, who can quickly fold up their tents before moving on to fresh pastures." Isaiah 38:12 speaks of the suddenness of death as resembling the plucking up and removal of a dwelling "like a shepherd's tent."

The fact that Peter speaks of his body as a "tent" suggests his recognition that life is transitory, and it prepares us for the reference to his death in verse 14.

The description of refreshing the memory of his readers in verse 13 is expressed by Phillips as "to stimulate you by these reminders." A similar structure of this phrase (using the Gr., *diegeirō* and *en hypomnēsei*) appears in 3:1.

*3. Pressing Demand for the Testament (1:14, 15)*

Peter's impending death made the preparation of a testament mandatory. Peter again emphasizes in verse 15 that preparing such a testament would allow his readers to have a reminder of the high moral demands and determined effort required of Christian pilgrims.

Peter expressed the conviction that his death would be an event that would come "soon" ("swiftly," ASV). The difference in translation between NIV and ASV points out the issue in interpretation. Is Peter's death to come soon, or does it come "swiftly" (i.e., violently) when it occurs? Peter was already in advanced years when he wrote this letter, and it would not be out of place for him to consider that his death was imminent. It is possible that some ominous event unknown to us had convinced Peter of the nearer imminence of his death. Also, there may be the possibility that a special revelation from Christ had conveyed to Peter new information about his death (cf. Acts 18:9, 10). There is likely some reference to Jesus' words to Peter in John 21:18, 19,[8] but the words in John disclose the violent manner, not the time of Peter's death. The spirit of this present passage seems more imbued with a sense of urgency so that the meaning of the word (Gr., *tachinē*) is better expressed with the idea of "soon." Somehow the words of Jesus had convinced Peter that his physical death was a near event.

In speaking of "putting his bodily tent aside" ("the removal of my bodily tent," Williams) Peter is slightly shifting metaphors. The previous reference to the "tent of this body" in verse 13 presented the picture of folding a tent. The reference here is more in line with removing a garment. Both metaphors are vivid pictures of death, and the mixing of such metaphors appears elsewhere in Scripture (cf. 2 Cor. 5:1–4).

In verse 15 Peter again emphasizes the value of a testament

[8]Gundry (*A Survey of the New Testament*, rev. ed., p. 196, n. 14) comments that the statement that Peter would stretch out his hands and that another would gird him and carry him where he would not want to go may describe the preparation of a condemned man for crucifixion.

in reminding his readers of the high call and challenging demands that lay before them (cf. v. 12). In light of Peter's emphasis in verses 16–18 concerning a historical basis for the Transfiguration, Peter may also have desired to communicate that the teachings and appeals that he had given were not based on mere myths but on historical facts. Peter's use of a future tense with "I will make every effort" suggests not a reference to 2 Peter but to a testament yet to be produced.[9] Some have felt that Peter was promising a succession of teachers who would keep the truth alive even after his death (Huther), but the most obvious meaning for Peter's statement is that he would prepare a document to which his disciples might be able to turn for confirmation of their belief (Bigg). Peter does not suggest that the document will be written after his death but that it would be of use in reminding Christians of sound teaching even after Peter has died. Early Christian tradition identified this document with the Gospel of Mark, and the suggestion was that Mark was the accurate interpreter and organizer of Peter's reminiscences of Jesus Christ.[10] Bigg suggests that "no document would redeem the apostle's promise so well as a gospel; and if a gospel is meant, the reference can hardly be to any other than that of St. Mark." Many later pseudonymous Petrine writings (e.g., *Apocalypse of Peter, Gospel of Peter, Preaching of Peter*) were probably suggested by these words. Bigg sees this fact as a point in favor of Petrine authorship of 2 Peter and says, "It seems hardly likely that such extensive liberties would have been taken with the name of Peter unless there were a phrase, in a writing generally recognised as his, which gave plausibility to the forgery."

The word for "departure" (Gr., *exodon*) is a very rare word for death, but it was used by Luke of Christ's death that was mentioned at the Transfiguration (Luke 9:31). It was also used by Irenaeus in a discussion of the authorship of Mark's Gospel. He used the word to refer to the deaths of Peter and Paul (*A.H.*

[9]The translation, "I will make every effort" (Gr., *spoudasō*), shows earnest, intense effort, not merely a casual desire.

[10]The tradition linking Mark with Peter is recorded in Eusebius's *Ecclesiastical History* where it is attributed to Papias, who was born about A.D. 70 (*H.E.* 3.39), and is attributed in the same source to Clement (*H.E.* 6.14) and to Irenaeus (*H.E.* 5.8).

3.1.1). It seems possible that Irenaeus knew the passage from 2 Peter and saw it to refer to the writing of Mark's Gospel. Certainly the appeals to Christian growth and discipleship in Mark's Gospel (Mark 1:17; 8:34–38) would remind Peter's readers of truths of development and maturity that they might carelessly neglect.

### C. The Power and Glory of Christ (1:16–18)

It is likely that Peter's readers were encountering false teachers who mocked at the idea of a powerful, heavenly Christ who could strengthen them for present godly living (2:1). Peter now turns his attention to convincing his friends that these mocking views of Christ are erroneous. He asserts that he himself was an eyewitness of the Transfiguration and that Christ received honor and glory from the Father in that event. The implication is that this powerful, majestic Christ was available to empower them in their daily life. It is also likely that these false teachers were denying the literal sense of the gospel miracles and seeing them as teaching some vague spiritual principles. With such a view they would obviously deny a future physical return of Christ (3:3, 4). Peter states clearly that the appearance and glory of Jesus in the Transfiguration foreshadow the revelation of His glory in His return. One historical event calls for another.

#### *1. An Eyewitness of Christ's Power (1:16)*

Some accused Peter of spinning out "cleverly invented stories" ("fictitious stories," Goodspeed; "fables of man's invention," Knox) concerning Jesus. Peter denies this and indicates that he was describing for his readers events that he had seen.

"Power" is a reference to the divine might that Jesus has as the resurrected Lord. Jesus had demonstrated this power at the Transfiguration and will again demonstrate it in His return. The "coming" is the term (Gr., *parousia*) normally used of the future return of Jesus, but here it is chiefly a reference to His coming in the Transfiguration and in other powerful events of His first advent. The words "power" and "coming" are a figure of speech known as a hendiadys and should be translated together as "powerful coming." The suggestion of Peter is that the "powerful coming" of Jesus in the Transfiguration and in other gospel events is an anticipation of His Second Coming in might and glory.

The events of the Transfiguration were seen by Peter and the other apostles as "eyewitnesses" (Gr., *epoptai*).[11] The noun was used in the mystery religions to designate the higher-grade initiates who were admitted to view the sacred objects of the religion. Peter is suggesting that he had enjoyed a "privileged admission to a divine revelation" (Kelly). "Majesty" is used in the New Testament (Luke 9:43; Acts 19:27) in reference to divine majesty, and it expresses the divine majesty of Jesus as revealed in the Transfiguration.

### 2. *The Honor and Glory of Christ (1:17, 18)*

These verses justify Peter's claim to be an eyewitness of the "power and coming" of Jesus. Peter refers to what he saw and to what he heard.

Peter saw the Son receive "honor and glory" (Gr., *timēn kai doxan*) from the Father. "Honour denotes the exalted status which the proclamation of Sonship implies" (Kelly). "Glory" is a description of the heavenly radiance of the transfigured Jesus. Such a radiance is often seen in the Bible as belonging to the very being of God (John 1:14; 1 Peter 1:7; Jude 25). The phrase, "the Majestic Glory," is a periphrasis for God, a method of referring to the Divine Being without mentioning Him by name. Specifically it is an allusion to the bright cloud that overshadowed Jesus at the Transfiguration. That cloud was the dwelling place of Jehovah (Matt. 17:5).

What Peter heard was a voice expressing pleasure in the work of the Divine Son. The words are not identical with the text of Matthew 17:5, but should probably read, "This is my Son, my Beloved" (Goodspeed).[12] "Beloved" was an early title for

[11] The noun is used only here in the New Testament, and the corresponding verb is found only in 1 Peter 2:12; 3:2. This might be another indication of common authorship.

[12] Matthew 3:17; 17:5 read, "This is my beloved Son." There is evidence that some scribes altered the actual text of Peter so as to agree identically with that of Matthew. The slight difference from Matthew in the text here adopted renders the same sense as the Matthaean text, but "Beloved" becomes a substantive instead of an adjective ascribing a quality to "Son."

the Messiah and should not be seen as an adjective modifying "Son." The phrase, "with him I am well pleased" ("in whom I delight," Rotherham), shows the good pleasure of the Father as it comes upon and remains with Jesus.

In verse 18 Peter stresses further that he had heard the voice of verse 17 as a witness of the Transfiguration. The plural subject (i.e., "we") is a reference to the disciples who witnessed the Transfiguration with Jesus—Peter, James, and John. The Mount of Transfiguration is called "sacred" because Peter had seen there the divine glory of Jesus.[13] Peter is using this incident to emphasize his complete knowledge of the historical Jesus and to put aside any talk about myths. There was no myth or fabrication to Jesus, for Peter had actually seen Him. A knowledge of the power of this Christ could strengthen Peter's readers in their daily struggles. A recognition of His glory could provide an incentive to endure in godly living until they might see Him personally at His return (Titus 2:12, 13; 1 John 3:2, 3).

### D. The Divine Message of Scripture (1:19–21)

Peter moves to conclude his discussion of divine provisions for the spiritual growth of his readers.

In addition to the calling of the individual Christian, the testament of Peter, and the glorious presence of Christ, there is also the divine message of Scripture. Peter indicated that the purpose of Scripture was to provide light for those who walked in the darkness of this world. The message of Scripture was certified as trustworthy because it had a divine, not a human origin.

#### *1. The Purpose of Scripture (v. 19)*

This verse can be understood in two different ways, and the crucial word in interpretation is "more certain" (Gr., *bebaioteron*). Is Peter saying that the Scriptures confirm the apostolic

[13]Some commentators have felt that the phrase, "sacred mountain," assumes a later time when the Transfiguration had been "taken up into and sanctified in the religious consciousness of the Church" (Strachan). However, the term for "sacred" (Gr., *hagios*) suggests the idea of "belonging to God," and Green notes that the mount is holy because it was visited by God. The mount where Moses met God was seen as holy for this reason (Exod. 3:5). In later times there was disagreement over whether the Mount of Transfiguration was Tabor or Hermon.

witness (KJV), or is he saying that the apostolic witness of the Transfiguration authenticates Scripture (ASV, RSV, NEB, NIV)? Many commentators (Bauckham, Kelly, Huther, Strachan) feel that the Transfiguration and other events of Jesus' life make the unfulfilled Old Testament prophecies about the coming of Jesus more certain and sure. Green, Bigg, and Cranfield feel that Peter is referring to a second witness (the Old Testament) that is seen as a stronger witness than the first (the Transfiguration and other gospel events). In favor of his view Green indicates that it is difficult to derive the meaning, "we have the prophetic word made more sure," out of the Greek *echomen bebaioteron* (literally: "we have more sure"). Another structure of the Greek could have said this more explicitly. Green also cites the normal tendency of the first-century Jew to prefer prophecy to a voice from heaven. As a Jewish Christian Peter would have a deep appreciation for the prophetic statements of the Old Testament, and he made frequent references to this in his speeches in Acts (cf. Acts 2:14–36; 3:11–26). In Green's words Peter is saying, " 'If you don't believe me, go to the Scriptures.' " The statement of Peter here may then be viewed as an expression of full confidence that Scripture is reliable. But why does he make this point?

Peter wants his readers to pay close attention to God's message. By the phrase "the word of the prophets" he is speaking of the Old Testament, and he compares it to "a light shining in a dark place." It is like a torch illuminating a murky room. This light will show up the dirt and make its removal possible. In application the "dark place" is the world as it exists, and Peter is saying that the prophetic declarations of Scripture illuminate the darkness of the world so that Christians can avoid the defilement and dirt of sin as they pass along. The darkness may also refer to the heresies of perdition that Peter's Christian friends were encountering.

The latter part of verse 19 indicates that Christians are to listen to this "word of the prophets" until its light is replaced by the brilliance of the return of Christ. The "dawning of the day" and "arising of the morning star" refer most naturally to the return of Christ. The "morning star" is applied in Greek literature to royal and divine persons. The Messiah is seen with the symbolism of a star in Numbers 24:17, and He is called the "morning star" in Revelation 2:28; 22:16. However, the references in Revelation do not use the same Greek words to describe the "morning star."

The concluding phrase of verse 19, "in your hearts," should not be seen as an attempt to speak about Christ's return as occurring only in the hearts of the readers. In light of Peter's emphasis in chapter 3 on the objectivity of Christ's return, it hardly seems likely that he would spiritualize that return here. The phrase may refer to the glow of anticipation in Christian hearts when they see clear signs that the day of Christ's coming is approaching. It may also refer to the inner transformation now begun by the Spirit through the study of Scripture (2 Cor. 3:18) and brought to completion on the day when believers will be made as He is (1 John 3:2). Some have also taken the phrase as linked with the opening words of verse 20, and they understand Peter to be calling upon his readers to "know in their hearts."

The exact details may be difficult to piece together, but the chief emphasis is clear. Peter is presenting Scripture as a lamp for guiding lives in this dark world. If we hide it in our hearts, heed its warnings, seek its guidance, we shall live safely. If we neglect it, we will walk in darkness and will lack the light that gives life. The Word of God is a source of counsel for our entire lives (Ps. 119:9, 11).

2. *The Trustworthiness of Scripture (1:20, 21)*

Peter presents the reliability of Scripture with the explanation that it comes not of human but of divine origin. Men moved by God's Holy Spirit produced the prophetic statements of the Old Testament.

The term "prophecy of Scripture" is a reference to the prophecies of the Old Testament. At this time in the writing of the New Testament Peter used the term "Scripture" as essentially a reference to the Old Testament, but note that he calls the writings of Paul "Scripture" (3:16, q.v.). The declaration is that Scripture does not come of "the prophet's own interpretation" ("a matter of one's own interpretation,' NASB). In interpreting this statement it is possible to see it as describing the origin of Scripture (i.e., from God) or the interpretation of Scripture (i.e.

not from man). The noun "interpretation" (Gr., *epilyseōs*) appears here only in the New Testament although the verb appears in Mark 4:34 and Acts 19:39. In both of these instances it means to unravel a problem. Kelly feels that the meaning is that "no individual is entitled to interpret prophecy, or scripture generally, according to his personal whim." In the context of the false teaching that Peter will shortly introduce (chapter 2; cf. 3:16) this is an apt warning. However, the context of verse 20 features a discussion of the authentication of Christian teaching rather than its interpretation. In verses 16–18 the authentication of the events of the Transfiguration is mentioned. It would be a proper emphasis to see Peter discussing the divine origin of Scripture here. "The same God whom the apostles heard speak in the transfiguration spoke also through the prophets" (Green). Particularly in verse 21 Peter is emphasizing the divine source of Scripture, and the statement there has less significance if it is seen as discussing the interpretation of Scripture. It appears, then, that Peter is discussing the divine source of Scripture. In verse 20 he states its divine source, and in verse 21 he provides a reason for believing that it comes from a divine source.

In verse 21 Peter asserts that "prophecy never had its origin in the will of man" ("no prophetic teaching ever came in the days of old at the mere wish of man," TCNT). In contrast, the true source or origin was "men . . . carried along by the Holy Spirit." Some manuscripts call these men "holy," but the adjective is omitted in the best manuscripts. It is obvious that those men led by God's Holy Spirit would be holy. Peter uses a maritime metaphor in describing the relation between human and divine in the production of Scripture (cf. Acts 27:15, 17, where the word "carried along" [Gr., *pheromenoi*] is used of a ship moved along by wind). "The prophets raised their sails, . . . and the Holy Spirit filled them and carried their craft along in the direction he wished" (Green).

This is one of the most complete biblical references to the inspiration of the authors, and yet there is no explicit description of the psychology of inspiration. Peter does not describe how they felt, but he states that they carried the message of God. The Holy Spirit used men dedicated to His services who uttered truths in a certain background and life situation. Upon these men God moved. They did not lose their consciousness or normal mental functions in the act of inspiration. There was not mere passive reception, but there was active cooperation. The result was that these men could be seen as speaking "from God." The Scripture was trustworthy. A proper doctrine of the inspiration of Scripture must carefully note the roles of both God and man. The neglect of either of these will lead to distortion and imbalance.

**For Further Study**

1. By use of a dictionary or the *Zondervan Pictorial Encyclopedia of the Bible* define the terms faith, virtue, knowledge, self-control, patience, godliness, and love as they appear in 2 Peter 1:5–7.
2. Consult commentaries on the meaning of Jesus' words to Peter in John 21:18, 19. What do these words tell about the manner of Peter's death as mentioned in 2 Peter 1:14?
3. Consult the description of the Transfiguration of Jesus as mentioned in Luke 9:28–36 and other gospel parallels. What had the Transfiguration taught Peter concerning Jesus?
4. Consult Paul's words in 2 Timothy 3:16, 17 about the source and usefulness of Scripture. Write out Paul's description of the source of Scripture and the uses to which it is to be put. What does Peter add about the source or origin of Scripture in 2 Peter 1:21?

# Chapter 3

## Danger Ahead—False Teaching

(2 Peter 2:1–22)

In chapter 2 the message of 2 Peter focuses intently on the very real problem of false teaching. Peter unleashes a strong warning and a strong verbal attack on the heretics who are disturbing his Christian readers. Peter's vocabulary is filled with words that are bombastic and pictorial. Many of these words appear rarely elsewhere in the New Testament.

Some years ago a young friend, wanting to impress me with his growing verbal ability, asked me with tongue in cheek, "Have you the audacity to doubt my veracity, or would you insinuate that I would prevaricate?" In simpler English he was saying, "Are you calling me a liar?" The first example is bombastic, but the second is plain and straightforward. Peter's words in Greek are bombastic and somewhat pretentious, but they communicate arresting word pictures.

In verses 1–3 Peter describes the immorality and greed of the false teachers. These heretics used people as a means of reaching their own selfish goals. In verses 4–10a Peter pictured the judgment reserved for these false teachers by describing the Old Testament examples of the sinning angels, destruction in the time of Noah, and the destruction of Sodom and Gomorrah. An insolent, disrespectful attitude toward divine commands was displayed by the false teachers (vv. 10b, 11), and the spiritual ignorance of these errorists led to arrogance, lust, and self-indulgence (vv. 12–16). Those who followed their teachings would find emptiness and spiritual slavery as a result (vv. 17–19). Because the false teachers ignored God's commands, they would eventually suffer separation from Him (vv. 20–22). There is much similarity in this section with Jude 5–16. Parallels will be pointed out during the process of discussion.

**A. A Self-centered Emphasis on Immorality and Greed (2:1–3)**

Peter's reference to "false prophets" who arose "among the people" indicated that false teaching had always been a problem among God's people. The false prophets who were affecting his readers were fulfilling the prophecies of both the Old Testament and of Jesus (cf. Deut. 13:2–6 and Matt. 24:24). It was nothing new to face heresy in Peter's generation.

The "false prophets" probably falsely claimed the office of prophet and pretended to have revelations from God that were of their own making. As "false teachers" they would lead others to both doctrinal and moral errors. Doctrinally they may have formally rejected Christ as God's Son (1 John 2:22, 23), but evidence from the rest of this chapter also indicates that their base, ungodly lives were a denial of Christ.

Peter states three things about these false prophets and teachers. First, they "will . . . introduce destructive heresies." Peter uses the future tense here, but from 10b onward he uses frequently a present tense in reference to the false teachers. The alternation between present and future may suggest that these men are at work elsewhere and will arrive speedily where he is (Bigg). The verb "introduce" carries with it the suggestion of smuggling or introducing something in an underhanded way. The "heresies" were false opinions that destroyed true godliness. The term is likely a reference to false doctrine rather than merely to divisive opinions."[1]

Second, the false teachers were "denying the sovereign Lord who bought them." Again, the denial could be doctrinal, moral, or a combination of both. The term "sovereign Lord" (Gr., *despotēs*) suggests absolute, unrestricted power, and it is

[1]The term "heresies" (Gr., *haireseis*) can be used of an exaggerated sectarianism in which one group broke off from another because they regarded the other as being perhaps spiritually, intellectually, or socially inferior. The term can also refer to an exaggeration of doctrinal views. Mayor feels that the primary idea behind the word here is a false opinion that became a source of great danger for the readers of 2 Peter.

frequently used in the New Testament in reference to the Father (Acts 4:24). Here, however, the reference to "bought" appears as a description of the atoning death of Jesus Christ. Peter is describing Christ as "sovereign Lord" (cf. Jude 4 where the same word is used and may refer to Christ). Since the Lord bought even these false teachers, they should have been committed to a life of purity, but "they did not recognize the obligation of holy living imposed by the Crucified" (Green).

Third, these false teachers will be those "bringing swift destruction on themselves." The term "swift" refers to a quickly working, unexpected manner of approach rather than to a destruction that was imminent. "The man who attempts to serve God and self is on the high road to *swift destruction,* for either death or the parousia will cut him off in mid-course" (Green).

In verse 2 Peter spotlights the immorality of these false teachers. Many among the believers will be taken in by the glib talk of the heretics and will be induced to follow their wicked lifestyle. The "shameful ways" ("dissolute practices," NEB) suggest sexual license by comparison with verses 7, 18 where the same word is used (cf. Jude 4 where the word [Gr., *aselgeia*] also appears). The term provides a strong description of reckless and hardened immorality, and the plural form denotes repeated acts of sensual excess. Because many believers follow the wicked doings of the false teachers, the Christian message will be vilified. The term "way" was an early name for Christianity (used in Acts 9:2). Christianity can be called "the way of truth" when its form of living is in harmony with the divine truth revealed in Scripture.

In verse 2 Peter shows that the effects of the doctrinal and ethical denial of the false teachers spread quickly to infect those who profess to follow Christ. When they defect from commitment to Christ, the character of God is discredited among the heathen (cf. 2 Sam. 12:14; Isa. 52:5; Rom. 2:24). Green indicates that the future tense in "will follow" is used to indicate that the defection of God's people is a frequently prophesied theme of Scripture.

In verse 3 Peter mentions the greed and materialism of the heretics and asserts again the certainty of judgment upon them. The expression, "in their greed," is a causal expression. The idea is that because of their greed they will exploit their hearers. Their covetousness may also include hankering after honor, prestige, or sexual promiscuity. They use "made-up" (Gr., *plastois*; "cunning," Moffatt; "manufactured by themselves," Williams) stories. They employ specious arguments designed to buy over converts. To "exploit" is a commercial term (Gr., *emporeuomai*) suggesting that the false teachers viewed their hearers as a source of personal financial gain to them. "The false teachers make a good financial profit out of their followers, who are taken in by their teaching and contribute to their support" (Bauckham).

Peter, however, feels that the judgment pronounced long ago in the Old Testament against false teachers is still pending (Ps. 73:18, 19). To say that their judgment "has . . . been hanging over them, and . . . has not been sleeping" effectively states the certainty that judgment will eventually consume them. The use of "has not been sleeping" is an expression describing drowsiness, and it pictures their evil deeds waiting for them with unsleeping eyes. Peter will illustrate their judgment with specific Old Testament examples in the following section.

### B. A Certainty of Judgment for Those Following False Teaching (2:4–10a)

This section bears some similarity to Jude 5–7 where examples of Old Testament judgment on the disobedient are mentioned. Both Peter and Jude describe God's judgment on the sinning angels (2 Peter 2:4; Jude 6) and the destruction of Sodom and Gomorrah (2 Peter 2:6; Jude 7). In addition, Peter describes the destruction of Noah's world (2:5), and Jude portrays the destruction of the generation of Israelites who came out of Egypt (v. 5). Peter also discusses the example of Lot's deliverance from judgment upon Sodom and Gomorrah (2:7, 8). The content of verses 4–10a forms a long conditional sentence in Greek. Peter begins with an "if" expression in verse 4, and he does not draw the conclusion from it until verse 9. In between, Peter mentions the judgment of the sinning angels (v. 4), the destruction of the world of Noah (v. 5), the doom of Sodom and Gomorrah (v. 6), and the deliverance of Lot from this destruction (vv. 7, 8). Verses 9, 10a form the conclusion to Peter's words.

*1. God's Judgment on the Sinning Angels (2:4)*

Here Peter does not mention specifically the sin of the fallen angels, but it was common for Jews of this time to understand their sin as either rebellion or sensual lust as in Genesis 6:1–4. Jude 6 (q.v.) makes reference to the same angelic incident, and the view that their sin consisted of sensual lust will be followed for both passages. In mentioning the judgment of the angels, Peter's argument is from the greater to the lesser. If even angels, great in magnificence and power, did not escape judgment at the hands of God, much less can mortal men expect to escape.

There is textual disagreement concerning whether the reading should be "chains" (Gr., *seirais*) or "dungeons" (Gr., *sirois*). Metzger cautiously adopts "chains," indicating that it is both the oldest reading and the most widespread. Jude 6 uses "chains" (Gr., *desmois*; "bonds," ASV), but the word in 2 Peter is more elegant than the more commonplace expression of Jude. Bigg sees Jude's usage as possible evidence for the priority of 2 Peter in that he feels that Jude may have seen the less common word in 2 Peter and altered it to the more familiar word used by him.

"Sent them to hell" is a single word in the Greek, and it occurs here alone in the Bible. Its meaning is to "consign to tartarus," a location viewed in Greek mythology as the place for punishment of the departed spirits of the very wicked. Alford sees it as equivalent to Gehenna, the place of punishment for the unrighteous dead. The implication is that these unrighteous angels are held in a location of temporary punishment until the arrival of the day of their final doom. Peter is using a word with which a pagan audience would be familiar, and the word's appearance may be an effort on his part to relate more effectively to the converted pagans who would read his message. His information about these angels should pose no more problem than Paul's information about judging angels in 1 Corinthians 6:3. The underlying thought in the verse is that God will act, as He always does, to punish sinners.

It is possible that Peter's discussion on fallen angels is an allusion to passages in the apocryphal Book of Enoch (10:4–6; 18:11–21:10), but, if Peter refers to this at all, he is quite cautious and discreet. Jude clearly refers to Enoch in verses 14, 15, and he may also use that book as a background for his emphasis in verse 6.

It will be noted that the historical examples of judgment that Peter introduces in verses 4–6 are arranged in chronological order. Jude's order in verses 5–7 does not include the same examples of judgment and is not in chronological order. Jude may have wanted to begin his examples of judgment with the obvious failings of the generation of Israelites who perished in the wilderness.

2. *God's Judgment on the World of Noah (2:5)*

The thought here is that God did not spare the generation involved in such grievous sin in Noah's time. He did show mercy in His deliverance of Noah, but He brought the Flood upon the world of the ungodly.

The implication from the Greek is that God kept Noah safe because he was a preacher of righteousness. The Old Testament presents Noah as a righteous man (Gen. 6:9) but not as a preacher. However, Josephus, drawing upon Jewish tradition, describes Noah as disgusted by the behavior of his neighbors and urging them to amend their ways (*Ant.* 1.3.1). The phrase, "Noah, . . . and seven others," is the translation of a single word (Gr., *ogdoon*) that does not refer to Noah as being in the eighth generation from Adam but as one of a group of eight who was delivered. He, his wife, their three sons, and their wives were rescued (cf. 1 Peter 3:20).

The mention of mercy shown to Noah introduces a comforting thought amidst the denunciation and judgment that Peter has mentioned. This preservation of the righteous will be further explained in the reference to Lot in verses 7, 8. The righteousness of Noah is not so much a reference to Noah's being justified as it is to Noah's godly service toward Jehovah. Noah was righteous in that he proclaimed a message about God so that the ungodly might come to repentance and receive the righteousness of God. For his readers Peter has mentioned Noah as an appeal to them to choose apostolic orthodoxy and commitment over contemporary heresy.

*3. God's Judgment on Sodom and Gomorrah (2:6)*

Here destruction by fire follows destruction by water, and the same sequence of destruction appears in 3:6, 7. The destruction of Sodom and Gomorrah is depicted with a participle, "burning them to ashes," a word mentioned nowhere else in the New Testament. However, the word does appear in an account by Dio Cassius (66) of the eruption of Vesuvius in A.D. 79 when Pompeii and Herculaneum were buried in lava. Some manuscripts add the words "with an overthrow" in the text after "condemned." If the presence of the word is accepted (the NIV omits it), it may suggest that Peter meant that God destroyed the cities by fire and sentenced that they should not be rebuilt (Bigg).

This destruction of Sodom and Gomorrah served as an example to the ungodly. The perfect participle for "made" (Gr., *tetheikōs*) shows that the wicked example of these cities served as lasting evidence of what befalls those who indulge in ungodly living. There is a question again concerning the proper text of verse 6, for competing readings appear to suggest either that the destruction served as "an example of what is going to happen to the ungodly" or that "it served an example to those about to do wrong." Metzger cautiously adopts the former reading, but the intent of Peter is not significantly altered with either text.

*4. God's Deliverance of Lot from Destruction (2:7, 8)*

The mention of God's protection for the righteous at this point in 2 Peter does not appear in Jude 5–7. There the emphasis is to underscore the judgment of God upon sinners. This account of the deliverance of Lot affords the encouragement and hope for Peter's readers that God can similarly deliver them from the heresy surrounding them.

The picture of Lot in the Old Testament (Gen. 13:10–13; 19:1–22) is anything but favorable to designating him as "righteous." However Jewish extra-canonical tradition did picture him as "just" (Wisdom 10:6; 19:17). It may be that in comparison with the men of Sodom, he can be seen as a good man. He may also be seen as righteous in that he accepted God's intervention on his behalf.

Lot was "distressed" ("wearied out," ABUV; "shocked," NEB) by the lifestyle surrounding him. The word suggests that he was "knocked about" morally by what he saw and heard so that he became dull to sin, apathetic about moral standards, and unwilling to look to the Lord for deliverance. The behavior of these people is described as the "filthy lives of lawless men" ("immoral conduct of unprincipled men," Goodspeed). "Filthy" is the same word that is translated as "shameful ways" in verse 2. It denotes a shameless indulgence in a style of living that violates even pagan moral standards. The word "lawless" is a description of those surrounding Lot as "without principles." These were men who had ignored the divine law and had trampled upon it.

Verse 8 enlarges upon the manner in which Lot's resistance to evil was worn down. There is an interpretive question concerning the word to which "saw and heard" are to be related. Some will relate the phrase with "righteous man" and will understand that Lot is called righteous in what he saw and heard (Strachan). The suggestion from this is that Lot was of nobler spiritual stock than those about him. However, the arrangement of the Greek seems most easily understood when "saw and heard" are linked with the verb "was tormented." This connection suggests that Lot's soul was tortured by what he saw and heard. The lawless deeds of the Sodomites tortured Lot's spiritual nature. Although he may have come from a different heritage and can be called "righteous," his opposition to their iniquity was finally worn down. The portrayal of Lot provides a warning to a generation of people who will view without protest television material that, a generation ago, they would never have considered seeing at a movie.

### 5. *The Principle of God's Working (2:9, 10a)*

The statement beginning in verse 9 can be seen as the apodosis or conclusion from the conditional statements that began in verse 4. The principle is that God knows to deliver the godly and to preserve the ungodly for punishment. The reference to the deliverance of the godly from trials indicates that the rescue is "out of" and not "away from" trials. God continues to allow trials to befall the Christian, and there is no promise that Christians are exempted from them. In the midst of such trials God meets, strengthens, and then delivers the Christian. Both Noah and Lot endured some years of difficulty before they experienced deliverance, and yet God delivered them both.

The "trials" out of which the believer is delivered refer to outward circumstances and not to inner desires. The presence of inner desires to evil is a product of one's own lust (James 1:14), and God never promised deliverance from these. Instead Paul ordered that they be "put to death" (Col. 3:5). Similarly God does not deliver the believer away from all external circumstances for evil, but He preserves a committed believer in the midst of such circumstances. The testing induced by outward trial is the atmosphere in which faith can be fully developed (James 1:2–4). Such an opportunity for testing is not to be carelessly sought or entered into (Luke 11:4), but these trials and temptations can be used to develop staying-power in the believer (James 1:12).

Just as the Lord knows to deliver the righteous, He also knows to keep the unrighteous in the process of being judged until the final great judgment. The present Greek participle for "continuing" the punishment of the unrighteous suggests that the wicked experience punishment during the time when they are awaiting the final judgment. They are in the process of being punished.[2] The phrase "day of judgment" is a reference to the final judgment at Christ's Parousia, and the wicked will experience then a finalization of that punishment that is already their own.

In verse 10a Peter describes those who are being kept in punishment. He singles out their sexual immorality and their spiritual rebellion. Those who are being kept in punishment are "particularly those who fall in with the polluting appetites of the flesh" (Moffatt). The phrase bears a resemblance to Jude 7 ("gave themselves up to sexual immorality and perversion") and Jude 8 ("pollute their own bodies"). Sensuality has become the

---

[2]Kelly observes that the parable of the rich man (Dives) and Lazarus (Luke 16:19–31) agrees with Jewish accounts that emphasize the wretched existence of the wicked during the interval between their death and the final judgment.

dominant power in these false teachers who are so deserving of punishment. These have a lust for pollution; they seem to desire impurity for its own sake, even apart from the satisfaction of the sensual appetite.

Further, these who are being punished are those who "despise authority" ("despise the powers Celestial," Moffatt). The phrase is similar to the description in Jude 8, and it is a reference to the denial of the authority of God or Christ (Bigg, Kelly).[3]

**C. Insolent Attitudes toward Divine Commands (2:10b, 11)**

In this section Peter continues his description of the dangerous attitudes of the false teachers. Primarily he describes their insolent self-willed attitudes. The denunciation of this attitude is paralleled by a similar section in Jude 8–10.

In 10b Peter heaps together three descriptive terms to picture the contemptuous attitude of the heretics. First, they are "bold" ("rash," Goodspeed). The term pictures an attitude that defies God and man. The verbal form of the word is used in Jude 9 to describe the restrained attitude of Michael the archangel in not daring to bring a word of judgment against Satan on his own. Michael did not duplicate the arrogant attitude of the heretics. Second, they are seen as "arrogant" ("headstrong," Goodspeed). The word pictures an obstinate person who is determined to please himself at all costs (Green). Third, they are pictured as those who "are not afraid to slander celestial beings" ("they think nothing of scoffing at the glories of the unseen world," Phillips). The "celestial beings" (Gr., *doxai*) may refer to either good or evil angels. Verse 11 implies that these "beings" merit condemnation, and Kelly feels that these are the evil angels mentioned in verse 4. It is difficult to know what form their slander took. Perhaps they were belittling the powers of Satan over them. "What remains clear is that their attitude . . .

[3]Two other ways of interpreting this phrase are to refer it to a denial of the authority or existence of an angelic hierarchy (cf. Col. 1:16) or the refusal to give authority to church leadership. There is little evidence of the interest of the false teachers in angels, and the interpretation given above in referring "dominion" to that of God (either Father or Son) seems preferable.

betokens a blasphemous rebellion against the divinely established order of existence" (Kelly).

In verse 11 Peter provides a contrast of the behavior of angels with that of these headstrong heretics. The false teachers do not hesitate to bring bitter accusations against their superiors whereas angels do not "dare to impugn their inferiors in such terms in the Lord's presence" (Green). Even though this interpretation seems generally sound, there is much ambiguity in the verse. First, to whom are the angels superior—church leaders, other angels, or the blaspheming false teachers? In the context it appears that Peter is citing the superiority of the angels to the fallen angels of verse 4. Also, who are those against whom the angels are fearful of bringing an accusation? It seems most natural to suggest that the angels do not bring a "slanderous accusation" against the fallen angels. There is also a textual question as to whether the phrase, "in the presence of the Lord," should be included. In the context it fits well in suggesting that the angels, unlike the careless false teachers, live their lives in God's presence so that no insulting language comes from their lips.

Peter's background for the statement of verse 11 is unclear. Some will note the similarity to Jude 9 (q.v.) and suggest that Jude and Peter use the same source at this point. Others may suggest that Peter has read Enoch 9 or is aware of the words of Joshua the high priest in Zechariah 3:1, 2. Peter's source is not clear, but the principle is that these false teachers were freer with their language than the angels themselves. An awareness of the presence of God had contributed to taming the tongues of the angels in verse 11, and the false teachers needed that!

### D. The Arrogance, Lust, and Greed Due to Spiritual Ignorance (2:12–16)

Here Peter continues his discussion of the dangerous false teaching of the heretics, citing their arrogance (v. 12), lust (v. 13), and greed (v. 14). In verses 15, 16 he cites Balaam as an example of some of these traits. Peter's assault on the heretics becomes direct, and he burns with righteous anger at the wickedness that they display.

*1. The Arrogance of the False Teachers (2:12)*

Peter compares the heretics to irrational animals who follow their instincts and eventually fall victim to their passions just as the animals do. The opening words, "But these," put the false teachers and their victims in contrast to angels (mentioned in v. 11), who show restraint. Lacking any moral discipline, these teachers have "no more sense than the unreasoning brute beasts" (Phillips). They had physical but not intellectual life and were no better than brutes that perished. Just as wild animals come to their end at the knife of a hunter, these false teachers will be destroyed in the corruption of their own passions. To "blaspheme" ("abuse," Goodspeed; "scoff," Phillips) is not so much verbal as moral. Their lifestyle indicates that they pour abuse on the Christian way of restraint that they fail to understand. The result of this "blasphemous" lifestyle is that they "too" (Gr., *kai*; an emphatic asseveration) will be destroyed. Some interpreters view the expression for "perish" (Gr., *phtharēsontai*) as meaning "corrupted," but it should be understood as a reference to the destruction of the false teachers by their yielding to the lusts of the flesh (Gal. 6:8).[4]

These false teachers demonstrate their arrogance in that their words and deeds abuse a way of life that they do not understand. Claiming to be wise, they are acting as fools. Their sole future expectation is misery in this life and retribution at the final judgment.

*2. The Lust of the False Teachers (2:13)*

Here Peter brings together three phrases to picture the immorality and lust of the heretics. These phrases, plus the further descriptions in verse 14, amplify what is involved when the heretics are accused of living a "blasphemous" lifestyle in verse 12.

[4] Bigg compares this verse with Jude 10 and finds evidence of the priority of 2 Peter, indicating that Jude has rewritten the sentence of 2 Peter to make it more correct and less forcible. Also, the Greek word for "destruction" (Gr., *phthora*) appears twice in 2 Peter 2:12 although it is not so reflected in the NIV translation. It was a common word of Peter, and repetition was a favorite practice of the apostle. The word, however, is omitted in Jude. Kelly, exhibiting an opposite view, feels that the writer of 2 Peter is expanding material taken almost word for word from Jude 10 and is rearranging it rather clumsily.

First, the false teachers are "being cheated of the profits of their wrong-doing" (Cranfield). Various manuscripts have variant readings of this phrase (e.g., "going to receive the wages of wrong-doing"), but Metzger feels that the author used this unusual grammatical construction to contrive a play on the verb for "cheat" ("paid back with harm," NIV) and the noun, "wrong-doing," ("harm," NIV) from the same word root. If Metzger's view is accepted, Peter is using a commercial metaphor to indicate that the false teachers will fail to collect their hoped-for wages from sin, and he is stressing that immorality is not worthwhile. In the end it will rob, not pay (Green).

Second, the false teachers count it pleasure "to carouse in broad daylight." Peter is underlining the extreme dissipation of people who do not get their fill of riotous, lascivious living at night. They must continue their wickedness throughout the day. Such daylight debauchery was frowned on even in a degenerate Roman society.

Third, they were "blots and blemishes, reveling in their pleasures while they feast with you." "Blemishes" (Gr., *mōmoi*) referred to moral imperfections (used in Lev. 21:17 [LXX] of bodily imperfections), and it was the opposite trait of the "unblemished" Christ (1 Peter 1:19). The word "pleasures" (Gr., *apatais*) is replaced in some texts with *agapais*, "love-feasts" (cf. Jude 12 for discussion of "love-feasts"). Metzger prefers "deceivings," but even if this term is used, it still could refer to the occasion of a "love-feast," but a feast that was actually a mockery of the real thing. The description of the behavior of the heretics in verse 13 might refer not only to social withdrawal but also to licentious activity at a feast that was originally intended as a memorial to Jesus.

### *3. The Greed of the False Teachers (2:14)*

The greed of these false teachers is described with possible references to both sexual and economic greed. Peter uses four descriptive phrases to picture the extent of their degradation.

First, they have "eyes full of adultery" and "they never stop sinning" ("eyes for nobody but adulterous women—eyes insatiable in sin," Goodspeed). They cannot look at a woman without reflecting on her likely sexual performance, an attitude that leaves a man restless, always longing for more. Second, they are guilty of seducing "the unstable" ("know how to win wavering souls to their purpose," Knox). To "seduce" is a fishing metaphor describing "to catch with bait." The unstable souls would be those easily caught because their life had not been firmly anchored in Christ. Third, they were "experts in greed" ("Their hearts are trained to be greedy," Beck). The suggestion is that these heretics had trained themselves in the unbridled desire for more and more of the forbidden. The word "greed" (Gr., *pleonexia*) may be used either in reference to money or to sexual desires. Fourth, they were "an accursed brood," an expressive Hebrew idiom meaning that "God's curse is on them" (NEB). Their wicked moral extremism had led them to a position of being under God's curse.

*4. The Wicked Example of Balaam (2:15, 16)*

Here Peter compares the false teachers to the hireling Old Testament prophet Balaam. The greed of Balaam can be inferred from Numbers 22–24, and his immorality is mentioned in Numbers 31:16. He becomes the prototype of an unprincipled false teacher seeking gain.

The incident of Balaam's quest for reward and the nature of the prophet's sin is discussed in Jude 11 (q.v.). Peter declines to reflect on the examples of Cain and Korah who are also mentioned by Jude. The name for Balaam's father in Numbers 22:5 is Beor, but Metzger indicates that here almost all Greek manuscripts spell the name Bosor. Green suggests that "Bosor" might be a "grim allusion to their sins, by paranomasia with *basar* ('flesh')." It may also represent the Galilean mispronunciation of the Hebrew name and in this instance could be a pointer to Peter's authorship, for he had a noticeable Galilean accent (Matt. 26:73).

In describing Balaam's sin Peter refers to the incident of the rebuke administered by Balaam's ass (Num. 22:21–35). The Numbers passage indicates that the angel of the Lord blocked the path of the ass so that the animal turned aside and "crushed Balaam's foot against the wall." Balaam did not see the angel and attempted to prod the reluctant animal with a blow. Eventually the animal, with divine aid, protested the unjust treatment, and Balaam received a personal rebuke from the angel of the Lord. Peter mentions this incident in order to warn the orthodox among his readers who might be misled by the pretentious arguments of the false teachers. His word for "spoke" is "used of important, portentous utterance" (Green). The suggestion is that the oracular speech of a donkey is contrasted with culpable "madness" ("folly," Lamsa) of the prophet. The intent of Peter's message is that his readers should heed the weighty messages of God rather than the specious arguments of the heretics.

### E. The Emptiness and Spiritual Slavery from Following Their Teachings (2:17–19)

In verse 17 Peter pictures the unsatisfactory content of the false teaching with a metaphor from the world of nature. It was teaching incapable of fulfilling its promises. In verse 18 Peter described the heretics as verbal bombasts who "baited" their hearers with deceptive words. Those who listened to these pretentious words would fall into slavery (v. 19).

#### *1. Empty Speaking (2:17)*

Peter compares the errorists to "springs without water" ("waterless fountains," Moffatt) and "mists driven by a storm" ("clouds driven before the storm," Goodspeed). The thirsty traveler or concerned farmer in the East might view a well or a cloud as a potential source of water. However, that well might prove dry, and the cloud could be driven away by the wind before it had an opportunity to deposit its life-saving liquid among those who needed it. In the same way, these heretics may have promised new springs of life to the naive, but in reality there was nothing to their promises. Their teaching was a dry well. Only those in firm touch with Christ would experience any lasting satisfaction. Jude 12 combines portions of both images from Peter and speaks of "clouds without rain."

As punishment for their empty teaching, the heretics are going to be consigned to "blackest darkness." Jude has the identical expression in verse 13. Calvin sees the term as referring to the thick, eternal darkness that will be prepared for the heretics to replace the momentary darkness in which they now live.

2. *Pretentious Talking (2:18)*

The false teachers used "empty, boastful words" ("big, empty words," NEB). The suggestion of Peter is that these ponderous words amount to nothing but folly or nonsense. The word for "mouth" (a verb in English) is the same verb used for "spoke" in verse 16, and here it describes the attempt by the heretics to appear weighty and important in their pronouncements. Pretending to utter oracular announcements, they spoke plain stupidity. However, their speaking did trick some who were "enticed" (for this word see "seduce" of v. 14, same word but different form) by the "lustful desires of sinful human nature." The idea is that the false teachers used shameless immoral appeals as a bait on their hook to attract the untaught and the unwary.

What was the argument of these false teachers? It may be that they maintained that the salvation of the immortal soul was all that was important. Once they had secured this by the superior knowledge that the false teachers promised, they could live morally as they pleased. Also, the false teachers may have suggested that the body was of such an insignificant nature that they might abuse it (cf. 1 Cor. 6:12–20). Paul countered this argument by appealing to the glorious future of the body and warning of the potential for ruining the body by bringing it into slavery. Peter follows this last-mentioned argument in verse 19.

The audience whom these false teachers attracted were those "who are just escaping from those who live in error." "Just" (Gr., *oligōs*) occurs nowhere else in the New Testament, but its rarity inclines Metzger to view it as the correct reading. If that word is allowed to stand, the suggestion is that the false teachers were attracting those who had just a brief time ago begun to escape the wickedness of a pagan background. The ones who "live in error" were the pagans from whom these relatively new Christians were escaping. These young Christians were escaping a former pagan background but were coming under the domination of the grandiose sophistry of the heretics.

### 3. *Enslaving Teaching (v. 19)*

Here the thought of Peter is that the false teachers promise freedom to their listeners, while they themselves are the servants of corrupting habits. Their slavery is seen in that they have been overcome by their evil habits and are in bondage to them.

The Greek present participle is used for "promise" and indicates that the false teachers continued to chatter on with promises about liberty even though they were imprisoned amidst lust. Here were prisoners talking to others of a freedom that they didn't have! This "freedom" may have been an exemption from offering loving service to the Lord Jesus, a "freedom" that would only plunge them back into bondage (Gal. 5:13; John 8:34). The heretics could have based their appeal on an inner voice of the spirit and visions received from the Lord (cf. Jude 8). The true freedom that Peter's readers needed was to be found in knowing Christ (1:3, 4).

Peter drove his argument home with a proverb that a man becomes a slave of whatever overpowers him. The Greek perfect tenses for "mastered" and "is a slave" suggest a condition of complete slavery. Whenever a man is ultimately vanquished by gradual spiritual and moral decay coupled with wilful indulgence, he is finally and completely a slave!

## F. The Ultimate Separation from God (2:20–22)

Peter argues that the false teachers appeared to have been delivered from the corrupting influence of the world by their knowledge of Christ but have eventually been overcome by sin (v. 20a). The result of this condition is that their final end is worse than their beginning (vv. 20b, 21). As a comparison in understanding this situation he uses two proverbs (v. 22).

### 1. *The Assumption (2:20a)*

In verse 19 the false teachers were called "slaves of depravity," and in verse 20 this group is being discussed again. The "corruption of the world" ("the world's contaminations," Phillips) refers to the staining moral influence of society alienated from God. The method of their escaping this corrupting influence was by a knowledge of the Lord Jesus that had set them free from the pollutions of the world, but they had been again entangled (another fishing metaphor like "entice" in v. 18) and overcome. The result of such a defection is mentioned in verses 20b, 21. Whatever "knowledge" of Jesus these heretics had, only affected them temporarily. Perhaps their knowledge of some Christian truth and adoption of some Christian actions had given them a short victory over the corruption of the world. True knowledge of Jesus would have affected the intellect and the will permanently. Their imperfect knowledge only caused a brief change.

*2. The Conclusion (2:20b, 21)*

The false teachers had understood the claims of Christ and had turned from them. The result was that they were "worse off at the end" than they had been at the beginning. "Peter considered their former condition of sin in a state of ignorance preferable to their present condition in a state of having repudiated the Christ whom they had come to know as the only way out of sin" (Summers). In what sense is the last state worse? Previously they had learned that the only way out of sin was by the knowledge of Christ. They had now rejected that. They were more culpable for having known and rejected the truth (Luke 12:47, 48). Further, their return to sin might be made more boldly. Having claimed some knowledge of Christ and some freedom from sin, they had returned to their old practices. Cynicism and bitterness multiply in the soul of individuals who turn from God's grace back to sin. Re-entanglement with evil produces scoffers and skeptics.

Because their last state of wilful rejection is worse than their initial state of uninformed ignorance, "it would have been better for them not to have known the way of righteousness." The "way" is a reference to salvation as it comes by faith in Jesus Christ. They had known about this way; they were fully aware of it (this seems the significance of the perfect infinitive "have known"), but they finally spurned it. The text here has variants that show three different words for "turn their backs" and two prepositions for "on," but there is little difference in sense with any of the combinations. Green understands the "sacred commandment" to be a reference to the laws of God delivered to man for his good (Deut. 10:13). He feels that the first stage in the apostasy of these false teachers was their rejection of the category of law. They saw themselves as enlightened believers without any need for a commandment to provide guidance. This rejection of God's law led them to a rejection of Him personally, for God is holy (1 Peter 1:16). These heretics, who had at one time a grasp of Christian truth, had sinned against knowledge. They called darkness light, designated bondage as liberty, and they thus practiced an unforgivable sin because they had no basis to acknowledge their sinfulness before God (cf. the unpardonable sin in Mark 3:21–30).

*3. A Comparison (2:22)*

Peter concludes this chapter of forceful denunciation of the heretics with two proverbs that correctly describe their situation. Peter designates both of these expressions as proverbial. The first resembles Proverbs 26:11, but the second does not appear to have a biblical parallel (its source may be a popular collection of Jewish sayings). The dog and the pig (the Greek uses "sow") were both animals regarded as unclean to the Jew, and the use of them in this expression would be loathsome to the Hebrew mind. Both proverbs show in a shocking manner the folly and disgrace of voluntarily reverting to the moral squalor of paganism after having learned how to leave that lifestyle through faith in Christ. Jesus unites both dogs and pigs in Matthew 7:6 as pictures of mankind out of touch with God.

Just as the nature of a dog leads him to eat again what he has vomited up in his sickness and the nature of a sow is to return to her filthy mud hole, these false teachers reverted to what their natures preferred. The dog was not "cured" by his emission, nor was the sow "cleaned" by her washing. Their natures were unchanged. The false teachers perhaps temporarily had followed the ways of Christianity, but they ultimately repudiated Christ by returning to their old way of life. By the use of these two examples Peter "concluded that the teachers had simply demonstrated their true nature as sick (the dog proverb) and filthy (the hog proverb)" (Summers).

It seems unlikely that Peter would ever have used such

terms as "dog" and "sow" of those who were true believers. It appears that his description of the heretics as those who "have escaped the corruption of the world" (v. 20) and who have "known the way" (v. 21) is based only on their appearance. They once appeared to be renewed, and they claimed to be such. The passing of time had demonstrated that their natures were not changed, and they had returned to what they preferred.

This passage touches on the teaching of the eternal security of the believer, also described as the doctrine that the saints of God will persevere to the end (Matt. 10:22). The suggestion followed in this interpretation is that these false teachers showed by their defection that they were not believers. Their profession was false. They had been mistaken about their own spiritual condition.

**For Further Study**

1. Familiarize yourself with the Old Testament background for the incidents mentioned in 2 Peter 2:4–7. Passages that you should investigate are Genesis 6:1–4; Genesis 6:9–9:29; Genesis 19:24–28, and Genesis 19:1–22. These verses are arranged respectively with reference to 2 Peter 2:4, 5, 6, 7.

2. In order to understand better how the Lord delivers the godly from temptation (2 Peter 2:9) read the following New Testament passages and observe how God cared for His people: 2 Corinthians 12:7–10; James 1:2–4; 1 Peter 1:6–9.

3. Use a standard work on theology or read the article on "Perseverance" in the *Zondervan Pictorial Encyclopedia of the Bible*. Relate what you have read to the interpretation of 2 Peter 2:20–22 given in the text.

# Chapter 4

## A Reminder of Divine Hope

(2 Peter 3:1–13)

In chapter 2 Peter has discussed at length the moral and spiritual failings of the false teachers. He has touched briefly on their doctrinal errors (2:1). Now he launches into a fuller discussion of their doctrinal failings, focusing on their denial of the Lord's Parousia. The recipients of 2 Peter lived among those who issued a strong denial of the return of Jesus Christ, and Peter initially merely reminds them of this precious truth (vv. 1–4). He proves the certitude of the Lord's return by a reference to God's control of history (vv. 5–7), an allusion to Scripture to describe God's unique relation to time (v. 8), a description of the mercy of God in delaying the return (v. 9), and a reference to Christ's own words concerning the unexpectedness of the return (v. 10). Peter concludes his discussion of the Second Coming by applying the idea of the Lord's return to produce holy living among his hearers (vv. 11–13).

### A. The Promise of the Lord's Return (3:1–4)

In introducing the promise of Jesus' return Peter first describes his purpose in mentioning it (vv. 1, 2). He wanted to remind his readers of a truth that they might easily forget. Second, he warns his readers of the forerunners of the event itself (vv. 3, 4). Prophets of denial would appear, and Peter's Christian friends must not be unsettled by their vigor in attacking the Christian doctrine of Jesus' Parousia.

### *1. The Purpose for Mentioning It (3:1, 2)*

The key emphasis here is "reminder." Deceitful heretical teaching and adamant denial might cause these recipients to lose sight of the hope of Jesus' return. Normal human carelessness and spiritual indolence could also contribute to laying aside the truth. Peter takes up his pen to correct this.

First, he addresses his readers as "dear friends." This term of affection would affirm his pastoral concern for the recipients. The vigorous denunciations in chapter 2 might have made readers feel that Peter could be personally harsh, but here he expresses love and earnest concern for their spiritual development.

Second, he speaks of his "second letter." This mention of a "second" writing implies a "first" letter, but what letter would this be? Peter does not state that both his first and second letters were "reminders," and Green feels that 1 Peter cannot fit this description. He suggests that the "first" writing may have been lost (cf. 1 Cor. 5:9, that may refer to a lost writing of Paul). Bigg feels that 1 Peter "will satisfy the conditions [of being a reminder] fairly well," and he supports his belief by noting that prophets and evangelists are mentioned in 1 Peter 1:10–12 and that the Parousia is frequently pointed out (1 Peter 1:7, 13; 4:7; 5:4). Either interpretation above leaves a satisfactory view of Peter's reference to a "second letter," and it is impossible to distinguish dogmatically between them.[1]

If the reference in verse 1 is seen as speaking of 1 Peter, then the recipients of the letter are obviously the same people to whom 1 Peter was sent (1 Peter 1:1, 2). If the reference is to a lost writing, then the location of the recipients is less certain. Asia Minor, however, is still a good probability for destination, for it was one of the chief sources for the Gnosticism of which 2 Peter provides a possible early example.

Third, Peter states that he wants to "stimulate" his readers to "wholesome thinking" ("revive in your sincere minds certain memories," Weymouth). Peter may have used this phrase to

[1] Bauckham sees the "second epistle" as an effort by a pseudonymous writer of 2 Peter to refer back to 1 Peter. The pseudonymous writer did this "to remind the readers that they should be reading this passage as though it were written by Peter."

convey to his readers that he believed that their minds were free of the lust and heresy spreading about them. The phrase may show a wise pastor at work among his flock.

Fourth, Peter reminds his Christian friends of the words of the prophets and the commandments of the apostles. Peter's chosen wording expresses the link between the Old Testament prophets who anticipated Christian truth, Jesus Christ who demonstrated it, and the apostle who provided an authoritative interpretation of it. In referring to the apostles as "your apostles" Peter may have described those apostles of Jesus Christ "with whom the readers had come into personal contact" (Lenski). Contact with both Peter and Paul is suggested by verse 15, and the phrase would at least include these two, and perhaps others. The "command" may be a reference to God's revelation in general through apostles and prophets, or it may speak of explicit warnings concerning the dangers of false teachers.[2] The warnings might refer to the Parousia, but this would not be the total content of it. Peter also uses the full title "Lord and Savior" in reference to Jesus Christ. This may have appeared because Peter was about to emphasize the future element in salvation that was ridiculed by scoffers. Jesus saved from the past (1:1–4), in the present (2:20), and for the future. A denial of the Second Coming is a denial of Jesus as Savior.

### 2. *The Forerunners of Its Occurrence (3:3, 4)*

Peter's chief emphasis here is the presence of "scoffers." His readers lived among false teachers who would unsettle and disturb them by ridiculing the idea of Jesus' return. Peter wanted his friends not to be turned aside from belief in the Parousia by the carping criticism of those who opposed the idea.

The time of the appearance of these opponents was the "last days." Jesus' appearance in history was "when the time had fully come" (Gal. 4:4) or the "last days" (Heb. 1:2). The suggestion is that the appearance of Jesus had opened the final section of human history but had not yet completed it. Between Christ's First and Second Advents lies a period of grace that would also be filled with opposition and difficulty. The appear-

[2]A parallel passage in Jude 17–19 warns against false teaching, not merely against the denial of the Parousia.

ance of the phrase here does not mean that Peter viewed the return of Jesus as "just around the corner," but that he felt Jesus' First Advent had opened the final days. These days would be concluded by Jesus' personal return (Matt. 24:3–5).

The personalities involved in opposition are called "scoffers" who will come "scoffing and following their own evil desires" (cf. Jude 18 that omits the pleonastic "scoffing"). These men "scoff" in that they ridicule the idea of the Parousia and live by "going where their own passions lead" (Goodspeed). They were cynics, and they practiced self-indulgence. They mocked at the very idea of a return of Christ, not merely the fact of its delay. Probably they were opposed to the idea of judgment that the Parousia would inaugurate, and they sought some excuse for living a hedonistic life. Green adds that "if we are right in seeing something of a proto-Gnostic flavour in this heresy, this particular characteristic [self-indulgence] would fit well with what we have already seen in chapter ii."

The accusations of the scoffers were deduced from the stability of the universe. Perhaps this argument was that the universe was a closed system not subject to outside interruption from an event like the Parousia. Evidence of impatience at the delay of Christ's return appears in many New Testament documents from this period (Luke 12:45, 46; Heb. 10:36, 37; James 5:7, 8), and Jesus' words in such passages as Matthew 10:23; 16:28, and 24:34 must have led to much wonder concerning the apparent postponement.

The mockers buttressed their disbelief concerning God's entrance into history through Jesus' return by emphasizing the immutability of the world. If they had lived today, they might have referred to natural laws that prevent the occurrence of miracles. To the "scoffers" the regularity of nature taught that nothing was going to change. "Their mistake was to forget that the laws of nature are God's laws; their predictability springs from His faithfulness" (Green).

The "fathers" may refer to the Old Testament fathers (Green), the first generation of Christians including their own parents and relatives (Kelly), or such specific early Christian leaders as Stephen, James the son of Zebedee, and others (cf. Heb. 13:7). In favor of viewing it as a reference to Old

Testament fathers Green points out that most New Testament references to "fathers" are to Old Testament fathers (Rom. 9:5; Heb. 1:1). Also, the *terminus a quo* of Peter's reference is not the First Advent of Christ but the "beginning of creation." These mockers were twisting Old Testament Scriptures, and Peter draws out of these Scriptures to refute his opponents.[3]

Peter used the Greek verb for "sleep" as a euphemism for death in verse 4. The pagan world of Peter's day was filled with a morbid horror of death, and the fact that Peter could refer to the event as "sleep" indicated the extent to which Christianity was supplying its followers confidence in the face of death. Jesus (Mark 5:39) and Paul (1 Thess. 4:13, 14) had spoken of "death" as "sleep," and when Stephen died, he was said to have fallen asleep (Acts 7:60).

Those who ridiculed the idea of Christ's return were ready to call the entire suggestion a delusion, an unfounded belief. Such a denial would free them to live in accord with their own passions and desires.

### B. The Proof of the Lord's Return (3:5–10)

The chief argument of the "scoffers" against the return of Christ was the apparent immutability of the world. Peter argues from history to indicate that present regularity should not be mistaken for permanent immutability (vv. 5–7), and by this he prepares the way for God's entrance into history at Christ's return. In verse 8 Peter cites an Old Testament Scripture to indicate that God's character and purpose are not altered by the passing of time. In verse 9 Peter suggests that the postponement in Christ's return is due to God's mercy in providing an opportunity for many more nonbelievers to come to faith in Christ. Finally, Peter refers specifically to a promise of Christ to indicate the certainty of Jesus' Parousia despite its unexpectedness (v. 10).

---

[3]In referring to the "fathers" some interpreters feel that the entire first generation of believers had passed away, and this would include the apostle Peter. Obviously such an interpretation would exclude Peter from the authorship of 2 Peter. Kelly says, "Evidently the first Christian generation at any rate lies well back in the past."

*1. Argument from History (3:5–7)*

The mockers had asserted that this was a stable, unchanging world. Their conclusion was that it would remain stable, and there would be no interruption from a Parousia. Peter moves to show that their premise is false, and thus their conclusion is invalid. To do this, he refers to Creation (v. 5), destruction (v. 6), and preservation (v. 7).

**a. Creation (3:5).** Peter describes the culpability of the false teachers by saying that they "deliberately" ignore the fact that Creation was a divine act by a sovereign God. Peter applies this act of creation to the original formation of the heavens (Strachan)[4] and to the subsequent creation of the earth.

In describing the Creation Peter views water as the material "out of" (Gr., *ek*) which the earth was made and also the material "with" (Gr., *dia*) which the earth was made. Alford distinguishes between these prepositions by indicating that the earth was formed "out of" water "because the waters that were under the firmament were gathered together into one place and the dry land appeared: and thus water was the material, *out of* which the earth was made." He feels the phrase "through" ("with," NIV) water indicates that the water supplied moisture and rain as the means for sustaining the creative process.

All of this act of creation was carried out "by God's word." The phrase might refer either to the creative fiat of God that called things into existence or to God's Eternal Word—Jesus Christ—who was an agent in creation (Col. 1:16). In this context it appears more likely that Peter's reference is to the divine fiat of Jehovah.

The false teachers had assumed constant and immutable order throughout the created universe. Peter takes his audience back to God's work in creation to demonstrate the source of this order and perhaps to remind them that there had not always been order.

**b. Destruction (3:6).** The opening words of verse 6 are smoothed out by a "whereby" in the KJV although the Greek has an ambiguous *di hōn* (literally: "through which things"). Some

[4]In describing the term "long ago" (Gr., *ekpalai*) as referring to the heavens as they existed before the creation of the world Strachan refers to a Jewish view that the heavens were in existence before God's work of creation started.

versions (NIV, NEB) see the plural form to refer to the two types of water mentioned in verse 5. Bigg says, "The fountains of the deep spouted up from below and the rain streamed down from above." Another possibility is to understand the combination of water and the word of God. Green says, "At God's decree, the very element from which this earth had its origin and by which it was maintained, was used to destroy it." This view seems more acceptable because it suggests that nature is not itself independent but can be created and destroyed only by the word of God.

The term "world" (Gr., *kosmos*) is a subject of much debate among commentators. Were the heavens also or the earth only destroyed in the judgment of God upon Noah? Jewish apocalyptic contains stories of the destruction of the entire universe.[5] In this apocalyptic view it is implied that the effects of the Flood extended throughout the universe and not just among mankind. Green suggests that "perhaps *kosmos* simply means 'the world of men,' as it does in an identical context in ii.5. Peter would then mean that human life perished."

To counter the unbelieving suggestion that the order of nature was a permanent feature, Peter has clearly referred to the flood of Noah's time (Gen. 7:1–24). His use of the phrase "that time" makes this clear. The "scoffers" might feel that nothing had changed, but they had wilfully neglected the disturbance of mankind in the flood of Noah. Nothing was to prevent that from happening again at the return of Christ, and the confident mockers should beware.

**c. Preservation (3:7).** Here Peter speaks of the fiery destruction of "the present heavens and earth." Does he refer to the entire universe or merely to the world of man? It is impossible to be sure which is correct, but there is no compelling reason why he should not believe that the entire universe will be destroyed by fire. Such an idea has an honorable Christian background. Some have found that Peter's description here of the destruction of "heaven and earth" by fire betrays Stoic influences, but Green indicates that Stoicism had a pantheistic program while Peter's program is monotheistic.

[5]In 1 Enoch 83:3–5 there is the story that the heavens crumble and collapse onto the earth, and the earth itself is swallowed up into a vast abyss.

Also, Stoicism expected a world of the same quality as the last to emerge from the destruction. The Christian hope calls for a transformed world and the redemption of the created order (Rom. 8:19–21; Rev. 21:1). The concept of fiery judgment appears throughout the Old Testament (Deut. 4:24; Mal. 4:1), and it describes the return of Jesus Christ in the New Testament (2 Thess. 1:7–9).

The phrase "by the same word" would apply to the same word of God that was active in Creation (v. 5). This word was also active in the preservation of the world for a final destruction. The word of God could create, preserve, and destroy. The false teachers had no adequate concept of any of this.

The imagery of fire is taken from apocalyptic sources, and it refers to the purification and destruction of evil to be undertaken when God comes to judge the world. Peter may indeed believe that the entire universe will be destroyed by fiery conflagration (a not impossible idea after Hiroshima), but all that he states is that the heavens and earth are reserved for fire in anticipation of the judgment of the ungodly. The present tense of the participle "being kept" is suggestive of the fact that only the power of God holds the present state of things together until He determines to end it.

In the Jewish conception of the rainbow promise (Gen. 9:8–17) water would not again be the agency of destruction used by God. Here Peter states that the destruction will be caused by fire. Whatever destruction is caused by that fire will not annihilate the present system totally, for there is to be a new heaven and a new earth filled with righteousness (v. 13).

*2. Argument from Scripture (3:8)*

Here Peter refers to Psalm 90:4 in an effort to show that God, who is omnipresent in time, views all times as equally near. Because of God's omnipresence and sovereignty He will reckon time differently from man. Since time for God is valued differently from time for man, the delay in the return of Christ is no proof that it will not occur. God views time with both an intensity and a perspective that human beings lack. A day is important to God. All time must be used for His glory. However, a delay of 1,000 years in executing the plan of God is unimportant from His perspective. By using these words Peter is contrasting the eternity of God's plans with the impatience demonstrated in mere human speculations. Having stated here that time seems long only because of our mortal time perspective, Peter will move to indicate that the delay proves purposeful in that it provides an opportunity for men to repent and be saved (v. 9).

This verse had a significant influence on the chiliasm of the second century, the view that the dawning of the Day of the Lord at the Parousia would bring a thousand years of rule by God's people in an earthly Jerusalem. Justin Martyr (*Dialogue* 81) and Irenaeus (*A. H.* 5.23.2) apparently refer to this passage. Irenaeus took the verse to support the belief that the world would last for as many thousand years as there were days of creation, and he arrived at 6,000 years as the length for world history (A. H. 5, 28, 3). Peter does not use this verse from the Old Testament to speculate at all about the end of the world, and he is reserved in its application to his proof of the Lord's return.

*3. Argument from God's Character (3:9).*

Peter is combating the idea that God has made a promise that He has not kept. He shows that God's plan is actually better than the bare promise, for the additional element of God's long-suffering and mercy are brought to the front. The delay of Christ's return is not due to impotence but to mercy. In speaking thus, Peter has opened the door to all repentant sinners, even to repentant scoffers.

The "some" may include some of the scoffers, but it will also refer to Christians who have been infected by their skepticism. The description of God as "not wanting anyone to perish" uses *boulomenos* as the Greek word for "wanting." Huther suggests that this describes an attitude arising with and from conscious reflection. It is not merely the preference but the conscious choice of God that none perish. Despite God's merciful desire some will unfortunately choose otherwise. God's patience is pictured with the verb *makrothumei* ("long-suffering," KJV). Trench describes the term as referring to a man who, having the power to revenge himself, yet refrains from the exercise of this power (*Synonyms of the New Testament*, 183). It supremely expresses the patience of God toward wayward persons. The reference to the "longsuffering of God" (KJV) in 1 Peter 3:20 provides a possible evidence of identity of authorship for the two epistles. A pressing application of these words of Peter is that Christians must use the time before the return of Christ in the preaching of the gospel to bring men to repentance.

### *4. Argument from Christ's Promise (3:10)*

Verses 8 and 9 countered apathy about Christ's return. Verse 10 can prevent excessive enthusiasm. The time of Christ's return must be left with God, but Christians can watch and be morally prepared (1 Thess. 5:6–8). In speaking of the "day of the Lord" Peter is using thoughts similar to those of Jesus in Matthew 24:43, 44 and Luke 12:39, 40. For Peter there is no distinction between the Day of the Lord and the coming of Christ.

The comparison of the coming of the Day of the Lord to that of a thief refers not so much to its suddenness or imminence as to its unexpectedness. Committed Christians will be prepared for this return, but the indolent and the wicked will not escape God's judgment (1 Thess. 5:3).

Peter mentions three things that will accompany the arrival of the Day of the Lord. First, "the heavens will disappear with a roar." Peter's language is taken from that of Jewish apocalyptic, and he uses apocalyptic to portray the indescribable. He wants the eyes of his readers to settle on the climax of history. The heavens are viewed as an envelope above the world, and "roar" (Gr., *rhoizēdon*) "is a colorful, onomatopoeic word that can be used of the swish of an arrow through the air, or the rumbling of thunder, as well as the crackle of flames" (Green). In choosing this word Peter has united many horrible events under one term.

Second, the physical elements (Gr., *stoicheia*) will "be destroyed by fire." The "elements" may refer to the physical elements of earth, air, fire, and water, out of which all things were felt to be composed. It may also refer to the heavenly bodies such as sun, moon, and stars. The view of Mark 13:24–26 points to more than merely physical elements. Third, Peter anticipates that everything in the earth will be "laid bare." This final verb in verse 10 varies so widely in Greek manuscripts that Metzger is hard pressed to determine the original. Alternate readings are "disappear" or "burn up," but Metzger decides in favor of "laid bare" as the oldest reading and the one that best explains the origin of the others that are preserved. The expression of "laying bare" the earth may point to a form of divine judgment that ends in a pronouncement of penalty by God. Peter spends no time in speculating on the meaning of the apocalyptic imagery, but he moves to apply the moral implications of the Parousia of Christ.

### C. The Application of the Lord's Return (3:11–13).

Having stated firmly the truth of Jesus' return, Peter uses this teaching for the encouragement of his readers. His friends were to develop an attitude of godliness in all their behavior (v. 11). They were to engage in the action of cooperating with God for the redemption of society (v. 12). They were to anticipate the new heavens and earth as the location of righteousness (v. 13).

#### *1. A New Attitude (3:11)*

Peter affirms that everything is to be destroyed in connection with the return of Christ. He uses an eschatological imperative as the basis for a moral imperative. The "everything" would be a reference to the "heavens and the earth" (v. 7), and it likely refers to a destruction of the entire universe, not merely the world of men. The "destruction" is expressed by a present participle (Gr., *luomenōn*). Some interpreters understand this tense structure to refer to a process of dissolution of the universe that is already underway (Kelly; cf. "are in the process of dissolution," TCNT), but more likely it is an instance of the present used for the future (Zerwick; "will be destroyed," NIV). The expression "what kind of" contains a hint that great things are expected of the readers. "How outstandingly excellent" these people ought to be (Kelly). The verb for "to be" (Gr., *huparchein*) suggests a permanent and enduring state. The idea is that a belief in the transitoriness of all that one can see on earth should lead to a life founded on the realities of truth and holiness. In verse 11 Peter urges that holiness of life and the worship of God should be practical responses to the knowledge of the return of Christ. The fact that both of these words are in the plural (lit. "holy behaviors and godlinesses") suggests that this response should take different forms and examples. In the next verse Peter adds that committed action affecting others is to be inspired by a knowledge of Jesus' return.

Barclay provides three examples from heathen tombs of what occurs when men reject the view that creation has a goal or climax to which it is moving. It can lead to hedonism: "I was nothing: I am nothing. So thou who art still alive, eat, drink, and be merry." It can lead to apathy: "Once I had no existence; now I have none. I am not aware of it. It does not concern me." It can lead to despair: "Charidas, what is below?" "Deep darkness." "But what of the paths upward?" "All a lie." . . . "Then we're lost." He concludes that without the truth from the doctrine of the Second Coming that life is going somewhere, there is nothing left to live for.

2. *A New Action (3:12)*

The anticipation of the return of Jesus does not call for pious inaction but earnest endeavor. Christians are to "look forward to the day of God and speed its coming." There is a hint that Christ's Second Advent is related to the response of God's people (cf. Acts 3:19–21). Christians are to be God's agents to involve themselves in the redemption of human society. Specifically this calls for efforts in evangelism (Matt. 28:19, 20); prayer (Rev. 8:4); godly living (1 Peter 2:12), and obedience.[6]

Peter's use of the unusual "day of God" in place of the more common "day of the Lord" (v. 10) is a reference to the return of the Lord Jesus. At that return the judgment is expressed in terms of fire that destroys (v. 10; also note discussion of "heavens" and "elements" there) and purifies (1 Peter 1:7). The present

[6]Cranfield rejects the idea that repentance and good works can speed the Parousia and suggests that the verbs beginning verse 12 should read "looking for and seeking earnestly." Although the timing of Christ's return is fixed, one may understand that repentance and holy living are prerequisites for Christ's return (cf. Acts 3:19–21) and can thus be viewed as leading to the occurrence of the event.

tense for "melt" (Gr., *tēketai*) is another example of the prophetic present (cf. "destroyed" in v. 11), the use of the present for the future.

The fire of judgment will strike terror into the hearts of mockers, but a knowledge of it can be an incentive to the faithful (cf. 1 Cor. 3:10–15). The committed Christian can face the destruction of all things with courage and even with joy.

*3. A New Anticipation (3:13)*

Here Peter provides a positive result of the day of God with reference to the church. The final "new heaven and a new earth" will result from fire just as the flood changed the old earth. Peter does not provide a detailed program of what God will do in providing a new creation, for the exact details of this program are not revealed.[7] The language of Scripture is a figurative description of what God will do, and it assures us that God has a purpose and a future for both the soul and the body. There are to be redeemed individuals and a redeemed society. The new earth is to be the permanent home (that is the meaning of the Greek *katoikei*) of righteousness. Wickedness will face destruction, and the will of God is to be done. Peter does not attempt to describe the new world with symbols borrowed from the present world, and his only emphasis is that morally this new order will be the opposite of the present order that is ruled by evil desire and corruption (1:4).

**For Further Study**

1. In 2 Peter 3:5–10 Peter provides four arguments in proof of the Lord's return. Notice the discussion of them as given in the text and summarize the four arguments in your own words.

2. In 2 Peter 3:11–13 Peter applies the fact of the Lord's return to the lives of his readers. Read again his words in these verses and summarize his argument. Compare this usage with the manner in which the return of Christ is mentioned in Titus 2:12, 13 and James 5:7.

---

[7]Green aptly reminds those prone to speculation that no group got the details of Christ's First Advent right.

# Chapter 5

# Closing Admonitions

(2 Peter 3:14–18)

Some truths bear repetition and frequent mention. Such is the truth of Christ's return, and Peter again uses the belief in this return as an incentive to encourage his readers to holy living (v. 14). He also reminds them of Paul's words describing God's patience with mankind, and he encourages them to see this patience as leading to salvation for more of mankind (vv. 15, 16). Even though these recipients are knowledgeable and informed concerning the heresies that they will encounter, they still could be misled and deceived. Peter encourages them to prevent this by steady growth in grace and the knowledge of Jesus Christ (vv. 17, 18).

**A. An Appeal for Moral Purity (3:14)**

A hopeful look to the future must produce a holy life. The false teachers had severed the link between belief and practice, and Peter was restoring it. "Peter never tired of stressing the this-worldly consequences of the other-worldly 'look'" (Green).

Peter used the same verb but in a different form for "looking forward" in verses 13, 14 and "look forward" in verse 12, and here "looking forward" provides a reason for the encouragement to make an effort. Since they expected the Advent of Christ to usher in fire and judgment, Christians must persevere in the process of sanctification and strive to produce a life of purity.

Peter had called the mockers "blots" ("spots," KJV) and "blemishes" in 2:13. He had also referred to the Lord Jesus in

1 Peter 1:19 as "without blemish or defect" ("spot," KJV). Here "spotless" is used of the moral purity expected of committed Christians. "Blameless" ("above reproach," NEB) has a similar reference to moral purity. Both words are taken from the religious language of sacrifice to describe animals perfectly suited physically for an offering to God. Peter was calling for these Christians to be the reverse of the false teachers.

To be "at peace" includes every element of blessedness, both peace with God and with man. It is likely that Peter's appeal that his readers "be found" in a state of peace encourages them to live in this state at the present time and anticipates that they shall also be found in this condition at the time of Christ's return.

**B. A Reminder of Paul's Words (3:15, 16)**

Peter had emphasized that the delay in the time of Christ's return was due to the long-suffering of God in allowing greater opportunity for more to trust Christ (v. 9). Peter here called upon his readers to acknowledge this as one of God's purposes in the delay.

Such a theme as this had also been addressed by Paul, but what teaching of Paul does Peter mention in verse 15? If Peter's theme is the idea that God is delaying the Parousia out of motives of mercy so that more can be saved, Paul makes this point in Romans 2:4 (cf. Rom. 9:22). Peter, however, may be referring to Paul's steady appeal for holy living especially in the light of Christ's return (Rom. 13:11–14). Notice also that Peter indicates that Paul had written to Peter's recipients—the intent of the "you" in the latter half of verse 15. These observations raise questions concerning which book(s) of Paul is (are) intended by Peter and also the destination of that book and of 2 Peter.

Some commentators see Romans as the book involved here (Mayor, Plummer). Green, who opposes seeing a reference to Romans, suggests that Romans might have had at least one edition sent to Ephesus. This idea would fit in with the suggestion that 2 Peter was written to Christians in Asia Minor. Kelly suggests that the Pauline letters were seen as the "common property of Christians everywhere" and "were in effect addressed to the world-wide Church."[1]

It is interesting to remember that there had once been a confrontation between Paul and Peter (Gal. 2:14). Apparently any conflict between them was of short duration, for there is a picture of concord in Galatians 2:8–10 and Acts 15:7–11. Peter's warm description of Paul as "our dear brother" would be expected as a proper response to the Christian emphasis on brotherly love and forgiveness.

Peter's mention of Paul's writings led him to mention their difficulty of interpretation and also their use as Scripture. In the first statement the word "hard to understand" (Gr., *dusnoētos* was used in antiquity of "oracles, whose pronouncements were notoriously capable of more than one interpretation" (Green). To "distort" (Gr., *strebloō*) was a vivid word that referred to twisting with a windlass. The use of "ignorant" ("ill-informed," Phillips) is a reference to people who lack the moral qualities that make for balanced judgment. Peter is warning that there are teachings in Paul's writings that the undisciplined and unstable can pervert so as to cause their own destruction. These teachings need not be the same as those of verse 15. What were these teachings? Many understand "these matters" to refer to the eschatological subjects mentioned earlier in the chapter (Mayor, Zerwick). Alford particularly feels that there is a possible reference to 2 Thessalonians 2:1ff. Green feels that "Peter is alluding to Paul's doctrine of justification by faith which was, we know, twisted by the unscrupulous to mean that once justified a man could do what he liked with impunity." Evidences of such teaching in Paul that could be misunderstood would appear in Romans 3:5–8; 6:1; 7:4; 8:1, 2; 1 Cor. 6:12–20; Gal. 3:10; 5:13. Kelly harmonizes these two emphases by suggesting that the twisting was done in the area of ethical libertinism and defective eschatology.

Despite the difficulty of interpreting Paul's writings, Peter

[1] Bigg feels that "if we judge both that the recipients of 2 Peter were Asiatics, and that the Pauline letter in question dealt explicitly with disorders rising out of doubts about the Parousia, we are forced to conclude that St. Peter is speaking of a Pauline Epistle which, . . . no longer exists." Dogmatism about the specific Pauline book intended is unwarranted, but the likelihood points to Romans, both because of its doctrinal content and evidence of its widespread acceptance.

indicates that they can be compared to "the other Scriptures." The phrase (Gr., *tas loipas graphas*) can be understood in two ways. First, it may distinguish Paul's letters from Scripture. In 1 Thessalonians 4:13 Paul uses a similar phrase (Gr., *hoi loipoi*) to describe others who were not Christians. Peter may be stating here that Paul's writings are twisted just as they twist the other Scriptures, i.e. the Old Testament. Such a statement would indicate a high view for Paul's writings, but it would suggest that they may not have been called "Scripture" this early in Christian history. On the other hand, Peter's statement may include Paul's letters in Scripture. Sometimes "Scripture" was used in a broad sense to refer to material not in the Old Testament but that was hallowed by long usage (e.g. James 4:5, a verse that has no specific Old Testament source). Green feels that before A.D. 60 Christian writings were being read in church alongside the Old Testament and were on their way to being rated as equal in value to it. The apostles were aware that they spoke the word of the Lord as surely as any of the prophets (1 Cor. 14:37; 1 Thess. 2:13), and it would not be unusual to see them placing each other alongside the Old Testament prophets (cf. the quote of Luke 10:7 in 1 Tim. 5:18). Peter thus may be viewed as putting Paul alongside the Old Testament writers in his reference here. The latter interpretation seems more likely in this context although the former option does preserve a high view of the authority of Paul's writings.

### C. Growth in Grace and Knowledge (3:17, 18)

Here Peter issues a warning against stumbling (v. 17) and prescribes how to avoid stumbling by mature Christian growth (v. 18). The verb for "guard" (Gr., *phylassō*) is a middle imperative in form and suggests that Peter's readers should guard themselves. The opponents of Peter's readers had previously been described as "lawless" (lit. "unprincipled") in 2:7. Peter's friends had a "secure position," but their opponents, the heretics, had no foundation whatever. Peter does not assume that the awareness and commitment of his friends would exempt them from spiritual failure, and he urges them to watch carefully lest that happen.

Peter was recognizing here that forewarning was a means of preparing his friends for what lay ahead. He wants his readers to avoid a purely private religious experience and to demonstrate their commitment by their endurance. He desires stability and steadfastness without compromise. Jesus had used the verbal form of the word for "secure position" ("steadfastness," KJV) with Peter in Luke 22:32 ("strengthen your brothers"), and it is instructive to see Peter's concern for this trait. "It is not surprising that he who had been so mercurial and had been changed by the grace of God into a man of rock should be so concerned about stability" (Green).

The recipients would best protect themselves by mature Christian growth. Peter's use of a present imperative in "grow" denotes that the readers are to continue their growth. It must not be a one-time emphasis but a developing experience. "Grace" is a reference to the spiritual strength that Jesus Christ supplies to the needy sinner. "Knowledge" can refer either to that knowledge that Christ supplies (understanding, practical knowledge) or to the personal knowledge and acquaintance with Him. If the latter is followed, then knowledge here (Gr., *gnōsis*) could not be distinguished from the other word for knowledge (Gr., *epignōsis*) appearing in 1:2, 3, 8; 2:20, that normally refers to personal knowledge of Jesus Christ. Since the words appear to be used differently by Peter, they should be separated in meaning here, and "knowledge" here thus becomes Christian instruction or practical wisdom.

"Glory" is a reference to the greatness of God expressed with a word that refers to the radiance of light. Peter desired that Christ experience this glory both "now" and "forever" (lit., "unto the day of the age"). This "day" is the same as the "day of judgment" (vv. 7, 10, 12), and it is the day that begins eternity.

**For Further Study**

1. In 2 Peter 3:15, 16 Peter demonstrates a deep appreciation for the writings of Paul. Read the following verses and notice in them the manner in which Paul views his own awareness of the authority of his writings: 1 Corinthians 7:12, 14:37; 1 Thessalonians 2:13.

2. Realizing that Christians should honor the Son even as they honor the Father (John 5:23), compare the manner in which Peter renders glory to Christ in 3:18 with the glory that is attributed to God in Romans 11:36 and Jude 25.

# Introduction to Jude

Unlike 2 Peter the Epistle of Jude has early, good attestation. Later, however, it seemed to fall into disfavor primarily because of its reference to apocryphal material in verses 9 and 14.

### A. Authorship

Jude identifies himself as a servant of Jesus Christ and brother of James (v. 1). The author obviously intended this as a reference to James the Lord's brother (cf. Mark 6:3 where both James and Jude are mentioned). In relation to Jesus, Jude chose to identify himself only as a servant, and gave no claim of a flesh relationship to the Lord. This would be a token of his humility. The fact that Jude was seen as a brother of Jesus would gain quite quickly a wide respect for the writing.

Such early Christian writers as Clement of Alexandria, Polycarp, and Tertullian knew of Jude. Some from later centuries, such as Eusebius of Caesarea, were less certain of its authenticity, but the conviction of the church grew that this was Scripture and that it was written by the Lord's brother.

### B. Occasion and Date

If Jude, the Lord's brother, is the author, the dating must be confined within the reasonable limits of his lifetime. Assuming that Jude was a younger brother of Jesus (the most likely interpretation of Mark 6:3), Jude would have been born in the early part of the Christian era. Under this assumption the epistle would normally be dated no later than A.D. 70 or 80. Some have attempted to date the writing in the second century by defining the false teaching as Gnosticism, but this is not a certain method of interpreting the false teaching. It is impossible to be precise in the dating of Jude, but Guthrie puts it between A.D. 65 and 80.

Jude had begun his writing as a treatise on the salvation he shared with his readers, but he quickly moved to deal with the problem of the false teachers. Perhaps Jude learned of this problem even as he was beginning to write the letter, and this may explain his blunt, passionate appeals. Jude's purpose in writing becomes primarily practical, and he does not provide a reasoned refutation of the teachings of the heretics. He does conclude his writing with a series of exhortations that would provide some direction and strength for his readers in their opposition to heresy. His chief purpose was to provide a warning for his readers.

**C. Destination**

No specific address is given, and those who are "called" and "loved" might be Christians living anywhere. Jude has such detailed acquaintance with specific false teachers that it seems unlikely that his letter is a circular writing intended to warn all Christians against heresy. He had a concrete situation in mind. Information on a specific geographical location is difficult to find. There is a likelihood that verses 17, 18 suggest that the readers had heard some of the apostles. The use of Jewish apocryphal writings might point also to a Jewish setting. With information such as this, some have pointed to a Palestinian setting, but such an opinion cannot be firmly held.

**D. His Use of Apocryphal Writings**

Jude certainly makes reference to the apocryphal book of 1 Enoch and quite probably also to the Assumption of Moses. His reference in verse 14 to Enoch indicates that he holds the book in high esteem and feels it legitimate to cite it in support of his views. However, it cannot be proved that he views the work as Scripture. Guthrie feels that Jude may be saying that what Enoch uttered has turned out to be a true prophecy in the light of the ungodly conduct of the false teachers (*New Testament Introduction,* III, 239).

In verse 9 there is a likely reference to the Assumption of Moses. Here the original text of the writing has been lost, but Clement of Alexandria and Origen assume that Jude used this book. Jude refers to the story of Michael in the Assumption of Moses as an illustration of the arrogance of the false teachers whom he is denouncing. Again, his reference to apocryphal writings may not tell us anything specifically about his view of their inspiration. Tertullian felt that Jude's reference to Enoch was evidence that Enoch was inspired (*Idol. 15*). Jerome expressed that doubts about Jude had arisen because he referred to the apocryphal writings in an authoritative way (*De Vir*, Ill.4).

It should be remembered that Paul occasionally refers to noncanonical books in his writings. In 1 Corinthians 10:4 he appeals to a rabbinical midrash, and in Acts 17:28 he refers to a heathen poet. In 2 Timothy 3:8 he draws on a noncanonical source to name the magicians who withstood Moses as Jannes and Jambres. These practices by Paul did not lead to a rejection of his writings.

**Outline of Jude**

I. Introduction
II. The Letter of Jude
  A. Greetings (vv. 1, 2)
  B. The Occasion for Writing—Entrance of False Teachers (vv. 3–4)
  C. A Description of the False Teachers (vv. 5–16)
  D. Advice to Committed Christians (vv. 17–23)
  E. Doxology of Praise to God (vv. 24, 25)

# Jude

Jude wrote his epistle to warn his Christian friends of the pernicious ways of false teachers who were already working in their midst. He was not content merely to denounce the heretics as troublemakers, but he provided instructions to his readers on how they could contend for the Christian faith by godly living. His brief letter provides an example of pastoral concern, pungent writing, and practical spiritual advice, plus praise and worship to God.

In the opening verses (vv. 1, 2) Jude identifies himself and wishes Christian graces for his readers. These brief words provide our only significant internal clue to the identity and background of the author.

Jude's words in verses 3, 4 show the occasion for writing. He had intended to pen a letter to his readers on the theme of salvation, but the knowledge that false teachers had begun their work among his friends led him to change the subject. With vigor and clarity he turned his attention to describing and opposing these heretics.

In verses 5–16 he provides a description of the false teachers. He portrays them as deserving of such judgments as God had given in the past to Israel, the sinning angels, and the cities of Sodom and Gomorrah (vv. 5–7). He portrays them as arrogant (vv. 8, 9) and shows that they delight in such corruption as greed, idolatry, self-centered living, and shameless immorality (vv. 10–13). These false teachers can expect the future punishment that he describes in verses 14, 15. Their complaining, boastful lifestyle provides further reason for God's righteous judgment (v. 16).

Jude prepares his readers for the onslaught of false teaching by reminding them of the detailed warnings about heretics, that had come from apostolic teaching (vv. 17–19). By growing in their grasp of Christian faith, fervent prayer, and obedient living, these Christians can receive the strength to endure their time of testing (vv. 20, 21). Yet, these growing Christians must keep constant watch for believers who would err, and must seek to reclaim them from the clutches of heresy (vv. 22, 23).

Jude's doxology in verses 24, 25 provides his recipients with a model of praise that can keep their spiritual eyes fixed on the power of the almighty God rather than on the deceitful activities of misguided heretics.

**A. Greetings (vv. 1, 2)**

Jude's writing follows the form of the typical letter of the day by including a writer, readers, and a greeting. Writing as a committed Christian, Jude naturally adds features in his introduction that would be absent from secular letters. He omits a destination in his greeting, and this has caused some to view the writing as a "catholic letter," addressed to all Christians. However, a closer reading of Jude indicates that he wrote for a particular situation in which false teachers were active even though he does not mention a specific church or geographical location.

Jude describes himself in two ways. He is "a servant of Jesus Christ" and a "brother of James." In the Introduction (q.v.) Jude was identified as the half-brother of Jesus. He has made a significant change from viewing Jesus as deranged (see Mark 3:21), to becoming his follower. "Now that he had become a believer, Jude's aim in life was to be utterly at the disposal of the Messiah Jesus" (Green). The unqualified reference to James could refer to only one person in the apostolic church—James, the brother of the Lord and leader of the church in Jerusalem (Acts 15:13–21; Gal. 2:9). Just as Andrew is known as the brother of Simon Peter, Jude is content to be known as the brother of James. Jude could have described himself as the "brother of the Lord," but probably "shrank from what might have seemed boastfulness of so describing himself" (Plumptre).

Jude uses three terms to refer to his readers. They are "called," "loved," and "kept." In Greek "called" is a substantive, and the participles "loved" and "kept" refer to those who have been "called." The idea of calling "expresses the divine initiative to which man must respond in faith" (Bauckham), and in the New Testament it has practically become a synonym for "Christian." The process of calling refers to God's call to men and women by the gospel to enter His kingdom and belong to His family. The realization of being called by God should rest in the mind of every Christian, for as a result of this the Christian has "passed from sin and death into the redeemed life which Christ bestows" (Kelly).

The phrase, "loved by God the Father," is variously worded ("sanctified by God the Father," KJV; "beloved by God the Father," Williams; "dear to God the Father," Goodspeed), and this reflects some variety in both the text and in interpretation. The best texts use "beloved" or "loved." Kelly says, "What the writer means by this is, not that they are loved by himself with a love rooted in God, but rather that they are loved by God and that His love enfolds them. As a result of being called, they have fellowship with Him, and in that fellowship experience His love."

The phrase, "kept by Jesus Christ," is also variously worded ("kept through union with Jesus Christ," Williams; "preserved in Jesus Christ," KJV). Any of the above translations could be regarded as legitimate, but Bauckham suggests, "This phrase has an eschatological sense: Christians are kept safe by God for the Parousia of Jesus Christ when they will enter into their final salvation in his kingdom." The idea may be that Christians are the property of Jesus and will be safely preserved for Him until He returns to claim them. This emphasis seems especially appropriate since the concern of Jude is that his readers be kept safe from the influence of false teachers.

Jude's use of the triad "mercy," "peace," and "love" in verse 2 introduces the reader to his preference for threes. Three examples of judgment appear in verses 5–7. Three examples of false teachers are given in verse 11. "Mercy" is God's attitude of kindness toward His covenant people, and "peace" is the experience of well-being that results from this. Often the greeting of "mercy" appears in the New Testament (cf. 2 John 3; 1 Tim. 1:2) against a backdrop of false teaching. A Christian needs mercy not only at the final judgment (2 Tim. 1:16, 18) but during every day of his life. Only the unmerited mercy of God can meet the needs of constant sinners who might hanker after false teaching. A man who is conscious of this mercy experiences the deep inner peace that provides him stability. This peace is not merely pietistic and self-centered, but it reaches out in love to others. The love that Jude wants to be multiplied may refer both to man's love for one another and God, and also to God's love for man. Jude's reference to "love" leaves the specific type of love open.

### B. The Occasion for Writing—Entrance of False Teachers (vv. 3, 4)

Jude's explanation in verse 3 suggests that he was seriously beginning to write a letter on the theme of "salvation" when he learned that false teachers were invading the area to which he wrote.[1] His awareness of the peril of false teaching led him to take up his pen to write an urgent warning for his friends. Three phrases in this verse need careful explanation.

Jude's reference to "the salvation we share" speaks of "the corporate nature of salvation as understood by Judaism, with its consciousness of being the people of God, and even more vividly by Christianity, with its conviction of fellowship in Christ" (Kelly). Salvation was not merely a personal, private experience but a collective fellowship with Christ. The salvation mentioned here means past deliverance (v. 5), a present experience (v. 23), and a future enjoyment of eternal life and glory (vv. 24, 25).

Jude's term, "contend," is an athletic metaphor taken from the vocabulary of Greek games. The simple form of the verb appears in Colossians 1:29; 4:12, and there it implies a mag-

[1] Green implies that the first "write," a present infinitive, indicates that he was undertaking his original letter in a leisurely style and that the second "write," an aorist infinitive, suggests that he was driven to snatch up his pen by news of a dangerous heresy. See also Bauckham who notes the same tense difference in the infinitive but does not see them as reflecting a decisive contrast.

nificent labor in Christian discipleship and prayer that will contribute to the maturity of growing Christians. Paul uses athletic metaphors to describe his work as a struggle for the spread of the gospel, and not merely to refer to life as a moral contest. This contending for the faith, in both Paul and Jude, is not merely defensive, but it is offensive, aiding the advance and development of the gospel. Contending for the faith is not exclusively a verbal exercise. In Paul it involves a disciplined, Christ-centered lifestyle (1 Cor. 9:24–27; Phil. 1:27; 1 Tim. 6:11, 12). With Jude, contending for the faith involves following the exhortations of verses 20–23 in the service of the gospel. To contend for the faith is not merely to master apologetic arguments for Christianity but to live a godly, obedient life. The latter is more difficult than the former.

Jude's discussion of "the faith that was once for all entrusted to the saints" is "a body of doctrine, dogmatic and practical, which is given to them by authority, is fixed and unalterable, and well known to all Christians" (Bigg). It contained both intellectual and moral truth. This faith had not necessarily been written into a former creed, but it had been passed on orally to converts.[2] For Jude the teaching of the apostles, not the current theological fad, was the hallmark of genuine Christianity. "The test of progress is, for him, faithfulness to the apostolic teaching about Christ" (Green).

In verse 4 Jude provides a description of the false teachers who are disturbing his friends. His use of the phrase "certain men" has a contemptuous significance (Mayor). The fact that they have "secretly slipped in" shows subtle, deceitful action. Various translations give the term a sinister significance ("crept in unnoticed," Weymouth; "slipped in by stealth," Moffatt; "sneaked in among us," Goodspeed). Jude uses four phrases to describe these deceitful heretics.

First, they are mentioned as people "whose condemnation was written about long ago." Bauckham notes that the expression "written about long ago" may refer to having the condem-

[2]Paul's reference to "teachings" (2 Thess. 2:15; 3:6); the "pattern of sound teaching" (2 Tim. 1:13); and "what I received" (1 Cor. 15:3) indicates both doctrinal and moral portions of the Christian faith that he had received from his spiritual forebears and had passed on to his converts.

nation of the false teachers written in heavenly books (Rev. 20:12), prophesied in an apostolic prophecy (e.g., 2 Peter 2:1–3:4), or prophesied in pre-Christian prophecy such as the Old Testament. He feels that the latter option gives a full weight to the meaning of the term "long ago," and he decides in favor of this. The term "condemnation" can refer backward to portions of verse 3. Here the condemnation of false teachers in defense of orthodoxy is implied. It can also reach forward to the rest of verse 4 or to part or all of verses 5–16. The most natural reference is to understand that in verses 5–16 Jude utilizes prophecy to point out the sins of the false teachers and the condemnation that their sins will receive. These false teachers will receive judgment at the Parousia, and this condemnation is described typologically in verses 5–7, 11 and quite pointedly in verses 14–15.

Second, these false teachers appear as "godless men." They had an attitude of irreverence toward God that led to shameless desires (v. 18) and shameless deeds (v. 15). Bauckham notes that the term describes "unrighteous behavior stemming from an irreverent rejection of the moral authority of God's commandments. It describes not theoretical atheism, but practical godlessness."

Third, Jude mentions them as changing "the grace of our God into a license for immorality." They were using the fact that God graciously accepts sinners, as an excuse for wanton sinning. Such perversion of the intent of grace is universally condemned in the New Testament (e.g. Paul—1 Cor. 6:9–20; Peter—2 Peter 2; John—1 John 3:7–10). "It is hardly surprising that men accepted the indicative of pardon and forgot the imperative of holiness. It was an inherent risk in the proclamation of the gospel of free grace, and it has always been so since then . . . ; the apostolic conclusion was to attack lasciviousness, but to continue to preach the grace of God who accepts the unacceptable" (Green). The phrase, "license for immorality," refers to sensuality or debauchery (Eph. 4:19; 1 Peter 4:3), and it is sometimes used specifically to point to sexual indulgence (2 Cor. 12:21; 2 Peter 2:18).[3]

---

[3]Mayor refers to Lightfoot who indicates that a man may be impure and hide his sin, but when he practices lasciviousness, he shocks public decency.

Fourth, he pictures the heretical intruders as those who "deny Jesus Christ our only Sovereign and Lord." The Greek word for "sovereign" is *despotēs*, a term used most frequently in the New Testament to refer to God the Father (e.g., Luke 2:29; Acts 4:24; Rev. 6:10). Green, Mayor, and Kelly see the word as a reference to the Father, but Bigg, Bauckham, and Plumptre refer it to Christ. Bauckham cites the clear reference to Christ in 2 Peter 2:1 using *despotēs*, and he suggests the term is suitable for the image of Jesus as the master of His servants.[4] One can deny Christ both in doctrine (1 John 2:22, 23) and in lifestyle, but the context here suggests that it is the moral or ethical denial that troubles Jude. "Jude means that by refusing to obey Christ's moral demands the false teachers are in effect, though not in words, disowning him as Master and rejecting his authority as Sovereign and Judge" (Bauckham).

### C. A Description of the False Teachers (vv. 5–16)

Here Jude focuses specifically on the sins of the heretics. He shows them to be deserving of God's judgments, and he mentions their arrogance, sensuality, greed, self-interest, spiritual emptiness, and coming doom. They are constant complainers, smooth-talking braggarts, and they cunningly curry the favor of the wealthy. Jude's descriptions here are quite similar to the descriptions of the heretics in 2 Peter 2, and their similarity provides evidence of a mutual relation between the two sections.

#### *1. Deserving of Previous Divine Judgments (vv. 5–7)*

Jude's preference for triads is again in evidence here. In verse 5 he refers to the divine judgment on the unbelieving multitude of Israel in Numbers 14. In verse 6 he speaks of the divine judgment upon sinning angels mentioned in Genesis 6:1–4. In verse 7 he points to the destruction of Sodom and Gomorrah and their sister cities described in Genesis 19:24–28.

In verse 5 Jude wants to remind his readers of some facts of

[4]The Greek article is absent before "Lord" (Gr., *kyrion*), and this would normally call for "Master" and "Lord" to refer to the same person (i.e., Christ). However, the article is often omitted before *kyrios*, and this issue alone should not decide the question. Bauckham's reasons for referring "Master" and "Lord" to Christ seem most appealing.

judgment from biblical history. He has not previously mentioned these in his letter, and he is not presuming a general knowledge of biblical history by them. He is apparently assuming that they had received some apostolic tradition denouncing false teaching. These readers had been instructed in the "faith . . . entrusted to the saints." They had once for all known these truths, and Jude did not want them to neglect or forget them.

There is a question as to who did the saving and destroying. Jude has just completed a reference to the "Lord" in verse 4, and the references in verses 4 and 5 use *kyrios*. The writers of the New Testament rarely use *kyrios* of God the Father, and sometimes they even interpret the *kyrios* of Old Testament texts as Jesus (Rom. 10:13; Heb. 1:10; 1 Cor. 10:9). Jude has used *kyrios* here as a reference to Jesus, "not so much because he is concerned to explain the preexistent activity of Christ, but rather because in his typological application of these Old Testament events to the present it is the Lord Jesus who has saved his people the church and will be the Judge of apostates" (Bauckham).[5]

The point of the reference is that the people of Israel were delivered from Egypt only to perish in the wilderness for lack of faith. They failed to believe Moses' power and God's promises (Num. 14:11; Deut. 1:32), and as punishment all aged twenty years and upwards perished except Joshua and Caleb. The word "later" (Gr., *deuteron*) clearly goes with the destruction in the wilderness. The earlier occasion of deliverance is implied in the reference to the Lord's rescuing His people from Egypt.[6]

---

[5]The New Testament text varies widely at this point. Various manuscripts will read either "God," "Jesus," or "Christ God" in addition to "Lord." Metzger's full discussion ends with support for "Lord" (p. 726). Also varying is the position of the word "already" or "once for all" (Gr., *hapax*). Metzger feels that it originally stood after "know," but it makes better sense in the sentence if it is taken with "delivered" (p. 726). In this commentary we have linked it with "know."

[6]Commentators note that "later" means literally "the second time," and they puzzle over its meaning. Since God only saved His people from Egypt once and destroyed them then, some see "the second time" as a reference to the sacking of Jerusalem in A.D. 70. Some construe "the second time" with "delivered" and feel that the second saving is the rescue of the Christian community from Jerusalem in A.D. 70. Others link the phrase with "destroyed" and see it as the second destruction in the wiping out of the Jews in Jerusalem who did not

Despite the similarity between 2 Peter 2 and Jude in this section Peter alone mentions Lot and his rescue, and Jude alone describes the deliverance from Egypt. This is a surprising observation if one copied from the other, and it might point to the existence of a common source between them that was used to describe the false teachers.

The warning of Jude resembles that of Paul in 1 Corinthians 10:11, 12. He uses the fate of apostate Israel to warn of the punishment awaiting apostate Christians. Such Christians, who may only profess but not possess genuine Christianity, must not take comfort in their original faith or orthodoxy. If their faith has not produced endurance and good works, they will be judged along with unbelievers (James 2:14–20; Heb. 6:1–8).

Jude warns in verse 6 against the perils of lust and pride as seen among the sinning angels. Jude's picture here is influenced by a story concerning these angels appearing in 1 Enoch 6–19.[7] "Jude does not necessarily endorse its truth; he does, however, like any shrewd preacher, use the current language and thought forms of his day in order to bring home to his readers, in terms highly significant for them, the perils of lust and pride" (Green).

These angels showed pride by not keeping "their positions of authority" and leaving "their own home." The phrase "positions of authority" (KJV, "first estate"; Moffatt, "domain"; Goodspeed, "responsibilities") is a reference to the position of power and dignity that God had given them. Sexual immorality is not specifically mentioned in verse 6, but it is implied in the Jewish tradition and suggested by the reference to "sexual immorality" in verse 7.

The punishment of these fallen angels is that they are "kept in darkness, bound with everlasting chains for judgment on the great Day." The method of their punishment is with "everlast-

---

acknowledge the Messiah. The simplest solution is to follow the interpretation above (well explained by Kelly), for the punishment given to unbelieving Israelites in the desert was the event in Jude's mind.

[7]Bauckham indicates that the angels were known in Jewish tradition as Watchers, were filled with lust for the beautiful daughters of men, and descended on Mount Hermon to take human wives. Their children, the giants, ravaged the earth, and these fallen angels taught men forbidden knowledge and all types of sin. They were responsible for the corruption of the world for which God sent the Flood. This was an effort to interpret Genesis 6:1–4 and was a widely held view among Jews until the mid-second century A.D.

ing chains," a figurative expression that shows their impotence and confinement until they are delivered up for final judgment. The place of their confinement, "darkness," is the underworld, the nether world, a place of doom, gloom, and loneliness. The time of their confinement was until the "judgment on the great Day," a reference to final judgment as mentioned in Acts 2:20 and Revelation 6:17. Jude uses a Greek perfect tense for "has kept," an effort to emphasize with intensity that these evildoers are perfectly kept.

Just as arrogance and lust had ruined these angels, the false teachers would also be doomed. A privileged position and a full knowledge had not saved those angels who had rebelled against God. There is an implicit warning for the readers lest they too become prideful and lustful.

In verse 7 Jude concentrates on the judgment given by God to Sodom and Gomorrah. In the parallel section in 2 Peter 2:5, 6 Peter mentions both the flood of Noah and the destruction of the cities, but Jude concentrates only on the cities. The destruction mentioned by Jude came not only on Sodom and Gomorrah but also on other cities of the Plain including Admah and Zeboim, but excluding Zoar, spared at the request of Lot (Gen. 19:22, 25; Deut. 29:23). Jude describes the sin of these cities and outlines the divine vengeance upon them.

Their sin is that they "gave themselves up to sexual immorality and perversion." Green sees this as a reference to homosexuality, but Bauckham says that "as the angels fell because of their lust for women, so the Sodomites desired sexual relations with angels." He sees Genesis 19:4–11 as in the background.[8] "The sin of the Sodomites . . . reached its zenith in this most extravagant of sexual aberrations, which would have transgressed the order of creation as shockingly as the fallen angels did" (Bauckham).

The divine vengeance is seen in that the location of the cities on the south end of the Dead Sea provided an ever-present evidence of the reality of divine judgment. Josephus

[8]The translation of "gave themselves up to . . . perversion" means more literally to "go after strange flesh." Bauckham feels that the "strange (Gr., *heteras*) flesh" is a reference to a type of flesh different from human flesh, i.e., of angels.

indicated in his day that traces of the divine fire could be seen there (BJ 4.8.4), and other Jewish writers join in attesting to the presence of visible reminders of the ruins stemming from divine judgment.

The phrase, "eternal fire," should be taken in connection with "punishment." In this way Jude was saying that the site of the cities was a warning picture of the eternal fires of hell. Such a scene was a living reminder that the triumph of evil was not final. The judgment of God, though long delayed, would surely come.

### 2. *Displaying Arrogance (vv. 8, 9)*

Here Jude shows the false teachers as being contemptuous of all standards that God has established. In their arrogance they are really defying God Himself, and they are disdainful of angelic creatures whom they should treat with respect.

In verse 8 Jude arraigns the heretics for lust, rebelliousness, and irreverence. The opening words, "in the very same way," (Gr., *homoiōs*), compare the sins of these teachers to those mentioned in verses 5–7. These false teachers cherished empty dreams and were guilty of polluting their own bodies. The reference to "dreamers" could describe those who have voluptuous dreams or could refer to an imagination that has sunk into the stupor of sin. Against the former possibility is the fact that the word for "dreamers" is a Greek participle and relates to all three main verbs. A reference to erotic dreams would not be meaningful in connection with the other two verbs. Also, the normal reference of the verb is not merely to the imagination. Green and Bauckham refer the term to prophetic dreams, and Green feels that "it probably indicates that the false teachers supported their antinomianism by laying claim to divine revelation in their dreams."

Jude describes these "dreamers" as guilty of three arrogant sins. Kelly refers the first charge of "polluting their own bodies" to a general charge of sexual immorality, but he feels that a reference to homosexual activities cannot be excluded. Second, they "reject authority." The term "authority" should be distinguished from the "celestial beings" to be mentioned later in the verse. In its use, "authority" may refer either to human or divine authority, but in view of Jude's earlier mention of denying the Lord (v. 4), it seems proper to see a reference to a denial of the practical authority of the Lord Jesus. These false teachers were not teaching christological heresy, but in their undisciplined behavior they rejected the authority of the Lord. A third offense of these heretics was that they would "slander celestial beings." The term "celestial beings" (Gr., *doxas*) means literally "glorious ones," and in much early literature it was used to refer to angels.

These angels are called glorious because they embody the glory of God. The context does not mention whether the angels are good or evil, but it seems unthinkable that Jude would find it blameworthy for his opponents to slander the forces of Satan. Bauckham feels it more probable that these wayward opponents were deriding good angels as givers and guardians of the law of Moses or God's created order. Jews believed that the law was mediated by angels (cf. Heb. 2:2; Gal. 3:19), and saw them as guardians of the created order (according to a possible interpretation of 1 Cor. 11:10). These false teachers understood Christian freedom to speak of freedom from all moral authority and therefore from the authority of the angels. This is further evidence of their arrogance.

There is much similarity between Jude 8 and 2 Peter 2:10. One difference is that Jude is saying that the false teachers resemble the inhabitants of the Cities of the Plain in their rejecting dominion and belittling glorious beings. Peter does not compare the residents of Sodom to the false teachers at this point. This may provide further evidence that Jude and 2 Peter were not copying from one another but were heirs of another common source.

In verse 9 Jude contrasts the presumption of his opponents with the modesty and restraint shown by Michael the archangel in a dispute with the devil. Commentators agree that the reference to Michael is taken from a story in the apocryphal *Assumption of Moses*, a work of which only a partial text survives today. Mayor provides Charles's summary of the incident: 1) Michael is authorized to bury Moses; 2) Satan opposes his burial on the grounds that he is the lord of matter and Moses is a murderer; 3) In answer to Satan's first claim

Michael rejoins, "The Lord rebuke thee, for it was God's spirit which created the world and all mankind."[9] Michael appears only here and in Revelation 12:7 in the New Testament. It is noteworthy that 2 Peter makes no reference to the incident.

The point of contrast between the false teachers and Michael is not that Michael treated the devil respectfully so that others should do the same. The point is that Michael did not reject the devil's protests on his own authority. He recognized that the devil was motivated by malice and saw the accusation as slanderous, but since he was not the judge, he could not dismiss the devil's case. He asked the Lord, who alone is judge, to condemn the devil for slander. No one is then an autonomous moral authority, and these false teachers must remain subject to the moral authority of the Lord. Jude had exposed the spiritual conceit of his opponents, and he had shown that their attitude toward angelic creatures demonstrates a resistance to moral authority that swaggers before God (Bauckham).

Although such early Christian leaders as Clement of Alexandria and Tertullian (*Idol. 15*) viewed Jude as canonical, Jude's reference to an apocryphal writing later caused his book to come under suspicion. Augustine (*City of God 15.23.4*) later attacked the writings of the Apocrypha as "fables." Jerome indicates that the reason for which Jude was rejected by some and regarded suspiciously by others was based on its quotation from the apocryphal Book of Enoch (*De Vir. Ill.4*). The quotation from Enoch appears in verses 14, 15. This suspicious attitude toward the Apocrypha caused many to question Jude's position in the canon. However, the Council of Carthage in A.D. 397 accepted the present books of the New Testament. Jude, of course, was among them.

Jude may have used the Apocrypha because he recognized that his audience would be familiar with the writings. He quoted them as relevant to his situation. With reference to the *Assumption of Moses* Jude may not have viewed the writing as canonical, and he could have used the story of the dispute between Michael and Satan only as an illustrative argument.

---

[9]The story is based upon Deuteronomy 34:6, and the words of Michael are a partial quotation of Zech. 3:2, apparently inserted into the *Assumption of Moses* because of their appropriateness.

Paul made reference to heathen poets in this way (Acts 17:28; 1 Cor. 15:32, 33; Titus 1:12).

*3. Delighting in Corruption (vv. 10–13)*

Jude introduces this section with a statement of the corruption of his opponents, and in verse 11 he uses historical examples from the Old Testament to characterize their materialism, immorality, and rebelliousness. His vivid metaphors in verses 12, 13 are intended to stimulate his readers to recognize the subtle dangers, empty pretensions, and moral degradation of the false teachers.

In verse 10 Jude accuses the heretics of maligning the celestial powers that they fail to understand. The NEB says that they "pour out abuse on things they do not understand." They know naturally the physical appetites that they share with the animal world, and these desires contribute to their downfall. Their tendency to "speak abusively" may have taken the form of actual ridicule of the authority of God as seen in His angels, or it may have expressed itself in immoral behavior that could be termed "blasphemous." These men who regarded themselves as superior were actually on the level of animals and were corrupted by the practices through which they sought liberty and self-expression. Jude's provocative words show that a man who is persistently deaf to the call of God will reach a point when he cannot hear the call he has ignored. He will then be at the mercy of the deadly instincts that appeared to promise freedom but that actually are merciless tools of death (cf. Gal. 4:8; Eph. 4:22; Phil. 3:19).

Jude returns to his preference for triads in the use of Cain, Balaam, and Korah in verse 11. The actual errors of the false teachers appear in verses 12, 13, and Jude uses verse 11 to show that they conform to their Old Testament types. In later Jewish tradition Cain was not simply that first murderer (cf. Gen. 4:8), but he is "the archetypal sinner and the instructor of others in sin" (Bauckham). He was seen as the prototype of hatred and envy toward one's brother. Josephus (*Ant.* 1.2.1,2) saw him as a purveyor of greed, violence, and lust and a corrupter of mankind. His involvement in leading others into sin makes him a suitable type of Jude's opponents. The false teachers imitated Cain by their leading others into sin.

According to the biblical account Balaam declined to curse Israel for financial reward (Num. 22:18; 24:13; cf. Deut. 23:4; Neh. 13:2), but Jewish understanding of the incident portrayed him as accepting Balak's invitation out of greed for the promised rewards. Jewish tradition suggested that Balaam advised Balak to entice Israel into sin by using scantily clad women adorned with gold and jewels who would encourage the apostasy of Numbers 25:1–3 (cf. Num. 31:16). Thus, Balaam is pictured as a man of greed who led Israel into immorality and idolatry. Jude notes that the false teachers "rushed for profit into Balaam's error." Just as Balaam, attracted by the prospect of reward, hurried to provide the advice that led Israel into immorality, the false teachers, greedy for money, have imitated his example. This evil example of Balaam is also mentioned in 2 Peter 2:15, but there the use of Cain and Korah as types of the false teachers is omitted.

Korah was notorious for his rebellion against Moses and Aaron, God's appointed leaders of Israel (Num. 16:1–35). He defied constituted leadership. The story of Numbers and later Jewish tradition also show that Korah invented his own way of worshiping God and claimed functions for which he had no right. He further claimed holiness for himself and his followers. "In general, here was a man who delighted to kick over God's traces" (Green). Insubordination of this kind appeared frequently in the early church, and it is clear that Jude sees the false teachers as excellent examples of this malicious trait (e.g., Titus 1:10, 11; 3:10, 11; 2 Tim. 3:1–9; 3 John 9, 10).

The loveless corruption of Cain, the careless materialism of Balaam, and the prideful insubordination of Korah were all examplified in these errorists. All three came to ruin,[10] and Jude sees this as the future for the false teachers. These three characteristics are mentioned by Green as major traits of second-century Gnosticism, and he says that "clearly we have here in Jude the early signs of the specific Gnostic systems which were

[10] Bauckham sees the verb "destroyed" (Gr., *apōlonto*, an aorist tense) as equivalent to a "prophetic perfect," a view that the future judgment of the false teachers was as certain an event as if it had occurred.

to plague the subapostolic Church." Such claims to special knowledge made men indifferent to moral behavior, careless of the needs of their brethren, and unconcerned about the directives of church leaders. Those who make the same claims today often fall into the same trap.

In verses 12, 13 Jude portrays the errors of these false teachers so as to demonstrate that they conform to the types given in verse 11. Jude heaps together a list of six metaphors in a remarkable accumulation of vivid phrases. He begins with statements of the deceit and self-centeredness of the heretics and moves toward images that picture their impending judgment. The first two of Jude's metaphors describe their activities in the fellowship of believers, and the last four, all derived from the world of nature, describe their spiritual emptiness and moral culpability.

First, they are "blemishes" in the Christian "love-feasts." Translators differ on the proper meaning for "blemishes" (Gr., *spilades*)."[11] Green says, "In secular Greek it means 'rocks' or "sunken rocks," but by the time of the fourth century it had come to mean *spots*." He prefers the translation of 'sunken rocks,' and he feels that the term warns the readers of the subtle danger of the heretics. The phrase "love feasts" is replaced in some Greek texts with "deceits" or "pleasures" (cf. 2 Peter 2:13), but most commentators understand that Jude is referring to the love-feasts as the fellowship meal that provided an opportunity for the observance of the Lord's Supper in the early church. Jude's point is that close fellowship with these errorists, in the context of the Lord's Supper, is an occasion for greed, disorder, and even immorality. They are as dangerous as the rocks that can wreck a ship.

The phrase, "eating with you," with perhaps the expression "without the slightest qualm" added, describes the manner in which these lawless teachers observe the Lord's Supper. Their observance of the Lord's Supper was no reverent time of praise but a time in which they reveled fearlessly. Jude's indictment spotlights the arrogance of the heretics.

Jude's second metaphor describes the false teachers as

[11] A sample of the variety is seen in "spots," KJV; "blots," Williams; "sunken rocks," Weymouth; "hidden reefs," NASB.

"shepherds who feed only themselves." Some translators (KJV; Williams) link the previously mentioned phrase "without the slightest qualm" with the shepherding activity of the false teachers. In this connection the phrase shows the shameless nature of their selfishness, for they are "daringly caring for no one but themselves" (Williams). Other translators (Alford; NIV; NEB) place "without the slightest qualm" with the participle "feast with you." Green notes that "either makes good sense."

Jude's use of "clouds without rain, blown along by the winds" begins a series of nature metaphors that heighten the vividness of the descriptions of evil among these false teachers. This third metaphor relates to the claim of the heretics to be prophets and teachers. On summer days clouds are often seen approaching the coasts of Palestine and Syria, and their advent holds out the promise of rain to farmers whose lands are parched and dry. However, the winds blow these clouds on by without producing any rain. These false teachers were similarly only empty promises. They might claim great potential for their teaching, but no real value came from it. Jude's warning is especially solemn to those in a position of teaching and spiritual leadership who must always be careful that their studies and knowledge provide benefits for others.

A fourth metaphor employed by Jude pictures the heretics as "autumn trees without fruit and uprooted—twice dead." The phrase "autumn trees" seems "to refer to the end of the season of harvest, when any tree's fruit, if it has any, should be ripe" (Bauckham). These trees promise fruit, but are without it even though it is high time to expect it. Just like such barren trees, the false teachers provided only empty lives when they should have been fruitful.

The phrase "twice dead" may picture a tree that has died once when it stops bearing fruit and a second time when the sap stops circulating and there is no possibility of revival (Plumptre). This second death of the tree would occur when it was uprooted, an Old Testament metaphor of judgment (Ps. 52:5). Some commentators (Mayor, Bigg, Green) feel that the description indicates that the apostate teachers have returned to their preconversion condition of spiritual death, but Bauckham and

Kelly more aptly feel that it refers to their physical death and also to their death in the next world (Rev. 2:11; 20:6, 14; 21:8).

A fifth figure of speech used in this setting describes the false teachers as "wild waves of the sea, foaming up their own shame." The waves of the sea, either at high tide or in storms, deposit all sorts of refuse, rubbish, and litter on the beaches as they recede. Just as the waves defile the shore, the false teachers soil other Christians with the polluted products of their teaching and conduct.

Jude's concluding image describes the errorists as "wandering stars, for whom blackest darkness has been reserved forever." Peter has words similar to this in 2 Peter 2:17, but it may be that both Peter and Jude are influenced by a passage from 1 Enoch 18:13–16. In this passage there is evidence of a view that the irregular movements of the planets are attributed to the disobedience of heavenly beings. Also, such phenomena as comets and meteors were viewed as heavenly beings falling from heaven (cf. Isa. 14:12–15; Rev. 9:1). Jude has spoken of fallen angels in verse 6, and he may be thinking of their punishment as he speaks of the doom reserved for wandering stars. Just as the fallen angels are doomed to eternal judgment, so the false teachers will be extinguished forever in darkness. Both fire and darkness were used in Scripture as descriptions for the place of final judgment (Matt. 8:12; 22:13; 25:30, 41; Rev. 20:14, 15). Here the image of darkness is more suitable in connection with the fate of stars.

Jude's quick accumulation of metaphors has provided a gripping picture of the wickedness of the false teachers. He has seen them to be "as dangerous as sunken rocks, as selfish as perverted shepherds, as useless as rainless clouds, as dead as barren trees, as dirty as the foaming sea, and as certain of doom as the fallen angels" (Green).

### *4. Doomed to Future Punishment (vv. 14, 15)*

Jude has just shared his own opinion on the coming judgment of the unbelieving teachers. He now provides a prophetic statement from 1 Enoch 1:9 that shows the divine view that these errorists were deserving of retribution. Enoch was a special person in Hebrew thought, for he was the man who walked with God and was taken up to heaven (Gen. 5:24). His description as "the seventh from Adam" is based on the Hebrew method of calculation that would have included Enoch as one of the seven along with Adam, Seth, Enosh (Enos), Kenan (Cainan), Mahalalel, and Jared. Enoch was thinking of "the Lord" as Jehovah coming in judgment, but Jude understands "the Lord" to be the Lord Jesus. The coming is the Parousia of Jesus, and the Saints who come with Him are the angels (Matt. 25:31). The coming of Jesus will result in the bringing of judgment on the wicked because of both their words and deeds.

It is important to note from this passage that there is an identification of Jesus functionally with God, for as God's representative He will perform the divine act of judgment (cf. John 5:27). It is also significant again to observe the explicit use of the Apocrypha by Jude. Bauckham observes that the use of "prophesied" indicates that Jude "regarded the prophecies of 1 Enoch as inspired by God." However, he feels that "it need not imply that he regarded the book as canonical Scripture." Green indicates that the question of Jude's view of the inspiration of 1 Enoch is not the point, but he "is quoting a book both he and his readers will know and respect. He speaks to them in language which they will readily understand, and that remains one of the most important elements in the communication of Christian truth."

### 5. *Demonstrating Self-Will (v. 16)*

Jude concludes verse 15 with the promise of judgment on the wicked teachers for their words and deeds, but in verse 16 he will concentrate primarily upon their words. He has already focused on their deeds in verses 5–10, and he now moves to concern himself with the false leaders as teachers. Using an assortment of vivid expressions, Jude pieces together a fivefold description of the fault-finding, pompous, self-centered words of the heretics.

First, they are "grumblers." A form of this onomatopoeic word (Gr., *gongystēs*) was used in 1 Corinthians 10:10 to reflect the discontent of the Israelites in the desert. It may be that these false teachers complained about other Christian leaders in the church, but the chief references here in their complaints were directed at the authority of God. Instead of submitting to His will in their lives, they fought against it and complained about it (cf. vv. 8, 10). They may have viewed the commandments of God as a burdensome restriction.

Second, they are "faultfinders" ("ever complaining about their lot," Williams). Bauckham feels that this word adds little to the meaning of "grumblers," and it is probably to be regarded as an adjective with the word. It is used only here in the New Testament, but it seems to suggest an attitude of discontent with the plans and provisions of God in life.

Third, Jude describes the errorists as those who "follow their own evil desires" ("Their lives are guided by their evil passions," Weymouth). "The temper of self-indulgence, recognising not God's will, but man's desires, as the law of action, is precisely that which issues in weariness and despair" (Plumptre). Jude's point is not so much that they indulge particular sinful desires but that they follow their own desires rather than those of God.

As a fourth description Jude uses a finite verb to suggest that they "boast about themselves" ("Big words come rolling from their lips," NEB). Jude is not merely saying that these false teachers are boastful in the usual sense of the word, but "they express their arrogant, presumptuous attitude toward God, their insolent contempt for his commandments, their rejection of his moral authority which amounts to a proud claim to be their own moral authority" (Bauckham).

In a final description Jude points out that they "flatter others for their own advantage" ("they flatter men for the sake of what they can get from them," TCNT). The expression means literally that "they admire" or "show respect to faces." The idea is that they curried favor with the rich and influential in order to obtain personal advantage. In addition to Jude's condemnation, such partiality or favoritism is soundly condemned in James 2:1–9. The false teachers may have sought special favor by altering or setting aside some of God's moral demands in the hope that they might ingratiate themselves with the members of the Christian group who might contribute most liberally to their greedy wants.

**D. Advice to Committed Christians (vv. 17–23)**

Jude moves the focus of his directions from the false teachers to his Christian friends who were his recipients. He reminds them of the apostolic warnings about false teachers, warnings that should be an incentive to discern and avoid such false teachers (vv. 17–19). He also describes the Christian actions that they are to display in a godly contending for the faith (vv. 20, 21). Instead of merely debating with the errorists, these Christian readers are to undertake positive actions that will foster spiritual growth. Further, they are to be watchful for other believers who might err and thus fall (vv. 22, 23). Their personal spiritual growth must include a collective concern for the welfare of other weaker, wavering Christians.

*1. Listening to Apostolic Warnings (vv. 17–19)*

Jude had clearly exposed the sins of the heretics in verses 5–16. He now reassures the faithful that this type of sin and opposition is exactly what they had been told to expect.

Jude's words in verse 17 are similar to those of 2 Peter 3:2. Jude omits the reference to "prophets" that appears in 2 Peter, and he speaks of "apostles" instead of using Peter's phrase "your apostles." Jude makes no claim here that he himself is an apostle.[12]

The chief emphasis of Jude here is that his readers should "remember." There was nothing novel about the current apostasy, for the apostles had foretold it. The reference to the words of the apostles is taken by some as evidence that Jude was written after the apostolic age, but Jude may be referring only to the initial period of Christian instruction of his readers. The predictions uttered by the apostles when they founded the church were being fulfilled in the experiences of the readers. The apostles mentioned by Jude need not be a reference to the entire group of apostles but only to those who had founded the churches to which Jude wrote.

Jude's reference to apostolic warnings in verse 17 may have

[12] Bigg makes the strong statement that Jude "here distinctly tells us that he was not an apostle himself." Bauckham indicates that most commentators would agree with Bigg, but he feels that Jude "need only be excluding himself with the number of those apostles who founded the church(es) to which he writes." He feels that this verse alone cannot settle the issue of Jude's apostleship.

referred to such material as Acts 20:29, 30; 1 Timothy 4:1–3; 2 Timothy 3:1–7.[13] The fact that Jude refers to warnings that were "told" or "said" suggests that the warnings were oral, but they could have been written down. The particular warning of verse 18 is similar to 2 Peter 3:3, but Green feels that the few differences between the verses favor a common source for both rather than copying by either Jude or Peter. Peter takes his description of 3:3 and applies it to mockers who were belittling the Second Coming, but Jude's discussions in verse 18 suggest that the false teachers laughed at those who would not walk with them in the path of their own lusts. Both Peter and Jude are giving accurate descriptions of the errors of the false teachers, but they focus on different errors.

The phrase, "in the last times," is a period in God's plan for the world that was partly accomplished in the coming of Jesus and also partly still to be consummated. In 2 Timothy 3:1 Paul speaks of the last days as future, but in 1 Peter 1:20 and Hebrews 1:2 the last time is already present.

The "scoffers" are a reference to "men who pour scorn on religion" (NEB). Their chief objects of scorn are the moral demands of a holy God. They are people who follow only where their own ungodly passions lead.[14] There is no attempt to listen to the laws of God, and depraved human insight alone becomes the standard for deciding conduct.

Jude brings together three terse descriptions of the spiritual condition of the false teachers in verse 19. First, these false teachers were those "who divide you." Green suggests that these people were acting like Christian Pharisees. Bigg indicates that they may have held a separate celebration of the "love-feasts," the Lord's Supper. The false teachers had also attached themselves to the rich (vv. 11, 16) and may have promoted divisions of class. They may have rebelled against

---

[13]Green feels that the Greek imperfect tense for "said" in verse 18 stresses the repeated nature of the warnings of the apostles.

[14]Green calls attention to Jude's frequent use of "ungodly" (cf. v. 15) and notes its absence at this point in 2 Peter. He feels the likelihood that this stress "shows the revulsion of a sensitive, godly man to those who make pious pretensions but utterly belie them in their behaviour." The word "ungodly" in verse 18 can be taken either as an objective genitive after desire (Gr., *epithumias*) so that it means "desire for ungodly things," or it may be seen as a descriptive genitive, "ungodly lusts."

authority of church officials who were not men of much earthly importance, and they may have assumed an intellectual superiority. Similar divisions were also at work at Corinth (1 Cor. 1:26–29; 11:17–34). Bauckham felt that the tendency of their teaching created an elitist group who regarded themselves as the true possessors of the Spirit.

Second, these false teachers were following "mere natural instincts" ("mere animals," Williams).[15] They were men governed by the natural life and not dominated by the Holy Spirit. They followed their mere innate instincts. They lived on the level of natural, earthly life. The meaning of these "natural instincts" is further explained by the third description that these heretics are among those who "do not have the Spirit." These errorists may have linked their claim to have the Spirit with visionary experiences and the revelations received in them (v. 8). As men who claimed to be spiritual, they felt that they were free from moral restraint and could live above moral judgments. Jude denied their claim because the outcome was immoral. Instead of being led by the Spirit of God, they followed their own ungodly lusts (v. 18). It is interesting to observe that Paul uses the same parallelism between those who are "natural" (Gr., *psychikos*) and those who are "spiritual" (Gr., *pneumatikos*) (cf. 1 Cor. 2:14–3:1). It is not certain that Jude had read Paul and obtained the idea from him, but it is certain that Jude viewed these false teachers as unqualified to wear the term "spiritual" because of their ungodly behavior. No amount of pious verbal claims to be "spiritual" can overcome the negative evidence of an ungodly life.

### 2. *Contending for the Faith (vv. 20, 21)*

Jude began his letter with an appeal to his readers to "contend" for the faith that they had received. He did not immediately launch into an explanation of the meaning of "contending," but he spent verses 5–16 and, to some extent, verses 17–19 in an explanation of the nature of the opposition. Having explained the dangerous situation that they faced, he now describes how to contend for the faith. His method (see

[15]This word is used in reference to "worldly wisdom" in James 3:15 to describe it as "unspiritual."

comments on v. 3) is not merely defensive, but it involves going on the offensive. The technique is not merely verbal, but it is primarily moral and spiritual.

He begins his series of exhortations with the words "dear friends," a term previously used in verse 17. By this word he contrasts his readers with the false teachers. His appeal has four elements, and if each part is followed, his readers can avoid contamination from the false teachers.

First, he gives the command, "Build yourselves up in your most holy faith." The "faith" is the system of Christian truth delivered by the apostles. Christians are to study and learn this system. Such a system of faith contains both doctrinal truths and moral appeals, and the New Testament provides frequent encouragement for Christians to study apostolic teaching (Acts 2:42; 20:32; Heb. 5:12; 2 Tim. 2:15). The faith is called "most holy" ("most sacred' " NEB) because it is completely different, entirely set apart from every other faith (Green). Jude's appeal is doubtless calling for individuals to master personally the truths and demands of the "faith," but it is also containing a collective appeal for each believer to contribute to the spiritual growth of the entire Christian community (Bauckham).

Second, he urges them to "pray in the Holy Spirit." The phrase refers to "the Christian's experience of abiding in communion with God through Jesus Christ by the Holy Spirit (cf. Rom. 8:9, 16, 26; Eph. 6:18)" (Wheaton). The battle against false teaching cannot be won by use of argument alone, but it depends on the use of God's mighty weapons to bring down "every pretension that sets itself up against the knowledge of God" (2 Cor. 10:5). Bauckham says that "praying in the Spirit includes, but is not restricted to, prayer in tongues," but Green says that if prayer in "tongues" is indicated, "it is hinted at very obscurely." Paul's appeal for prayer that the "message of the Lord may spread rapidly and be honored" and that "we may be delivered from wicked and evil men" (2 Thess. 3:1, 2) demonstrates the urgency of prayer for mature Christians in the most demanding circumstances. The "advanced" Christian who has outrun prayer has wandered far beyond his spiritual supply lines and is in danger of outrunning Christianity altogether.

Third, Jude gives the command to his readers to "keep

yourselves in God's love." This command is a complement to the statement that believers are "loved by God the Father" (v. 1). Here Jude urges that his friends fulfill their part of the covenant of love with God. However the phrase, "God's love," is to be interpreted,[16] the emphasis by Jude is upon their contribution to that relationship. Obedient behavior is the way to continue in the love of God. "It was by flagrant disobedience that the false teachers had fallen out of love with Him, and thus, inevitably, with men as well" (Green).

Fourth, Jude's readers must preserve the flames of Christian hope by waiting "for the mercy of our Lord Jesus Christ to bring you to eternal life." The act of "waiting" does not call for a passive "hanging around," but it demands that God's people erupt into an outburst of "holy living and godliness" (2 Peter 3:11; 1 Thess. 5:4–8). The "mercy of our Lord Jesus Christ" was especially seen at the atonement, and mercy is possible for the sinner only because of what Jesus has accomplished there. "Eternal life" has already begun in the believer (John 5:24), but it is to be experienced more fully in the resurrection life that Christ will give at His coming (1 Thess. 4:13–18). A deeper experience of this resurrection life in the present and a sublime hope for a richer future experience at the return of Christ will give the believer a proper balance between a this-worldly and an other-worldly faith. A Christian whose attention is riveted solely on the future will become so heavenly minded that he is of no earthly good. A believer who soft-pedals the future element in Christian hope can reduce Christianity to an adjunct of social service. A growing believer needs to hope for the mercy of God not only initially in his Christian life but daily and also at the last (2 Tim. 1:18).

### 3. *Looking Out for Erring Believers (vv. 22, 23)*

Jude has just defined Christian salvation in terms of faith, prayer, love, and hope. This salvation also involves service with others, and he now turns to this theme. The active practice of

[16]The phrase "God's love" has "God" in the genitive case. It may be seen as an objective genitive (their love for God), or it may also be viewed as a subjective genitive (God's love for them). Bauckham notes that the parallel in John 15:9, "remain in my love," shows that the love is certainly Christ's love for His disciples.

Christian evangelism and discipleship will provide the most proper way of learning the value of any theology. Jude calls upon his readers to become involved in this way.

The general drift of these verses is clear, but the textual tradition beneath them is varied, and it is difficult to determine what is the original. The main division lies between those manuscripts that speak of three groups of people and those that describe two groups.[17] If three groups are mentioned, the first group is a description of some who need mercy because they are in doubt. Green notes that the reading "confute the waverers" might be better rendered at this point than the command to "show pity on the waverers" ("Be merciful to those who doubt, NIV). Metzger, however, feels that the wording "confute" was a scribal change introduced in order to distinguish this statement from a later appeal to show mercy that appears in verse 23. He feels that the scribe wanted to produce a sequence progressing from a severe statement of reproof to a compassionate statement showing mercy, and he thus contends that the better reading is "show pity on the waverers." The idea of showing mercy is an appeal to watchful Christians to demonstrate concern for weaker Christians whose faith may give way and whose commitment may be compromised. One Christian is to be the keeper of his brother Christian (cf. Gal. 6:1, 2).

A second group will contain some who must be saved by snatching them "from the fire." This group differs from the first group in that they no longer restrain themselves but enthusiastically give way to the appeals of the false teachers. These are definitely on the wrong path and must be told boldly of their ultimate destiny. These will demand a frontal approach and a direct appeal to come to Christ (cf. James 5:20). The reference to "snatching them out of the fire" is taken by some to refer to the passion of sensual indulgence to which the heretics had given

---

[17]Kelly opts for two groups ("doubting souls who need your pity" and "others for whom your pity must be mixed with fear") because this version of the text is rougher and more difficult and more likely to be original. He feels that the text distinguishing three groups can be "explained as attempts to make sense of the abrupt shorter text" (cf. NEB). Green decides in favor of three groups, citing superior manuscript attestation and Jude's preference for triads (cf. RSV, NIV). Neither urges his position with dogmatism, but Green's arguments seem stronger and will be followed here.

way. The heretics were misleading others to follow them. It may also be a reference to the fire of judgment to which professing believers will be liable if they do not repent. One who professes Christ while living in iniquity shows that his profession is empty and wrong, and he demonstrates that he is heading for the fires of eternal punishment. Such a person is in reality in need of the evangelistic ministry of God's people. The view chosen here is that all three of these groups are friends of Jude who were being misled by the false teachers. Doubtless they professed Christianity, but their continued waywardness would belie their profession. Some were perhaps unbelievers who claimed to be believers. Still others were true believers who needed reclaiming.

The third group will be those who are to be shown "mercy, mixed with fear." Concerned Christians must demonstrate pity on even the most wayward unbeliever, but they must be quite cautious in their approach lest they defile themselves. They must retain a hatred of sin even while they demonstrate a love for the sinner (cf. 2 Cor. 7:1). Such rescue work must also be done in a spirit of gentleness, for a haughty spirit will only repel the wayward professing believer. "It must be done in fear, in recognition that 'there, but for the grace of God, go I'" (Green). The "clothing stained by corrupted flesh" describes the inner garment (Gr., *chitōn*) that was worn next to the skin. The suggestion is that those deceived by the false teachers had become so corrupt that their clothing was defiled. The term is still describing the unhappy dupes of the false teachers, and it utilizes much scriptural hyperbole.[18] The Christian must show pity on people so frightfully misled, but he must continually retain a hatred for the sin that they practice. Jude's use of "flesh" here is similar to that of Paul (e.g., Rom. 7:18; 8:3), and he sees the "flesh" as the seat of sin.

Jude has urged an attitude of mercy, urgency, and caution toward evildoers. The Christian leader must demonstrate compassion on those who wander into sin, must move quickly and

[18] In Leviticus 13:47–52 the garment worn by a leper is to be burned because it is unclean. Other passages using garments as an image of purity or impurity are Isaiah 64:6; 61:10. In the New Testament the believer is pictured as one who has not soiled his garments (Rev. 3:4).

boldly to rescue some, but must be wary and wise in his approach to others.

### E. Doxology of Praise to God (vv. 24, 25)

Jude has contemplated the errors of the false teachers in verses 5–16, and he has dealt with this by sharing advice for his Christian readers in verses 17–23. His mind now moves to the almighty God who alone can provide strength for the arduous journey in the Christian life. In verse 24 he praises God for His preserving, sustaining power toward believers, and in verse 25 he offers a fourfold peal of praise to God for His mighty salvation. This doxology of praise has some similarities to doxologies of Paul in Romans 16:25 and Ephesians 3:20, 21. The ending of the letter is unusual in that it completely lacks any personal references.

In verse 24 Jude offers praise to God who "is able to keep you from falling." The metaphor "keep" is not an appeal for personal action, but it suggests that the power of the mighty God is itself providing protection for believers. The word "falling" does not appear elsewhere in the New Testament, but "it is used by Xenophon of a horse which is surefooted and does not stumble, by Plutarch of the steady falling of the snow, and by Epictetus of a good man who does not make moral lapses" (Green). The idea is that God will watch over Jude's readers and keep them from falling into the sinful ways of the heretics.

Further, God is able to set believers "before his glorious presence without fault and with great joy." Not only can God protect Christians amidst difficult temptations to evil, but He can stand them before His open presence in heaven. There they will be "without fault" ("irreproachable," Goodspeed). The term was used with reference to animals fitted by their physical perfection for sacrificial usage, and was applied to Christ in 1 Peter 1:19. The phrase, "his glorious presence," is a reverential way to refer to God Himself, and the phrase, "with great joy," describes "the jubilation of God's people in the attainment of his purpose" (Bauckham). The term is frequently used of a peculiarly religious joy, and the verbal form describes the joy of Mary at the announcement of her conception (Luke 1:47).

In verse 25 God is noted as the only God. "In the Old

Testament it is emphasized that God is the Saviour of His people; there is none else (Is xlv. 15)" (Green). The only holy God created the world, supervises it, liberated it through Jesus Christ, and will be glorified in it. The phrase "through Jesus Christ our Lord" may mean either that it is by Jesus Christ that man is saved or that glory can be given to God properly only through Jesus. The words "glory, majesty, power, and authority" are attributes ascribed to God. This is not a prayer but an ascription of these traits to the Father because of the achievement of Jesus.

**For Further Study**

1. In Jude 1 notice the terms that Jude uses to identify who he is. What does the expression, "servant of Jesus Christ," tell us about Jude? Read Acts 15:13–21 to discover something about the identity and role of James in the early church. This is the James to whom Jude claims to be a brother.

2. What does Jude 4 tell us about the occasion for Jude's writing his letter?

3. In Jude 5–7 there is a description of God's judgment on three groups who had disobeyed Him. Who are these three groups? For further information about these groups see Numbers 14, Genesis 6:1–4, and Genesis 19:24–28 for the groups mentioned respectively in Jude 5, 6, and 7.

4. In Jude 8–16 the brother of the Lord describes some of the wicked traits of the false teachers. List some of the traits after a reading of the text.

5. Jude describes the actions that Christians need to use in strengthening themselves against these heretics in verses 20, 21. List these actions and apply them specifically to your own life.

6. The doxology of Jude in verses 24, 25 is one of the best known sections of the letter. Memorize these verses and use their promises to lead you to focus on the power that God can provide for the needs of the Christian life.

# Bibliography

Alford, Henry. *The Greek Testament*, vol. 4: *Hebrews—Revelation* Boston: Lee and Shepard, 1888.

Arichea, Daniel C., and Nida, Eugene A. *A Translator's Handbook on the First Letter from Peter.* New York: United Bible Societies, 1980.

Arndt, W. F., and Gingrich, F. Wilbur. *A Greek–English Lexicon of the New Testament and Other Early Christian Literature*, 2nd ed. Chicago: The University of Chicago Press, 1979.

Balfour, R. Gordon. "Christ Preaching to the Spirits in Prison," *The Expository Times*," vol. VII.

Barclay, William. *The Letters of James and Peter* in "The Daily Study Bible," 2nd ed. Philadelphia: Westminster Press, 1960.

Bauckham, Richard J. *Word Biblical Commentary*, vol. 50: *Jude, 2 Peter.* Waco, Texas: Word Books, 1983.

Beare, F. W. *The First Epistle of Peter, The Greek Text with Introduction and Notes.* Oxford: Basil Blackwell, 1970.

Best, Ernest. *I Peter*, in The New Century Bible. London: Oliphants, 1971.

Bigg, Charles. *A Critical and Exegetical Commentary on the Epistles of St. Peter and St. Jude* in "The International Critical Commentary." Edinburgh: T & T Clark, 1910.

Blum, Edwin A. *1, 2 Peter, Jude.* Vol. 12 in *The Expositor's Bible Commentary.* Grand Rapids: Zondervan, 1981.

Brown, John. *Expository Discourses on the First Epistle of the Apostle Peter.* Edinburgh: William Oliphants and Sons, 1848.

Calvin, John. *Commentaries on the Catholic Epistles.* Reprint. Grand Rapids: Wm. B. Eerdmans Publishing Company, 1948.

Clark, Gordon H. *II Peter: A Short Commentary*. Nutley, N.J.: Presbyterian and Reformed Publishing Company, 1975.

Cranfield, C. E. B. *I & II Peter and Jude* in "Torch Bible Commentaries." London: SCM Press, 1960.

Dalton, W. J. *Christ's Proclamation to the Spirits. A Study of I Peter 3:18–4:6*. Rome: Pontifical Bible Institute, 1965.

Dana, H. E. *Jewish Christianity*. New Orleans: Bible Institute Memorial Press, 1937.

Elliott, John H. *I–II Peter/Jude* in "Augsburg Commentary on the New Testament." Minneapolis: Augsburg Publishing House, 1982.

Erdman, Charles R. *The General Epistles*. Philadelphia: Westminster, n.d.

France, R. T. "Exegesis in Practice: Two Samples," *New Testament Interpretation*. Ed. I. H. Marshall. Grand Rapids: Eerdmans, 1977.

Green, Michael. *The Second General Epistle of Peter and the General Epistles of Jude* in "The Tyndale New Testament Commentaries." Grand Rapids: Wm. B. Eerdmans Publishing Company, 1968.

Grudem, Wayne. "Christ Preaching Through Noah: 1 Peter 3:19–20" in the "Light of Dominant Themes in Jewish Literature," *Trinity Journal*," vol. 7, 1986. This is an article adapted from an appendix to the author's commentary on 1 Peter in the *Tyndale NT Commentary* series.

Gundry, Robert H. *A Survey of the New Testament*, rev. ed. Grand Rapids: Zondervan Publishing House, 1981.

Guthrie, Donald. *New Testament Introduction: Hebrews to Revelation*, 2nd ed. London: The Tyndale Press, 1964.

Hart, J. H. A. *First Epistle General of Peter* in The Expositor's Greek Testament. Ed. W. Robertson Nicoll. Grand Rapids: Eerdmans, n.d.

Hiebert, D. Edmond. *First Peter: An Expositional Commentary*. Chicago: Moody Press, 1984.

Hort, F. J. A. *The First Epistle of St. Peter, I. l–II. 17. Expository and Exegetical Studies, Compendium of Works Formerly Published Separately*. Reprint. Minneapolis: Klock and Klock, 1980.

Hunter, A. M., and Homrighausen, E. G. *The First Epistle of Peter* in The Interpreter's Bible. New York: Abingdon, 1957.

Huther, John. Ed. *Critical and Exegetical Handbook to the General Epistles of James, Peter, John, and Jude* in "Meyer's Commentary on the New Testament," translated by Paton J. Gloag, D. B. Croom, and Clarke H. Irwin. Peabody, Massachusetts: Hendrickson Publishers, 1983.

Johnstone, Robert. *The First Epistle of Peter: Revised Text with Introduction and Commentary.* Reprint. Minneapolis: James Family, 1978.

Kelly, J. N. D. *A Commentary on the Epistles of Peter and of Jude* in "Harper's New Testament Commentaries," ed. Henry Chadwick. New York: Harper & Row, 1969.

Leighton, Robert. *Commentary on First Peter.* Reprint. Grand Rapids: Kregel Publications, 1972.

Lenski, R. C. H. *The Interpretation of the Epistles of St. Peter, St. John and St. Jude.* Columbus, Ohio: Wartburg Press, 1945.

Lillie, John. *Lectures on the First and Second Epistles of Peter.* Reprint. Minneapolis: Klock and Klock, 1978.

Luther, Martin. *Epistles of St. Peter and St. Jude.* New York: A. D. F. Randolph, 1859.

Masterman, J. H. B. *The First Epistle of St. Peter Greek Text.* London: Macmillan, 1900.

Mayor, Joseph B. *The Epistle of St. Jude and the Second Epistle of St. Peter.* Grand Rapids: Baker Book House, 1965.

Metzger, Bruce M. *A Textual Commentary on the Greek New Testament.* n.p.: United Bible Societies, 1971.

Moffatt, James. *The General Epistles: James, Peter, and Jude* in "The Moffatt New Testament Commentary." New York: Harper and Brothers, n.d.

Mounce, Robert H. *A Living Hope: A Commentary on 1 and 2 Peter.* Grand Rapids: Wm. B. Eerdmans Publishing Company, 1982.

Nisbet, Alexander. *1 and 2 Peter.* Reprint. Edinburgh: Banner of Truth Trust, 1982. First published in 1658.

Plumptre, E. H. *The General Epistles of St. Peter and St. Jude* in "The Cambridge Bible for Schools and Colleges," ed. J. J. S. Perowne. London: Cambridge University Press, 1899.

Polkinghorne, G. J. *The First Letter of Peter* in a New Testament Commentary. Edited by G. C. D. Howley. Grand Rapids: Zondervan, 1969.

Reicke, Bo. *The Disobedient Spirits and Christian Baptism.* Copenhagen: Munkegaard, 1946.

Robertson, Archibald Thomas. *Word Pictures in the New Testament*, vol. 6: *The General Epistles and the Revelation of John.* Nashville: Broadman Press, 1933.

Salmond, S. D. F. *Christian Doctrine of Immortality.* Fourth Edition. Edinburgh: T. & T. Clark, 1901.

Selwyn, E. G. *The First Epistle of St. Peter, The Greek Text with Introduction, Notes and Essays.* London: Macmillan, 1949.

Sidebottom, E. M. *James, Jude and 2 Peter* in "The Century Bible." New edition: Greenwood, South Carolina: Attic Press, 1967.

Stibbs, Allan M. *The First Epistle General of Peter* in Tyndale New Testament Commentaries. Introduction by Andrew F. Walls. London: Tyndale, 1959.

Strachan, R. H. *The Second Epistle General of Peter* in "The Expositor's Greek Testament," vol. 5. New York: George H. Doran Company, n.d.

Summers, Ray. *2 Peter* in "The Broadman Bible Commentary," vol. 12, ed. Clifton J. Allen. Nashville: Broadman Press, 1972.

Thomas, W. H. Griffith. *The Apostle Peter. Outline Studies in His Life Character and Writings.* Grand Rapids: Wm. B. Eerdmans Publishing Company, 1946.

Trench, R. C. *Synonyms of the New Testament.* Reprint. Grand Rapids: Eerdmans, 1947.

Wand, J. W. C. *The General Epistles of St. Peter and St. Jude* in Westminster Commentaries. London: Methuen, 1934.

Wheaton, David H. "2 Peter" in *The New Bible Commentary: Revised.* Grand Rapids: Wm. B. Eerdmans Publishing Company, 1970.

Williams, Nathaniel M. *Commentary on the Epistles of Peter* in an American Commentary on the New Testament. Reprint. Philadelphia: American Baptist Publication Society, n.d.

Zerwick, Maximilian and Grosvenor, Mary. *A Grammatical Analysis of the Greek New Testament,* vol. 2: Epistles-Apocalypse Rome: Biblical Institute Press, 1979.

All Scripture passages, unless otherwise identified, are quoted from the New International Version. Other translations referred to are as follows:

Beck, William F. *The New Testament in the Language of Today.* St. Louis: Concordia Publishing House, 1964.

Broadus, John A. *The New Testament of our Lord and Savior Jesus Christ,* improved edition. N.p.: United Bible Society.

Goodspeed, Edgar J. *The New Testament: An American Translation.* Chicago: The University of Chicago Press, 1951.

*Good News for Modern Man.* The New Testament in Today's English Version. New York: American Bible Society, 1966. Referred to in this book as TEV.

Knox, Ronald. *The New Testament in the Translation of Monsignor Ronald Knox.* New York: Sheed and Ward, 1944.

Lamsa, George M. *The Holy Bible from Ancient Eastern Manuscripts.* Philadelphia: A. J. Holman Co., 1940.

Moffatt, James. *The New Testament: A New Translation.* New York: Harper and Brothers, 1950.

Montgomery, Helen Barrett. *The New Testament in Modern English.* Valley Forge: Judson Press, n.d.

*New American Standard Bible.* Nashville: Broadman Press, 1960. Referred to in this book as NASB.

Norlie, Olaf M. *The New Testament: A New Translation.* Grand Rapids: Zondervan Publishing House, 1961.

Phillips, J. B. *The New Testament in Modern English.* New York: The Macmillan Company, 1962.

Rotherham, J.B. *The Emphasized Bible,* reprint edition Grand Rapids: Kregel Publications, 1967.

*The Holy Bible: King James Version.* New York: American Bible Society, 1964. Referred to in this book as KJV.

*The Holy Bible: Revised Standard Version.* New York: National Council of Churches of Christ, 1952. Referred to this book as RSV .

*The Holy Bible: Standard Edition.* New York: Thomas Nelson and Sons, 1929. Referred to in this book as ASV .

*The Modern Language Bible. The New Berkeley Version.* Grand Rapids: Zondervan Publishing House, 1959. Referred to in this book as MLB.

*The New English Bible.* Oxford and Cambridge: University Press, 1965. Referred to in this book as NEB.

*The Holy Bible: Standard Edition.* New York: Thomas Nelson and Sons, 1929. Referred to in this book as ASV.

*The Twentieth Century New Testament: A Translation into Modern English.* Chicago: Moody Press, n.d. Referred to in this book as TCNT.

Weymouth, Richard Francis. *The New Testament in Modern Speech.* Newly revised by James Alexander Robertson. New York: Harper and Brothers, n.d.

Williams, Charles B. *The New Testament: A Private Translation in the Language of the People.* Chicago: Moody Press, 1949.